Wrestling with the Violence of God

Bulletin for Biblical Research Supplements

Editor
RICHARD S. HESS, Denver Seminary

Associate Editor
CRAIG L. BLOMBERG, Denver Seminary

Advisory Board

LESLIE C. ALLEN
  Fuller Theological Seminary
DONALD A. CARSON
  Trinity Evangelical Divinity School
DONALD A. HAGNER
  Fuller Theological Seminary
KAREN H. JOBES
  Wheaton College

I. HOWARD MARSHALL
  University of Aberdeen
ELMER A. MARTENS
  Mennonite Brethren Biblical Seminary
BRUCE K. WALTKE
  Knox Theological Seminary
EDWIN M. YAMAUCHI
  Miami University

1. *Bridging the Gap: Ritual and Ritual Texts in the Bible*, by Gerald A. Klingbeil
2. *War in the Bible and Terrorism in the Twenty-First Century*, edited by Richard S. Hess and Elmer A. Martens
3. *Critical Issues in Early Israelite History*, edited by Richard S. Hess, Gerald A. Klingbeil, and Paul J. Ray Jr.
4. *Poetic Imagination in Proverbs: Variant Repetitions and the Nature of Poetry*, by Knut Martin Heim
5. *Divine Sabbath Work*, by Michael H. Burer
6. *The Iron Age I Structure on Mt. Ebal: Excavation and Interpretation*, by Ralph K. Hawkins
7. *Toward a Poetics of Genesis 1–11: Reading Genesis 4:17–22 in Its Near Eastern Context*, by Daniel DeWitt Lowery
8. *Melchizedek's Alternative Priestly Order: A Compositional Analysis of Genesis 14:18–20 and Its Echoes throughout the Tanak*, by Joshua G. Mathews
9. *Sacred Ritual: A Study of the West Semitic Ritual Calendars in Leviticus 23 and the Akkadian Text Emar 446*, by Bryan C. Babcock
10. *Wrestling with the Violence of God: Soundings in the Old Testament*, edited by M. Daniel Carroll R. and J. Blair Wilgus
11. *Wealth in Ancient Ephesus and the First Letter to Timothy: Fresh Insights from Ephesiaca by Xenophon of Ephesus*, by Gary G. Hoag
12. *Paul and His Mortality: Imitating Christ in the Face of Death*, by R. Gregory Jenks

Wrestling with the Violence of God

Soundings in the Old Testament

edited by

M. Daniel Carroll R. and J. Blair Wilgus

Winona Lake, Indiana
Eisenbrauns
2015

© Copyright 2015 Eisenbrauns
All rights reserved.
Printed in the United States of America.
www.eisenbrauns.com

Library of Congress Cataloging-in-Publication Data

Wrestling with the violence of God : soundings in the Old Testament /
   edited by M. Daniel Carroll R. and J. Blair Wilgus.
       pages   cm. — (Bulletin for biblical research supplements)
   Includes bibliographical references and index.
   ISBN 978-1-57506-828-2 (hardback : alk. paper)
   1. Violence in the Bible.   2. God—Biblical teaching   3. Bible. Old
Testament–Theology.   I. Carroll R., M. Daniel, editor.   II. Wilgus,
J. Blair, editor.
     BS1199.V56W74   2015
     221.6—dc23
                                                                  2015014139

The paper used in this publication meets the minimum requirements of the American National Standard for Information Sciences—Permanence of Paper for Printed Library Materials, ANSI Z39.48-1984. ♾™

Contents

Preface vii

Contributors ix

Abbreviations xi

1. Introduction:
   What Do We Do with the God of the Old Testament? 1
   M. Daniel Carroll R. and J. Blair Wilgus
       Doubting and Denying the God of the Old Testament   1
       The New Challenge   5
       Responding to Charges against the Old Testament   7
       The Purpose of This Volume   12

2. The Near-Sacrifice of Isaac:
   Monstrous Morality or Richly Textured Theology? 15
   Paul J. Kissling
       Introduction   15
       Insights from a Close Reading of the Hebrew Text   16
       Insights from the Wider Pentateuchal Context   19
       Insights from the
           Wider Old Testament Canonical Context   20
       Insights from the Social and Historical Background   20
       Insights from the Early History of Interpretation   22
       Engaging Modern and Contemporary Concerns
           about This Text   27
       Conclusion   29

3. How Can We Bless Yhwh?
   Wrestling with Divine Violence in Deuteronomy 31
   Daniel I. Block
       The Forms of Divine Violence in Deuteronomy   32
       The Targets of Divine Violence in Deuteronomy   33
       The Motivation for Divine Violence in Deuteronomy   36
       Conclusion   49
       Postscript   50

4. Taking the Land by Force: Divine Violence in Joshua 51
   Hélène M. Dallaire
       Introduction   51
       Joshua: A Brief History of Interpretation   53
       Joshua: Ideology   57

The Warrior God in Joshua 61
The Rhetoric of Violence in Joshua: The *Ḥērem* 63
Conclusion 71

5. Cries of the Oppressed: Prayer and Violence in the Psalms 75
DAVID G. FIRTH
Contexts for Violence 75
Which Psalms Are Imprecatory? 78
Communal Psalms 86
Conclusion 88

6. Suffering Has Its Voice:
Divine Violence, Pain, and Prayer in Lamentations 91
HEATH A. THOMAS
Introduction 91
Divine Violence and Lamentations 95
Retribution and Confession as Response 101
Complaint as Response 104
Conclusion 108

7. "I Will Send Fire":
Reflections on the Violence of God in Amos 113
M. DANIEL CARROLL R.
Amos and the Violence of God 117
Conclusion 132

8. Toward an End to Violence: Hearing Jeremiah 133
ELMER A. MARTENS
Divine Anger: Factoring in the Context of Covenant 134
Portrayal of a Benevolent God: A Challenge to the
    View that God Is Malevolent 138
Portrayal of a God Who Loves: A Challenge to a Violent
    and Solely Retributive God 140
A Portrait of God as Marital Lover Who Perseveres
    beyond Disloyalty: A Decisive Challenge to a
    Negative View of God 144
Conciliatory Messages in Jeremiah: Challenging Violence
    as a Divine Modus Operandi 145
A Scenario of "No Violence": Imagining a New Reality 146
Conclusion 149

Bibliography 151

Index of Authors 167

Index of Scripture 171

Preface

This volume began its journey at the 2012 annual meeting of the Evangelical Theological Society. The session topic of the Old Testament Theology study group that year was "The Old Testament and Violence." Both the papers presented and the discussions that ensued were lively and thought-provoking, and several committee members felt it was a worthy project to pursue as a published work. In the months that followed, we identified multiple texts that were either essential for a comprehensive treatment of the topic or that provided something unique to the discussion.

From the beginning, we had several goals in producing this book. Our first desire was to create something that was widely accessible. As the introduction will show, the discussion of God and violence is not confined to the academy. This is a question that plagues many lay Christians and one that is often raised by skeptics as a reason they will not embrace the faith. Because of this, the length of each chapter has been restricted to keep discussions clear and concise. Footnotes direct interested readers to more-detailed treatment of issues. We have chosen to avoid technical discussions as much as possible and have opted to transliterate Hebrew to accommodate a broader audience.

We also wanted to present a work that devoted attention to Old Testament texts and that was written by Old Testament scholars. As the introduction also will show, contemporary works on the topic are frequently written by scholars specialized in one area of Hebrew Bible study while addressing the whole corpus. This work addresses texts of violence in the Pentateuch, Joshua, Psalms, Lamentations, and the Prophets, and each chapter is contributed by a scholar who has made that section of Scripture his or her life's work.

Another goal we had in this project was to present an engagement with Scripture that was not bound to a single ecclesial tradition. The chapters in this book do not represent the teaching of one denominational body or the position of a specific educational institution. They represent thoughtful interaction with the text from a group of scholars of varied traditions who teach at different institutions. These religious traditions include Anglican, Baptist, Christian Church, Evangelical Free, Mennonite, nondenominational, and Messianic Judaism. The authors also represent diverse national and ethnic backgrounds. Four are from the United States, three are from different Canadian communities, one is Australian, and another is of Guatemalan heritage.

The core belief of the contributors to this volume, and perhaps the most important component of this work, is that the issue of God's participation in violence found in the Hebrew Bible can be addressed and understood without jettisoning belief in the Bible as the word of God. The contributors attempt to interact with the theologically complex character of God seen in the pages of Scripture. Each chapter seeks to engage its text attempting to discern how it contributes to a fuller understanding of the God depicted therein. It is this picture of God that we offer to the interested reader.

As with all projects, several people deserve thanks for help in reaching the final product. The editors would like to thank each of the contributors for their work and cooperation. Kayla White and Brandon Benziger, Danny Carroll's graduate assistants at Denver Seminary, were instrumental in formatting the essays and compiled the abbreviation list and the composite bibliography. Thanks are due especially to Richard Hess and the Institute for Biblical Research for accepting this volume into the series.

Contributors

Daniel I. Block (Ph.D., University of Liverpool) is Gunther H. Knoedler Professor of Old Testament at Wheaton College, Wheaton, Illinois (USA).

M. Daniel Carroll R. (Rodas) (Ph.D., University of Sheffield) is Distinguished Professor of Old Testament at Denver Seminary, Denver Colorado (USA), and adjunct professor at El Seminario Teológico Centroamericano in Guatemala City (Guatemala).

Hélène Dallaire (Ph.D., Hebrew Union College) is Professor of Old Testament at Denver Seminary, Denver Colorado (USA).

David G. Firth (Ph.D., University of Pretoria) is Lecturer in Old Testament and Director of Research Degrees at St. John's College, Nottingham (UK).

Heath A. Thomas (Ph.D., University of Gloucestershire) is Associate Professor of Old Testament and Hebrew and Director of Ph.D. Studies at Southeastern Baptist Theological Seminary in Wake Forest, North Carolina (USA).

Paul J. Kissling (Ph.D., University of Sheffield) is Professor of Old Testament at Lincoln Christian University, Lincoln, Illinois (USA).

Elmer A. Martens (Ph.D., Claremont Graduate School) is President Emeritus and Professor Emeritus of Old Testament at the Fresno Pacific Biblical Seminary, Fresno, California (USA).

J. Blair Wilgus (Ph.D., University of Edinburgh) is Chair, Online Undergraduate Ministry Program and Associate Professor of Biblical Studies at Hope International University, Fullerton, California (USA).

NICOT	New International Commentary on the Old Testament
NIDOTTE	VanGemeren, W. A., ed. *New International Dictionary of Old Testament Theology and Exegesis*. 5 vols. Grand Rapids: Zondervan, 1997
NIVAC	New International Version Application Commentary
NSBT	New Studies in Biblical Theology
OBO	Orbis biblicus et orientalis
OBT	Overtures to Biblical Theology
OC	Orientalia et classica
OP	Occasional Papers
OTL	Old Testament Library
OTS	Old Testament Studies
OTT	Old Testament Theology
PBM	Paternoster Biblical Monographs
RB	*Revue biblique*
SBLMS	Society of Biblical Literature Monograph Series
SBLSymS	Society of Biblical Literature Symposium Series
SBS	Stuttgarter Bibelstudien
SBT	Studies in Biblical Theology
SCJ	*Stone-Campbell Journal*
SHBC	Smyth & Helwys Bible Commentary
SOTBT	Studies in Old Testament Biblical Theology
SOTSMS	Society of the Old Testament Study Monograph Series
SPS	Studies in Peace and Scripture
SSN	Studia semitica neerlandica
TDOT	Botterweck, G. J., and H. Ringgren, eds. *Theological Dictionary of the Old Testament*. Translated by D. E. Green. 15 vols. Grand Rapids: Eerdmans, 1974–2006
TECC	Theological Explorations of the Church Catholic
TLS	The Terry Lectures Series
TOTC	Tyndale Old Testament Commentary Series
TynBul	*Tyndale Bulletin*
UBT	Understanding Biblical Themes
UCOP	University of Cambridge Oriental Publications
VT	*Vetus Testamentum*
WMANT	Wissenschaftliche Monographien zum Alten und Neuen Testament
WUNT	Wissenschaftliche Untersuchungen zum Neuen Testament
WW	*Word and World*
WWSup	Word and World Supplement Series
ZAW	*Zeitschrift für die alttestamentliche Wissenschaft*
ZBK	Zürcher Bibelkommentare

Chapter 1

Introduction: What Do We Do with the God of the Old Testament?

M. Daniel Carroll R.
and J. Blair Wilgus

Doubting and Denying the God of the Old Testament

Suffering generates crises of faith. Natural disasters, armed conflicts, and human cruelty in its multiple forms raise questions about the ability (and even the desire) of God to prevent such misery and about his role in these events. Theodicy, the effort to understand how a good God can countenance evil, is an ongoing challenge for the Christian faith, as it is for all religions.

Several historical moments have especially highlighted the complex issues of God and his connection to human violence and have triggered moments of significant theological and biblical reflection.[1] One of the most important, of course, was the unspeakable cruelty and the staggering numbers of deaths of the Holocaust, or *Shoah* ("calamity" in Hebrew). What is particularly shocking is the support given to the Nazi regime by certain sectors of the Christian church and by several prominent theologians and biblical scholars, who proclaimed a deity that legitimated that murderous nationalistic and ethnic ideology.[2] That horror of decades ago continues to foment Jewish deliberations on faith and religious practice, and many

---

1. Violence is a term with a wide range of possible meanings. The focus of this essay and of this volume is the violence associated with inflicting harm (directly and indirectly), most often in war and its aftermath, by God (whether directly or through human or natural instruments). This can include harm in multiple spheres, such as the physical, the emotional, and the cultural. Mark Douglas provides this useful definition: "a forceful action that intends to cause unwanted injury to another" ("Violence," in *DSE* 809-10).

2. Robert P. Ericksen, *Theologians under Hitler: Gerhard Kittel, Paul Althaus and Emanuel Hirsch* (New Haven, CT: Yale University Press, 1985); Doris L. Berger, *The Twisted Cross: The German Christian Movement in the Third Reich* (Chapel Hill: University of North Carolina Press, 1996); Cornelia Weber, *Altes Testament und völkische Frage: Der biblische Volksbegriff in der alttestamentlichen Wissenschaft der nationalsozialistischen Zeit, dargestellt am Beispiel von Johannes Hempel* (FAT 28; Tübingen: Mohr Siebeck, 2000); Susannah Heschel, *The Aryan Jesus: Christian Theologians and the Bible in Nazi Germany* (Princeton: Princeton University Press, 2008).

Christian thinkers contend that the *Shoah* must be considered in their own theologizing about life with God in the world.³ The magnitude of the campaign to exterminate the Jews in Europe has led some to have profound reservations about traditional beliefs. Within the Jewish community, one eloquent, powerful voice of such distrust is that of the Nobel Prize winning author Elie Wiesel.⁴

Others have marked the obliteration of the Twin Towers in New York City on September 11, 2001, as a turning point for the Western world. That act of terrorism truly was shocking, but human history is littered with such barbaric acts. From the last 100 years, one could mention the killing and destruction of two World Wars, the gulags of Stalinist Russia, the atrocities of the Pol Pot premiership in Cambodia and of the dictatorships in Latin America, the ethnic cleansing of the Serbian—Croatian conflict, the tribal massacres in Rwanda ... the list could go on. To these tragedies can be added the terrible impact of earthquakes, tornadoes, tsunamis, floods, drought, epidemics, and famine. Human atrocities and natural disasters oblige constant reassessment of theological convictions.

The current state of affairs, however, has shifted from wondering about the nature and purposes of God to sharp skepticism of the metaphysical.⁵ Recent attacks on God and faith, both in the popular media and in scholarly publications, tend to concentrate on the violence that is done in the name of religion. Critics argue that all religions are essentially violent, especially the monotheistic faiths of Christianity and Islam. It is asserted that this violence is due to their absolute, exclusionary claims that condemn those outside their circles. These monotheistic religions also are said to be irrational.⁶ Several individuals, who have been called the "New Atheists," have

---

3. For surveys of Jewish and Christian grappling with the *Shoah*, see Marvin A. Sweeney, *Reading the Hebrew Bible after the Shoah* (Minneapolis: Fortress, 2008) 1–22; idem, *TANAK: A Theological and Critical Introduction to the Hebrew Bible* (Minneapolis: Fortress, 2012) 5–36; Peter Admirand, *Amidst Mass Atrocity and the Rubble of Theology: Searching for a Viable Theodicy* (Eugene, OR: Cascade, 2012) 184–216; cf. Hemchand Gossai, *The Hebrew Prophets after the Shoah: A Mandate for Change* (Eugene, OR: Pickwick, 2014).

4. These sentiments are powerfully portrayed in Elie Wiesel's *Night* trilogy. Note the recent edition in three volumes with new prefaces by the author: *Night, Dawn,* and *Day* (New York: Hill & Wang, 2006).

5. Debates over theodicy are not new, but the pervasiveness of a broad skepticism about God and the Bible is. For introductions to the issue of theodicy in the Old Testament, see, for example, J. L. Crenshaw: *A Whirlpool of Torment: Israelite Traditions of God as Oppressive Presence* (OBT; Philadelphia: Fortress, 1984); idem, *Defending God: Biblical Responses to the Problem of Evil* (Oxford: Oxford University Press, 2005); R. P. Belcher Jr., "Suffering," and J. Davies, "Theodicy," in *DOTWPW*, 775–81 and 808–17, respectively; H. A. Thomas, "Suffering," *DOTP*, 757–66.

6. Note, e.g., Regina M. Schwartz, *The Curse of Cain: The Violent Legacy of Monotheism* (Chicago: University of Chicago Press, 1997); Hector Avalos, *Fighting Words: The Origins of Religious Violence* (Amherst: Prometheus, 2005); Mark Juergensmeyer and Margo Kitts, eds., *Princeton Readings in Religion and Violence* (Princeton: Princeton University Press,

done much to disseminate such an unfavorable view of the Christian faith. Well-known spokespersons of this perspective include Sam Harris, Richard Dawkins, Daniel C. Dennett, and the late Christopher Hitchens. The Old Testament[7] and its God are special targets of their disparagement. Their work presents Yahweh as the supreme sovereign over the actions of nations and as a judge who, they claim, indiscriminately uses excessive violence to advance his plans or simply out of malicious whim. An oft-quoted remark by Dawkins forcefully conveys this attitude toward Yahweh:

> The God of the Old Testament is arguably the most unpleasant character in all fiction: jealous and proud of it; a petty, unjust, unforgiving control-freak; a vindictive, bloodthirsty ethnic cleanser; a misogynistic, homophobic, racist, infanticidal, genocidal, filicidal, pestilential, megalomaniacal, sadomasochistic, capriciously malevolent bully.[8]

Accusations regarding the unpleasantness of the God of the Old Testament are not new. Complaints against the Old Testament and the violence associated with its God goes back to the first centuries of the early Church. Marcion of Sinope (ca. 85–ca. 160) is the crucial figure here.[9] In his view, the Creator, who is the God of the Old Testament and of the Jews, is to be distinguished from and is lesser than the universal Redeemer God manifested in Jesus. The former is primitive, jealous, and a cruel punisher of those he deems guilty. In sharp contrast, the message brought by Jesus and Paul was truly a new word, even though portions of the Gospels and the epistles still cling to the false God of the Old Testament and had been corrupted by Judaizers. Marcion lessened the value of the Old Testament and limited acceptable revelation to portions of the Gospel of Luke and of Paul's letters.

Modern-day critics contend that the Old Testament encourages and legitimates aggression by believers. On the one hand, it is undeniable that the biblical material *describes* ancient warfare—its weaponry, tactics, ideologies,

---

2011). Cf. the survey in William T. Cavanaugh, *The Myth of Religious Violence: Secular Ideology and the Roots of Modern Conflict* (Oxford: Oxford University Press, 2009) 15–56.

7. The label "the Old Testament" is used instead of "the Hebrew Bible." This discussion is self-consciously from the perspective of the Christian faith, in which the first testament is part of a larger canon. For helpful discussions of this option, see, e.g., Christopher R. Seitz, "Old Testament or Hebrew Bible? Some Theological Considerations," *World without End: The Old Testament as Abiding Witness* (Grand Rapids: Eerdmans, 1998) 61–74; Craig G. Bartholomew, "Listening for God's Address: A *Mere* Trinitarian Hermeneutic for the Old Testament," in *Hearing the Old Testament: Listening for God's Address* (ed. C. G. Bartholomew and D. J. H. Beldman; Grand Rapids: Eerdmans, 2012) 3–19.

8. Richard Dawkins, *The God Delusion* (New York: Houghton Mifflin, 2006) 31.

9. Sebastian Moll, *The Arch-Heretic Marcion* (WUNT 250; Tübingen: Mohr Siebeck, 2010); cf. Adolf von Harnack, *Marcion: The Gospel of the Alien God* (trans. J. E. Steely and L. D. Bierma; Durham: Labyrinth, 1924; repr., 1990); John Barton, "Marcion Revisited" in *The Canon Debate: On the Origins and Formation of the Bible* (ed. L. M. McDonald and J. A. Sanders; Peabody, MA: Hendrickson, 2003) 341–54. Sinope is located in modern-day Turkey. See the sustained, virulent refutation in five volumes by Tertulian (ca. 160–ca. 225), *Adversus Marcionem* (ed. and trans. E. Evans; Oxford: Clarendon, 1972).

rhetoric, and horrendous consequences—all of which can be disturbing. The issue, though, is that over the centuries some individuals and groups have interpreted Old Testament texts as *prescribing* or *endorsing* violence. Philip Jenkins even claims that the Christian faith (due in large measure to the influence of the Old Testament) actually may be more culpable of violence than other religions, in particular Islam.[10]

It is not difficult to find appeals to the Old Testament to justify armed conflict.[11] Well-known examples from long ago include the establishment of military religious orders, such as the Knights Templar and the Knights Hospitallers of St. John of Jerusalem, and the launching of the crusades.[12] Postcolonial scholars argue that the European colonial powers used the Old Testament to justify their territorial expansion and economic reach in Africa, Asia, and Latin America.[13] If one were to focus on the history of the United States, the sermons and pamphlets of the American Revolution, the Civil War, and the Great (or First) World War,[14] among many other instances, stand as evidence of the utilization of the Old Testament for war.

"Reading against the grain," recent ideological approaches to the Old Testament articulate what is felt to be a more fundamental difficulty. Beyond the fact that the Old Testament contains material dealing with war and the unfortunate biblical interpretations that on occasion have spawned violence is the inescapable problem that *the God portrayed in the text* appears to be violent. Distasteful character traits and unacceptable actions are presented in the Old Testament as integral to God's person and his ways. They also form the theological basis for petitions in prayer and the cursing of enemies and are celebrated in song. Sadly and dangerously, it is said, this perspective is picked up and perpetuated by some communities of faith.

---

10. Philip Jenkins, *Laying Down the Sword: Why We Can't Ignore the Bible's Violent Verses* (New York: HarperOne, 2011) 73–95.

11. For lists, see Jenkins, *Laying Down the Sword, passim*; Eric A. Seibert, *The Violence of Scripture: Overcoming the Old Testament's Troubling Legacy* (Minneapolis: Fortress, 2012) 15–26.

12. Michael Walsh, *Warriors of the Lord: The Military Orders of Christendom* (Grand Rapids: Eerdmans, 2003).

13. Michael Prior, *The Bible and Colonialism: A Moral Critique* (Biblical Seminar 48; Sheffield: Sheffield Academic Press, 1997); R. S. Sugirtharajah, *The Bible and the Third World: Precolonial, Colonial and Postcolonial Encounters* (Cambridge: Cambridge University Press, 2001); cf. Mark G. Brett, *Decolonizing God: The Bible in the Tides of Empire* (Bible in the Modern World 16; Sheffield: Sheffield Phoenix, 2008); Bradley L. Crowell, "Postcolonial Studies and the Hebrew Bible," *CBR* 7 (2009) 217–44.

14. James P. Byrd, *Sacred Scripture, Sacred War: The Bible and the American Revolution* (Oxford: Oxford University Press, 2013); Mark A. Noll, *The Civil War as a Theological Crisis* (Chapel Hill: University of North Carolina Press, 2006); and the relevant sections in idem, *America's God: From Jonathan Edwards to Abraham Lincoln* (Oxford: Oxford University Press, 2002); Jonathan H. Ebel, *Faith in the Fight: Religion and the American Soldier in the Great War* (Princeton: Princeton University Press, 2010); Philip Jenkins, *The Great and Holy War: How World War I Became a Religious Crusade* (New York: HarperOne, 2014).

In addition, certain feminists bring a specific charge against the Old Testament and its God. They decry its power to promote gendered violence, with its many social, political, economic, relational, and familial implications.[15] The exploitation endured by several female characters in the Old Testament is there for all to see, and interpreters of all stripes rightly condemn the brutality of those scenes (such as the rapes of Dinah and Tamar and the dismembering of the Levite's concubine in Judges 19). Some feminists employ a hermeneutic of suspicion to say that the biblical text consistently presents Yahweh as an abusive male. They assert that this portrayal naturally condones (and models) the mistreatment of women.[16]

In summary, the Old Testament is under attack from several quarters.[17] For some, it is a witness to the violence inherent in all religions. More specifically, the Old Testament is reviled because of the violence it contains (*content*) and the conflicts that some believe it has sanctioned (*function*), and because its God is a violent deity (*ideology*).

The New Challenge

Voices are being raised—even within more traditional circles—against what is considered to be a heartless, brutal deity and a religious text that is suspect and potentially dangerous. Recently, several scholars within evangelicalism, broadly defined, have joined the chorus of those who disapprove of the Old Testament's representation of God. Two of the more visible spokespersons of this trend are Eric Seibert and Kenton Sparks.[18] Both have produced book-length studies to sustain their arguments.[19]

---

15. Of course, there is a spectrum of attitudes toward the Old Testament in feminist circles, from guarded respect to outright rejection. For surveys, see Natalie K. Watson, *Feminist Theology* (Guides to Theology; Grand Rapids: Eerdmans, 2003) 1–24; Alice Ogden Bellis *Helpmates, Harlots, and Heroes: Women's Stories in the Hebrew Bible* (2nd ed.; Louisville, KY: Westminster John Knox, 2007) 3–34.

16. For treatments of particular texts, see, e.g., P. Trible, *Texts of Terror: Literary-Feminist Readings of Biblical Narratives* (OBT; Minneapolis: Fortress, 1984); J. Cheryl Exum, "The Ethics of Biblical Violence against Women," in *The Bible in Ethics: The Second Sheffield Colloquium* (ed. J. W. Rogerson, M. Davies, and M. D. Carroll R.; JSOTSup 207; Sheffield: Sheffield Academic Press, 1995) 248–71; J. M. O'Brien, *Challenging Prophetic Metaphor: Theology and Ideology in the Prophets* (Louisville, KY: Westminster John Knox, 2008).

17. There are many biblical scholars who condemn the violence of the Old Testament in addition to the examples already cited. For an accessible example, note (along with the works cited in his footnotes) John J. Collins, "The Zeal of Phinehas: The Bible and the Legitimation of Violence," *JBL* 122 (2003) 3–21.

18. Eric A. Seibert, *Disturbing Divine Behavior: Troubling Old Testament Images of God* (Minneapolis: Fortress, 2009); idem, *The Violence of Scripture*; Kenton L. Sparks, *Sacred Word, Broken Word: Biblical Authority and the Dark Side of Scripture* (Grand Rapids: Eerdmans, 2012).

19. Also note, e.g., the work by Mennonite J. Denny Weaver, *The Nonviolent God* (Grand Rapids: Eerdmans, 2013), and the popular-level book by Peter Enns, *The Bible*

These scholars say that the actions of the God of the biblical text are unacceptable and capricious, his wrath excessive and undifferentiating. The section headings of one of the chapters in Seibert's *Disturbing Divine Behavior* are provocative. Yahweh is called a Deadly Lawgiver, Instant Executioner, Mass Murderer, Divine Warrior, Genocidal General, Dangerous Abuser, Unfair Afflicter, and Divine Deceiver.[20] This biblical God, Seibert says, has a troubling legacy of (to reflect the headings of a chapter in his *The Violence of Scripture*) justifying war, legitimating colonialism, supporting slavery, encouraging violence against women, harming children, condemning gays and lesbians, and distorting the character of God. It is not just that texts have been misused; the text itself is a problem because of the offensive behavior it fosters and, more importantly, because of the kind of God it depicts.[21]

Christians always have struggled with how to deal with these potentially disquieting Old Testament texts. With different levels of success and viability, diverse strategies over the centuries have been developed to minimize their discomfort. Seibert surveys several and finds them inadequate.[22] These include the interpretive strategies of applying typology and allegory to troublesome texts, of Christians often acting like what he calls "functional Marcionites" (that is, having the propensity to ignore unpleasant passages), of defending God on the basis of his unfathomable ways and permissive will, and of appealing to the concept of progressive revelation. His suggestion is that these texts need to be appreciated as historically conditioned. Accordingly, their stances should be questioned and, if necessary, set aside. Seibert calls for embracing a Christological hermeneutic as a guide for discerning what can be embraced and what must be disallowed.[23] Sparks argues for a Christological hermeneutic as well, proposing four priorities for what he considers to be a more constructive approach to the Bible: an appreciation of mystery; the pursuit of spiritual, emotional,

---

Tells Me So: Why Defending Scripture Has Made Us Unable to Read It (New York: HarperOne, 2014). From Roman Catholic circles, see Matthew J. Ramage, *Dark Passages of the Bible: Engaging Scripture with Benedict XVI and Thomas Aquinas* (Washington, DC: Catholic University of America Press, 2013). The Church's Magisterium acknowledges the challenges of difficult texts and counsels their interpretation within "their historical-literary context and within the Christian perspective" (Pope Benedict XVI, *Verbum Domini* [Boston: Pauline Books & Media, 2010] §42).

20. Seibert, *Disturbing Divine Behavior*, 17–32.
21. Idem, *The Violence of Scripture*, 15–26.
22. Idem, *Disturbing Divine Behavior*, 59–88; cf. Eryl W. Davies, *The Immoral Bible: Approaches to Biblical Ethics* (London: T. & T. Clark, 2010); Emily Arndt, *Demanding Attention: The Hebrew Bible as a Source for Christian Ethics* (Grand Rapids: Eerdmans, 2011). For brief historical overviews, note Charles H. Cosgrove, "Scripture in Ethics: A History," in *DSE* 13–25; with his own proposal for appropriating the Bible, J. W. Rogerson, *According to the Scriptures? The Challenge of Using the Bible in Social, Moral and Political Questions* (BCCW; London: Equinox, 2007).
23. Seibert, *Disturbing Divine Behavior*, 183–207; cf. idem, *The Violence of Scripture*, 73–92, 147–57. Also note Weaver, *The Nonviolent God*, 129–50.

and psychological wholeness; the commitment to redemptive praxis; and a more missional approach to Christian life.[24]

Inevitably, as Seibert and Sparks are aware, their evaluation of the Old Testament raises the issue of the nature of Scripture and its authority.[25] Both continue to hold that the Old Testament at some level is a word from God, but classical, or traditional, formulations no longer will do.

Responding to Charges against the Old Testament

Responses to these disapproving criticisms of the Christian faith have come from many quarters, and not always from expected voices. Literary theorist Terry Eagleton, for example, takes the new atheists, the "Ditchkins" (his playful label that combines the surnames Dawkins and Hitchens), to task in characteristically humorous—yet pointed—fashion by contending that they do not understand the Christian faith (especially the exemplary self-giving person of Jesus), which they misrepresent and caricature; they are naïve, too, he says about the myth of human progress and ignore the destructive tendencies of humanity. Eagleton complains, ironically, that Hitchens supported the use of military force in the Middle East, even as he and others criticize the supposed inherent violence of religion.[26]

Yale theologian Miroslav Volf answers arguments of the opponents of Christianity and the Bible by pointing out how little these individuals comprehend of the significance of the life and cross of Jesus.[27] In an earlier, award-wining publication and speaking from his personal experiences as a Croat in the Serbian-Croatian conflict, Volf decries contemporary credulous confidence in human goodness and rationality, which trumpets that the elimination of God will bring the eradication of violence. Instead, he argues that, without the presence of faith, violence would have no moral filter or check and would become even more ubiquitous and ugly.[28] For his part, William Cavanaugh contends that the modern "myth" of religion as violent actually is an ongoing historical cultural construct to legitimate the

---

24. Sparks, *Sacred Word, Broken Word*, 132–41.

25. Seibert, *Disturbing Divine Behavior*, 263–80, *passim*; idem, *The Violence of Scripture*, 159–62, *passim*; Sparks, *Sacred Word, Broken Word*, *passim*.

26. Terry Eagleton, *Reason, Faith, and Revolution: Reflections on the God Debate* (TLS; New Haven: Yale University Press, 2010). This is not to say that Eagleton always gets it right in regards to Christian faith, but he repeatedly shows admiration for the life and self-sacrifice of Jesus (e.g., pp. 22, 27, 37) and points out Christianity's realistic assessment of human evil. Eagleton champions what he calls a Marxist, tragic humanism stance.

27. Miroslav Volf, "Christianity and Violence," in *War in the Bible and Terrorism in the Twenty-First Century* (ed. R. S. Hess and E. A. Martens; BBRSup 2; Winona Lake, IN: Eisenbrauns, 2008) 1–17. Interestingly, Eagleton points to the suffering of Jesus for others as foundational for providing meaning to human life.

28. Idem, *Exclusion and Embrace: A Theological Exploration of Identity, Otherness, and Reconciliation* (Nashville: Abingdon, 1996) 278–90. In this book, Volf develops an ethic grounded in the cross of Christ and the divine embrace of the Other.

contours of Western liberal democracy, even as it is used to justify military intervention in other parts of the world.[29] Both of these authors present sophisticated theological and philosophical discussions to counter the misinformed distortions of religion that are so prominent today in the academy and the public square. Their work is just a sample of the growing theological and philosophical debate.[30]

From these broader responses to recent disparagements of Christianity, we turn to engaging the negative appraisals of the more specific targets that are the Old Testament and its God. Volumes from different evangelical persuasions are appearing, from lay to more academic levels.[31] Of course, responses are not limited to evangelicals. Scholars from other traditions also are speaking out with their own solutions to the challenges; these, too, have been directed at various kinds of audiences.[32] A full set of arguments from within biblical studies that need to be brought to bear on these critiques of the Old Testament and Yahweh would require interaction with multiple fields of research. To name a few:

1. *Comparative Studies*. The contribution of this discipline would be in at least two areas. First, the study of similar kinds of texts in the ancient world that wrestle with the inexplicable contradictions and cruelties of life, such as *The Admonition of Ipuwer* of Egypt and the Sumerian *A Man and His God*,[33] would yield a sense of the religious world within which the Old Testament texts arose. Does this sort of material surface in certain religious genres, and how do these works compare with what is found in the Old Testament? Are there elements of a common humanity in these reflections that find an echo in the Old Testament, and is there anything different in the Old Testa-

---

29. Cavanaugh, *The Myth of Religious Violence*.

30. An interesting example that puts philosophers and biblical scholars in conversation is Michel Bergmann, Michael J. Murphy, and Michael C. Rea, eds., *Divine Evil? The Moral Character of the God of Abraham* (Oxford: Oxford University Press, 2011).

31. E.g., C. S. Cowles et al., *Show Them No Mercy: Four Views on God and Canaanite Genocide* (Counterpoints; Grand Rapids: Zondervan, 2003); Christopher J. H. Wright, *The God I Don't Understand: Reflections on Tough Questions of Faith* (Grand Rapids: Zondervan, 2008); Douglas S. Earl, *Reading Joshua as Christian Scripture* (JTISup 2; Winona Lake, IN: Eisenbrauns, 2010); idem, *The Joshua Delusion? Rethinking Genocide in the Bible* (Eugene, OR: Cascade, 2010); Paul Copan, *Is God a Moral Monster? Making Sense of the Old Testament God* (Grand Rapids: Baker, 2011); David T. Lamb, *God Behaving Badly: Is the God of the Old Testament Angry, Sexist and Racist?* (Downers Grove, IL: InterVarsity, 2011); Heath A. Thomas, Jeremy Evans, and Paul Copan, eds. *Holy War in the Bible: Christian Morality and an Old Testament Problem* (Downers Grove, IL: IVP Academic, 2013); Ian Provan, *Seriously Dangerous Religion: What the Old Testament Really Says and Why It Matters* (Waco, TX: Baylor University Press, 2014); Matthew Richard Schlimm, *This Strange and Sacred Scripture: Wrestling with the Old Testament and Its Oddities* (Grand Rapids: Baker Academic, 2015).

32. E.g., Thomas Römer, *Dark God: Cruelty, Sex, and Violence in the Old Testament* (trans. S. O'Neill; New York: Paulist Press, 2013); Jerome F. D. Creach, *Violence in Scripture* (Interp; Louisville, KY: Westminster John Knox, 2013).

33. For these texts, see *COS* 1: 93–98 and 573–75, respectively.

ment's view of God and the world? If so, why? What might the import of that be? A second area is research that compares and contrasts the national or imperial theologies and ideologies of warfare in the ancient world and the Old Testament.[34] Once again, the issues of genre, the degree and significance of shared ideological and theological views, as well as the differences, would be relevant to understand better and assess the Old Testament's view of the acts of Yahweh that now are under scrutiny.

2. *History of Reception*. The study of the effect of difficult Old Testament texts would entail investigating how and why they have been used inappropriately in certain historical contexts, some examples of which were cited earlier in this essay. An awareness of the full spectrum of available evidence yields a much more nuanced picture of the relationship between religion (including Christianity and its Scripture) and violence, which does not make a facile connection between faith and conflict. All sorts of factors come into play, and within religious traditions there exists a plethora of stances.[35] More specifically, a fuller appreciation of the influence of the Old Testament also needs to take a serious look at the role of the Old Testament within circles that self-consciously desire to avoid armed conflict—from the just-war tradition to pacifist circles.[36] Even more telling is that

---

34. The literature here is vast. Note, e.g., T. Raymond Hobbs, *A Time of War: A Study of Warfare in the Old Testament* (Wilmington, DE: Michael Glazer, 1989); K. Lawson Younger Jr., *Ancient Conquest Accounts: A Study in Ancient Near Eastern and Biblical History Writing* (JSOTSup 98; Sheffield: JSOT Press, 1990); Susan Niditch, *War in the Hebrew Bible: A Study in the Ethics of Violence* (New York: Oxford University Press, 1993); Richard S. Hess, "War in the Hebrew Bible: An Overview," in *War in the Bible and Terrorism in the Twenty-First Century* (ed. R. S. Hess and E. A. Martens; BBRSup 2; Winona Lake, IN: Eisenbrauns, 2008) 19–32; Michael G. Hasel, *Military Practice and Polemic: Israel's Laws of Warfare in Ancient Near Eastern Perspective* (Barrien Springs, MI: Andrews University Press, 2005); Brad E. Kelle and Frank Ritchel Ames, eds., *Writing and Reading War: Rhetoric, Gender, and Ethics in Biblical and Modern Contexts* (SBLSymS 42; Atlanta: Society of Biblical Literature, 2008); C. L. Crouch, *War and Ethics in the Ancient Near East: Military Violence in Light of Cosmology and History* (BZAW 407; Berlin: de Gruyter, 2009); cf. Charles Trimm, "Recent Research on Warfare in the Old Testament," *CBR* 10 (2012) 171–216.

35. R. Scott Appleby, *The Ambivalence of the Sacred: Religion, Violence, and Reconciliation* (Carnegie Commission on Preventing Deadly Conflict; Lanham: Rowman & Littlefield, 2000); cf. Admirand, *Amidst Mass Atrocity and the Rubble of Theology*.

36. Again the bibliography is extensive. E.g., see the essays (and their bibliographies) in R. S. Hess and E. A. Martens, ed., *War in the Bible and Terrorism in the Twenty-First Century* (BBRSup 2; Winona Lake, IN: Eisenbrauns, 2008). For more pacifist orientations to the Old Testament, in addition to what is mentioned in that source, note recently Patricia M. McDonald, *God and Violence: Biblical Resources for Living in a Small World* (Scottdale: Herald, 2004); David A. Leiter, *Neglected Voices: Peace in the Old Testament* (Scottdale: Herald, 2007); cf. Walter Brueggemann, *Peace* (UBT; St. Louis: Chalice, 2001). The discussions within the Christian tradition about God and war and violence has been enriched in the last few years by drawing on the theories and activities of both the just war and pacifist traditions to create a new paradigm. See Glen Stassen, ed., *Just Peacemaking: Ten Practices for Abolishing War* (Cleveland: Pilgrim, 1998).

experiences of horrific violence have led some individuals *to faith in the God of the Bible*, and not to the rejection envisioned by recent critics.[37] It will not do for critics of the Old Testament and its God to state boldly that the Old Testament necessarily generates violent attitudes and promotes injustice without considering carefully the many counter-narratives and the diverse theological and ecclesial constructs that do not point in this direction.

3. *Theological Foundations.* Discussions about the God of the Old Testament directly affect the field of Old Testament theology. Though the issue of violence, both human and divine, is of special concern in contemporary discussions (and in the Old Testament!), one is hard pressed to find substantive treatment of these matters in older theologies. This lacuna has begun to be filled in more recent works, such as those by Walter Brueggemann, Terence Fretheim, and Mark McEntire.[38] Another theological area affected by the debate—something recognized by all—is that of the meaning of biblical authority in light of these challenges. This issue was mentioned above in passing in relationship to Seibert and Sparks. Coincidentally, there has been a surge in interest in this topic in the last couple of decades because of matters such as those that concern this volume, as well as because of other recent trends such as changing sexual mores and the nascent field of the theological interpretation of Scripture and its coordination with critical studies. Scholars from across the theological spectrum, including within evangelical circles, are reconsidering the Bible's authority and reformulating how best to articulate its significance.[39]

A third theological issue concerns the relationship between the Old and New Testament. Authors such as Seibert and Sparks apply what they consider to be a Christological hermeneutic to the Old Testament to sort out

---

37. Appleby, *The Ambivalence of the Sacred*; Admirand, *Amidst Mass Atrocity and the Rubble of Theology*.

38. Walter Brueggemann, *Theology of the Old Testament* (Minneapolis: Fortress, 1997); Terence E. Fretheim, *God and World in the Old Testament: A Relational Theology of Creation* (Nashville: Abingdon, 2005); Mark McEntire, *Portraits of a Mature God: Choices in Old Testament Theology* (Minneapolis: Fortress, 2013).

39. For varied evangelical reflections on the Bible and its authority, see, e.g., John Goldingay, *Models for Scripture* (Grand Rapids: Eerdmans, 1994); Vincent Bacote et al., eds., *Evangelicals and Scripture: Tradition, Authority, and Hermeneutics* (Downers Grove, IL: InterVarsity, 2004); J. Merrick and Stephen M. Garrett, eds., *Five Views on Biblical Inerrancy* (Counterpoints; Grand Rapids: Zondervan, 2013). For broadly evangelical approaches to the theological interpretation of Scripture, note, e.g., John P. Burgess, *Why Scripture Matters: Reading the Bible in a Time of Church Conflict* (Louisville, KY: Westminster John Knox, 1998); Joel B. Green, *Practicing Theological Interpretation: Engaging Biblical Texts for Faith and Formation* (TECC; Grand Rapids: Baker Academic, 2012); Craig G. Bartholomew and David J. H. Beldman, eds., *Hearing the Old Testament: Listening for God's Address* (Grand Rapids: Eerdmans, 2012); Andrew G. Shead, *A Mouth Full of Fire: The Word of God in Jeremiah* (NSBT 29; Carlisle: Apollos and Downers Grove, IL: InterVarsity, 2012). On the issue of the violence of God and Joshua, note the respectful and constructive exchange between D. S. Earl and C. J. H. Wright in Earl, *The Joshua Delusion*, 139-56.

the acceptable from the questionable and unacceptable. The formulations of what this relationship looks like and its import for this topic will differ.[40]

4. *Textual Readings.* Because Old Testament books and individual passages play a central role in discussions about God, the treatment of the issues pertaining to Yahweh and violence require the reading and interpretation of specific biblical texts. Methodological issues come into play, such as the form of the text to be analyzed (the canonical shape or some sort of prior stage of redaction), the situation and stance of the reader, and the use of approaches that are, to the best of the exegete's judgment, appropriate to these texts' literary genre, particular literary features, context, and apparent purpose. Passages cannot all be taken in the same way, and reading strategies and explanations will differ, but having the textual data in hand at least allows for getting at these theological and ethical discussions on more solid ground. The resulting proposals based on these reading will move in differing directions, from more synchronic or canonical proposals to others that will seek some sort of historical development paradigm or that will understand certain passages more symbolically or ideologically than a straightforward method might yield.

5. *Virtuous Sensitivity.* The treatment of issues revolving around the violence of God must be thoughtful and respectful before the real suffering that raises such questions. Cruelty has marked human existence, and the literature of the world (whether religious or secular) since time immemorial has voiced the cries of the hurting. This cannot be a glib discussion, characterized by emotional aloofness or indifference. This is a painful topic at many levels and merits serious and compassionate engagement. Film and publications remind us of the unspeakable horrors of all the kinds of violence that permeate human existence.[41]

A second area of necessity in reading concerns the reading virtues. These are those that the Christian faith ideally seeks to inculcate for the character building that can be the fruit of the act of reading. At a time when critics of the Old Testament and its God claim that they engender cruelty and imperial callousness, others argue that the biblical text can work to create attentive, obedient, and peaceful readers. Again, what that looks like and what texts are suitable for such an enterprise will yield disagreement, but the goal should not only be to intellectually comprehend passages and their potential theological and ethical implications; what we seek are a different kind of people who will not perpetuate the very things all deplore.[42]

---

40. Note, e.g., Cowles et al., *Show Them No Mercy*; cf. p.6 nn. 26–27.

41. War, of course, is a major category of violence, but there are many more. Recent eyewitness sources that describe the sobering cruelty and dehumanization of war include, e.g., Chris Hedges, *War Is a Force That Gives Us Meaning* (New York: Anchor, 2002); Sebastian Junger, *War* (New York: Twelve, 2010); Benjamin John Peters, *Through All the Plain* (Eugene, OR: Cascade, 2014).

42. See esp. Richard S. Briggs, *The Virtuous Reader: Old Testament Narrative and Interpretive Virtue* (STI; Grand Rapids: Baker Academic, 2010); cf. Alan Jacobs, *A Theology of*

The Purpose of This Volume

The essays that follow concentrate on the fourth topic, the study of specific texts. Nevertheless, the other four fields of research occasionally surface or lie in the background. All of the chapters presuppose a high view of the authority of the Old Testament commensurate with thoughtful, generally conservative, generous evangelical scholarship.[43] This collection is motivated at least in part by the desire to offer an alternative voice to those who currently, in one way or another, diminish the theological and ethical value of the Old Testament and question its presentation of God. It offers studies on books from the spectrum of genres across the canon as samples of the extensive work that needs to be done to grapple substantively with such a difficult set of issues. These are only initial forays into a difficult subject. Views on aspects of the violence connected to God may differ to some degree across these essays, but a core commitment to the Old Testament as Scripture underpins them all.

Fundamentally, this volume is designed to function as a conversation starter. Readers may disagree with the some of the textual expositions or the theological reflections, but we hope that they might stimulate future interchanges among those of diverse opinions in regard to the violence of Yahweh and encourage close attention to the biblical text as the place for which to launch such dialogue.

To begin with, Paul Kissling offers an examination of the *Aqedah*, or the "near-sacrifice" of Isaac, in Genesis 22. He starts by drawing attention to literary elements such as narrative flow, repetition, wordplay, and the presence and absence of speech. These elements serve to focus attention on important elements within the story such as the test itself, Abraham's responsiveness, and God's oversight. Kissling then surveys pertinent material from the wider pentateuchal and canonical contexts, as well as modern, contemporary, and Jewish interpretations, some of which reveal the inadequacy of some of today's critiques of the passage. Kissling concludes by advocating an empathetic reading of the narrative, one that ultimately looks to the New Testament story of God the Father offering his own son as a sacrifice.

In chapter three, Hélène Dallaire examines the conquest account in the book of Joshua. She surveys ways the book has been interpreted across the centuries and atrocities it has been used to support. After refuting scholars

---

Reading: The Hermeneutics of Love (Boulder, CO: Westview, 2001). From a different perspective, Kevin J. Vanhoozer, *Is There a Meaning in This Text? The Bible, the Reader, and the Morality of Literary Knowledge* (Grand Rapids: Zondervan, 1998) 376–81, *passim*. Insightful secular voices in this vein include various works by Martha C. Nussbaum and Robert Coles.

43. It is difficult to assign adequate descriptors to the positions of the contributors, but these labels reflect the approach and tone of the essays. In addition to the sources listed in n. 42, also note the eight volumes of the Scripture and Hermeneutics Series (Grand Rapids: Zondervan, 2000–2007), which were spearheaded by Craig Bartholomew.

who minimize the theological problem of the conquest by categorizing it as an account created to buttress the reign of Josiah in the seventh century B.C.E., Dallaire locates the ideology and language of the conquest within ancient Near Eastern conceptions of divine participation in war. Proper appreciation of this cultural setting, she argues, reveals that the Israelites were not a barbaric horde following orders of a bloodthirsty God.

In the fourth chapter Daniel Block examines divine violence in the book of Deuteronomy. He highlights the forms and targets of both direct and indirect divine violence before systematically examining the motivations of this violence in response to both moral and religious conduct. Repeatedly, the issue is the holiness of the people of Israel before their holy God, though this election of Israel is an act of God's grace in the world. The election of Israel initiates Block's examination of the *ḥērem*, where he discusses several considerations when reading *ḥērem* texts today. Ultimately, while the key issue is the righteousness of God and the need for a holy alternative in the world, Block concludes by advocating consideration of the grace of God alongside texts of violence.

Addressing a portion of Scripture frequently absent from this discussion, David Firth turns our attention to the Psalms in chapter five. While noting that there are different types of violence in the Psalms, Firth concentrates on the imprecatory psalms. He provides a hermeneutic for approaching these psalms rather than attempting to address them all. Psalms must be read as Christian Scripture (though not exclusively), and each psalm must be read as part of the entire canonical Psalter. Together, these guidelines prompt the interpreter to recognize the belief that Yahweh's justice would prevail. The imprecatory psalms demonstrate an act of surrender on the part of the psalmist to the wisdom of God.

In chapter six, Heath Thomas examines the unique contribution of the book of Lamentations. He explores how God's people, Israel then and the modern church today, can react to the violence of God. Here, readers will find a template for the language and expressions of pain and grief. Those in the midst of suffering are encouraged to confess, but also to complain. At times the appropriate response to pain at the hands of God is penitential prayer. This repentance can bring about a reversal of judgment, but confession does not (always) alleviate pain. In these instances, Lamentations models prayers wherein the people of God pray against God himself.

In the seventh chapter, M. Daniel Carroll R. looks at divine violence in the book of Amos. He stresses that an awareness of historical and cultural context identifies the language of the book as hyperbolic and stereotypical. Importantly, God's violence is not arbitrary. It is a measured response to human violence. Carroll offers a helpful corrective to the popular trend of dichotomizing God's judgment and his mercy. These two need to be held in close approximation, and in Amos (and throughout the Old Testament) we see God himself tormented over the judgment that he sends. Finally, judgment has as its goal the salvation and restoration of all of creation.

In this volume's last essay, Elmer Martens looks at the character of God and his violence in the book of Jeremiah. He begins by framing God's judgment in terms of covenant, stressing that God's violence is not capricious. He challenges negative views of God, suggesting instead that God is ultimately good. He is disposed to love, seeks intimacy, and is compassionate toward his people. The conciliatory messages of the prophet Jeremiah move from depicting Yahweh as violent toward the new reality to which Jeremiah looks forward: the time when violence is no more. It is this picture of Yahweh that Jesus embodies and toward this end that modern believers should strive.

In conclusion, it is clear that readers throughout history have wrestled with the issue of divine violence in the Old Testament. It is unlikely that a solution that satisfies all interested parties will ever be found, and believers and nonbelievers will continue to debate this issue. The contributors to this volume do not minimize the difficult challenges to faith and the Bible, and indeed there may be shades of difference in the stances of some of the authors. The overriding concern, grounded in a solid commitment to the Old Testament as Christian Scripture, is that the engagement with specific texts in *Wrestling with the Violence of God* might be a constructive voice in this ongoing discussion that has garnered such particular resonance.

Chapter 2

The Near-Sacrifice of Isaac: Monstrous Morality or Richly Textured Theology?

PAUL J. KISSLING

Introduction

Regarding Gen 22:1–19, the narrative of the near-sacrifice of Isaac or, in Jewish tradition "the binding of Isaac" (*Aqedah*),[1] Eric Siebert in his often cited *Disturbing Divine Behavior* asks: "What kind of God asks a faithful follower to kill his own child?"[2] Similarly, Gunn and Fewell state:

> We are not told what God wanted or expected to find in Abraham's performance. Most readings assume that what Abraham did meet with God's approval. Abraham, on account of his radical obedience, becomes an exemplary character. Such a reading, on the other hand, leaves the character of God in a rather sticky situation. At the very best one might assert that God is simply unfathomable; at the worst, God is deranged and sadistic.[3]

Siebert concludes, "Thus, while this text can be regarded as one that encourages total devotion to God, it has a shadow side." Even more trenchantly, he adds:

> God is portrayed as acting in an emotionally abusive way toward both Abraham and Isaac—toward Abraham for having to contemplate and almost carry out this diabolical deed and toward Isaac for having to experience the trauma of being tied to an altar while his dad prepares to kill him.[4]

While the evangelical Christian interpreter of Scripture certainly can empathize with these readings, and who of us has not had similar thoughts, I would contend that ultimately readings of this sort come from failing to

---

1. The term *Aqedah* derives from the verb *'āqad*, "bind," which appears in the Old Testament only in Gen 22:9.
2. Eric A. Siebert, *Disturbing Divine Behavior: Troubling Old Testament Images of God* (Minneapolis: Fortress, 2009) 27.
3. David M. Gunn and Danna Nolan Fewell, *Narrative in the Hebrew Bible* (OBS; Oxford: Oxford University Press, 1993) 98.
4. Siebert, *Disturbing Divine Behavior*, 27.

read Scripture *empathetically* and, perhaps more significantly, from reading in a fundamentally decontextualized way. Surprisingly, ancient Jewish interpretation, up to and including the time of the New Testament documents, no matter how fanciful and speculative it may appear in some ways, actually does a better job of reading this rich but challenging text empathetically and within its historical, textual, and canonical contexts. In this chapter, we will first look at the text itself in the Hebrew for clues to its interpretation and then situate it in its literary context in the Pentateuch, the rest of the Old Testament, and in the early history of its interpretation in Jewish sources both outside and within the New Testament. Based on the insights gained, we will address the more recent interpretation of this text since the time of Kant.

Insights from a Close Reading of the Hebrew Text

Gen 22:1–19 is near the end of the Abraham narrative (Gen 11:27–25:11) and is in many ways its high point, both in terms of its narrative tension and in terms of its significance for understanding the primary message of that narrative. Near the beginning of the narrative, Yahweh tells Abram to "go" (*lek-lĕkā*) from his father's house (Gen 12:1). This exact phrase only appears elsewhere in the entire Hebrew Bible in Gen 22:2, where God told Abraham to go (*lek-lĕkā*) to the land of Moriah. These two texts thus form a bracket around the Abraham narrative, which invites the reader to read them together. This structure suggests a tension between the promise to make of Abraham's descendants a great nation and the command to offer up as a burnt offering the son, who will be the only approved heir and the one who will produce that great nation. In between these verses, we see Abraham struggle to try to facilitate the achievement of the promise of a great nation descended through him by means of his own strategies. Each of the strategies is focused on a potential male descendent, and each strategy fails to produce an heir of whom God approves. Lot, Eliezar, and Ishmael each fall by the wayside. Isaac, the only child of Abraham and Sarah, is to be the promised child, who will be the means of God fulfilling his promise.

The Order of the Telling

The potential horror of the text for the ancient reader is not the command to offer a child in sacrifice to a god, but the fact that this particular child is the only available and divinely approved means of God's fulfilling the promise. The narrator, however, precludes this sense of horror by starting his narrative with the declaration that "God tested Abraham."[5] By placing this comment first, the reader knows that this is only a test and that Isaac is not to be sacrificed, or at least that he will not in the end be dead. The reader is privy to this information, while the character within the narrative, Abraham, is not. Thus, the test has a poignant reality for him, which

---

5. All translations are mine unless otherwise specified.

it does not have for the reader. Of course, the reader already knows that Abraham had not killed Isaac, because the entire nation traces its lineage through Isaac. Without Isaac, there would have been no such readers, no nation descended from Abraham through Isaac to read the narrative, and no story to tell through the narrative.

Another instance of the importance of close attention to the order in which things are narrated is in the description of the preparations for the sacrifice. The customary order for a burnt offering would be to kill the animal before placing it on the wood (Lev 1:3–13). In the *Aqedah*, Isaac is bound and placed on the altar fully alive. Whether this is an example of Abraham stalling, hoping for a divine intervention, or for some other reason, the canonical reader knows that this is as abnormal as was the original command to sacrifice Isaac as a burnt offering.

Narrative Naming

Adele Berlin's classic analysis of the importance of careful attention to the way the Hebrew narrative refers to characters is especially pertinent in analyzing the *Aqedah*.[6] God refers to Isaac as "your son, your one and only, whom you love, Isaac" (Gen 22:2). This slows the narrative down to focus attention on the magnitude of the commandment that Abraham receives. The repetition of part of this formula in v. 12 in the angel's speech ties the narrative together, ending as it began. The son, whose name means "he will laugh" is at first a sign of the surprising joy of a child given by God's direct action without any human means of attaining it, has now become something of a divine joke. At a literal level, Isaac is not Abraham's only son, and he is not the only son whom Abraham loved. The Septuagint has captured this insight by translating the Hebrew *yĕḥîd* ("only") with *agapētós*, the same Greek word for "beloved" in the New Testament's description of God's speech at Jesus' baptism (Matt 3:17; Luke 3:22). Another example of narrative naming is the unnecessary repetition of "his son" or "your son" or "my son" to describe Isaac in the narrator's voice (vv. 2, 6, 9, 10, 13), God's voice (vv. 2, 12), and Abraham's voice (vv. 7, 8) as well as the narrator's and Isaac's use of "father" to refer to Abraham (v. 8). These words emphasize the close personal relationship between Abraham and Isaac.

Repetition

Repetition with variation appears in Abraham's response to the speech of others.

v. 1: "God . . . said to Abraham; and he said, 'Behold, here I am.'"
v. 7: "Isaac . . . said, 'My father'; and he said, 'Behold, here I am.'"
v. 11: "The angel . . . said, 'Abraham, Abraham': and he said, 'Behold, here I am.'"

---

6. Adele Berlin, *Poetics and the Interpretation of Biblical Narrative* (Sheffield: Sheffield Academic Press, 1983) 59–61.

Abraham is as attentive to his son's voice as he is to God's voice. The repetition of the name *Abraham* in the second divine speech shows the urgency of the situation. The fact that Abraham responds in exactly the same way to the divine voice at the beginning and at the climax of the narrative shows that he is ever willing to be responsive to the divine voice.

Word Play

The Hebrew verbs *yārē'* ("he was afraid") and *rā'â* ("he saw") and their cognates, especially in the imperfect, are homophonous and look quite similar in an unpointed text. Thus, for the Hebrew reader, Moriah (v. 2), Abraham's "seeing" the place from afar (v. 4), God will "see" to the sacrifice (v. 8), the angel's newly acquired knowledge that Abraham "fears" God (v. 12), Abraham "seeing" a ram caught in the thicket (v. 13), the name *Yireh*, which Abraham gave to the mountain (v. 14), and the narrator's statement about it being "seen" in the mountain of Yahweh (v. 14) are all interconnected by the wordplay between *yārē'*, *rā'â*, and cognate words.

There is another word play between the Hebrew words for one and only (*yĕḥîd*, vv. 2, 12) and for "together" (*yaḥdāv*, vv. 6, 8, 19). The fact that Isaac apparently does not return from Moriah with Abraham as earlier promised and that "together" in v. 19 refers to Abraham and his two young men without Isaac is probably significant, or at least the earliest interpreters thought so, as they attempted in various ways to explain Isaac's absence.[7]

The Presence and Absence of Speech

This narrative speaks volumes by not having the characters within it say very much, if anything at all. Both the exact words that the narrator puts in the mouths of characters and the characters' silence when saying something might be expected are important clues to the point of view of the narrator, especially in minimalist narratives such as those found in the Hebrew Bible. At two particular points in this narrative, characters say nothing when words might be expected. While Abraham responds to God's speech in v. 1 with "Here I am," when he is told what he is to do, he quite significantly says nothing (v. 2). Instead, he rises early in the morning to obey the divine command (v. 3). Here, there is no attempt to negotiate with God, no appeal to divine justice, no questioning of God. This is in stark contrast to the extended negotiation over the possibility of finding 50 or maybe only 10 righteous people in Sodom in Gen 18. Here, an innocent victim is about to be slaughtered in a sacrifice, but Abraham does not even attempt to negotiate with God. Given Abraham's intercession in that earlier chapter, this absence is exceptional. While the text does not answer the question, this absence certainly invites the reader to question why Abraham does not intercede on behalf of his son.

---

7. For instance, see *Genesis Rabbah* 55–56, discussed below.

A second time when speech is absent is at the time of the actual attempted sacrifice. Isaac had, quite understandably, questioned Abraham about the lamb on the way to Mt. Moriah. Abraham's enigmatic response evidently is accepted by Isaac, who never speaks again. What is noteworthy, however, is that when Abraham, having built the altar and laid the wood in order, bound Isaac and laid him on the wood, Isaac says nothing. What is sometimes missed in interpretations, which assume that Isaac is a young child, is that he was old enough to understand the need for a lamb for a burnt offering and yet makes no comment and offers no resistance when he is bound like a sacrificial animal and laid on the wood. If he is old enough to ask the initial question, he is old enough to at least question what exactly is about to happen. Isaac may not be as young as is sometimes assumed.

Insights from the Wider Pentateuchal Context

Within pentateuchal law the firstborn of every womb, including the human womb, belongs to God. Exodus 13:12b–15 relates this to the plague of the firstborn in Egypt. Firstborn humans are explicitly exempted from being offered as sacrifices by the payment of a monetary redemption price of five shekels. Within the pentateuchal narrative, the presumption prior to the golden calf episode (Exod 32) is that the firstborn son of each family would be offered to God in service as priests. The tribe of Levi, after their actions in defense of Yahweh's honor following the building of the golden calf, replaces the firstborn sons as priests. The difference in number between the adult male Levites and the number of firstborn sons throughout the families of Israel is compensated for in legal terms by a redemption through money (Num 3). The connection between the *Aqedah* narrative and the redemption of the firstborn within the canonical form of the Pentateuch is made by referring to Israel as God's firstborn son in Exod 4:22, 23 and by the blowing of the ram's horn at the Passover.[8] For the ancient reader, it is only to be expected that the firstborn is God's. Abraham, who anticipates the law in several ways, is, for the ancient reader of the Pentateuch, preparing the way for the later revelation of the Passover.[9]

---

8. In Jubilees, the date of the *Aqedah* is subtly related to the date of the Passover. Jon Levenson comments: "Prince Mastema renders his charge against Abraham on the twelfth day of the first month of the year. If we remember that it takes Abraham's party three days to arrive at the site of the sacrifice, we can reasonably infer that they did so toward the end of the fourteenth of the month. The late afternoon of the fourteenth of the first month is exactly the time when the Torah specifies that the Passover sacrifice must be offered" (*Inheriting Abraham: The Legacy of the Patriarch in Judaism, Christianity, and Islam* [Princeton: Princeton University Press, 2012] 92).

9. Levenson shows how the blowing of the ram's horn, at first related to the Passover and later shifted to Rosh Hashanah, becomes the basis for future acts of blessing and forgiveness of the Jewish people. He quotes b. Rosh Hashanah 16a: "Rabbi Abbahu said: Why do we blow the horn of a ram? The Holy One, blessed be He, said: 'Blow the horn

Insights from the Wider Old Testament Canonical Context

The Location of the Sacrifice

Playing on the wordplay in the *Aqedah* and its implicit message, 2 Chr 3:1 informs us that Solomon built the temple on Mount Moriah, the only other mention of Moriah in the canon. The near sacrifice of Isaac and Abraham's and Isaac's willingness to obey the divine command lead to the regular substituting of human sacrifice with the sacrifices of the temple. Just as God "saw to" the sacrifice in Gen 22, the location of the temple on Mount Moriah suggests his ongoing provision of a means and place of sacrifice.

Later Jewish sources also made the connection between Isaac's near sacrifice and the later temple sacrifices. The Mishnah (*Taanit* 2:5; *Tamid* 4:1; circa 200 C.E.) and the *Book of Biblical Antiquities*, also known as Pseudo-Philo (32:2–3; dated between the revolts of 70 and 135 C.E.), both note the way that the daily offering (the *Tamid*) was tied up foreleg to hind leg, which began to be referred to as *Aqedah* (binding).[10]

Insights from the Social and Historical Background

The intensity of the shock that contemporary readers experience with this text is partly due to the post-Enlightenment idealization of childhood and the historical distance between our contemporary world and the ancient world. While the literal sacrifice of children, particularly the firstborn son, was not common in the ancient world, it did happen. So, it would not have been surprising to ancient readers that a god would have commanded someone in the time of Abraham to make such a sacrifice and that he might obey that command.

But Gen 22, in its canonical form—and it is only in its canonical form that it is the object of later interpretation—is always to be read as part of the Pentateuch and is to be understood as such. The command that God gave Abraham is in direct violation of levitical and deuteronomic laws that strictly prohibit child sacrifice (Lev 18:21; 20:1–5; Deut 12:31; 18:10). The reader of Genesis knows this.

In an ancient Near Eastern context it is not shocking that someone would sacrifice a child to a deity; the practice was well known throughout many cultures. What is shocking for the original audience is that Abraham, the ancestor who first received the promises of Yahweh and founded the chosen nation, would act in violation of the laws which were later revealed to that very same nation. Even more shocking would be the fact that Is-

---

of a ram before Me so that I may remember for your benefit the Binding of Isaac, and I will account it to you as if you had bound yourselves before Me'" (ibid., 99).

10. Paul M. Flesher and Bruce Chilton, *The Targums: A Critical Introduction* (Waco, TX: Baylor University Press, 2011) 448.

rael's God, who would later strictly forbid child sacrifice, should demand it of Abraham in this text. The narrator defuses that reaction before it has a chance to manifest itself by alerting the reader at the beginning of the story with the comment, "God tested Abraham." Contemporary readers who are shocked by the ancient practice of child sacrifice, deeply affected by a relatively recent cultural idealization of children, and appalled by the idea that God would command such a thing are something like the person who turns on the television immediately after the warning, "this is a test of the emergency broadcasting system, this is only a test," and hearing only the blaring sound thinks that a real life-threatening emergency is occurring. The ancient reader knows that God has no intention of allowing Abraham to sacrifice Isaac. If he had so intended, there would be no nation descended from Isaac and no Torah in which to read about it. The tension for the original audience is not over whether the sacrifice will occur. They know it will not occur. The tension is not over whether a deity has the right to request such a thing from a human being. It was a common judgment that deities could quite reasonably make such demands. As Christopher Hays writes, "Efforts to show that the Bible does not portray actual child sacrifice in the Molek cult, but rather dedication to the god by fire, have been convincingly disproved. Child sacrifice is well attested in the ancient world, especially in time of crisis."[11]

That child sacrifice was pervasive and lasting and would have been part of the readers' cultural understanding throughout the early interpretation of this text also has been convincingly argued by Chilton in his recent book *Abraham's Curse*:

> The evidence of Carthaginian child sacrifice provides a case in point. During the first century B.C.E., Diodorus Siculus reported on the ancient practice at Carthage, revived during time of war, to offer children to the local god (History 20.14.6): "A bronze statue of Cronos among them extended its hands, palms up and inclining toward the earth, so that the children set on it rolled down and fell into a chasm filled with fire." According to Diodorus's account, two hundred children were selected for this treatment, and another hundred were volunteered for the rite. Here there can be no doubt but that child sacrifice was practiced ritually, and Diodorus refers to human sacrifice among Egyptians (1.88.5), Celts (5.31.3–4; 5.32.6; 31.13.1), and Messenian Greeks (8.8.2) as well.[12]

The tension in Gen 22 for ancient readers is not over whether a deity has the right to demand the death of a child; it is over whether Abraham is willing to obey and whether he will thus pass the test. That test demands of Abraham what any god might demand of his followers.

---

11. Christopher B. Hays, *Death in the Iron Age II and in First Isaiah* (FAT 79; Tübingen: Mohr Siebeck, 2011) 181.

12. Bruce Chilton, *Abraham's Curse: The Roots of Violence in Judaism, Christianity, and Islam* (New York: Doubleday, 2008) 39–40.

Insights from the Early History of Interpretation

The early post-Hebrew Bible interpretation of the *Aqedah* is full and rich and comes from both non-Christian Jewish and Christian Jewish sources. These two traditions of interpretation are intertwined, as Levenson notes:

> The parallels between the two traditions as they have interpreted this central text are so striking that to speak of the Aqedah in late Second Temple and rabbinic Judaism (that is, Judaism between about 200 B.C.E. and 500 C.E.) without reference to the parallel interpretations in early Christianity, or vice versa, is myopic and misleading.[13]

But it is not only that the traditions are intertwined; they are impressively perceptive in noticing details in the text and founding their interpretive speculations on those details.

The Age of Isaac

One of the great questions in the history of the interpretation of this text is the age of Isaac and thus whether and/or the degree to which he cooperated in his own near sacrifice. Modern translations do a disservice by using language that implies that Isaac is quite young, precluding the possibility that he is a mature, albeit young, man. JPSV, NRSV, ESV, and NIV all have "boy," while NASB, TLB, and RSV all have "lad." Many contemporary readings are based on these loose translations. Siebert refers to Isaac as a "child" and to Abraham as Isaac's "dad."[14]

Particularly instructive in this regard is Gen 22:5, where the "young men" or "servants" are described with the same Hebrew word (*naʿar*) used to refer to Isaac. The term has a broad semantic range in terms of age.[15] Only rarely is it used of young children, unless it is further qualified with a modifier such as "little." It is used in Genesis of the young men who defeated the kings who had taken Lot hostage (14:24), of Ishmael who is older than 13 (21:12, 17–20), of Shechem who raped Dinah (34:19), of Joseph at 17 and older (37:2; 41:12), of Benjamin when he visits Joseph in Egypt (43:8; 44:22, 30–34), and of Ephraim and Manasseh when Joseph takes them to the dying Jacob for a blessing (48:16). Both *Targum Onkelos* and *Targum Pseudo-Jonathan*[16] preserve the link between the age of the young men who accompanied Abraham and the young man Isaac, by using the same Aramaic word for both. *Targum*

---

13. Levenson, *Inheriting Abraham*, 66.
14. Siebert, *Disturbing Divine Behavior*, 27.
15. Victor Hamilton, *"naʿar," NIDOTTE* 3:124–27.
16. When we come to Jewish sources after 100 C.E., we face the dilemma of dating. While *Targum Onkelos* is dated to circa 130 C.E., the other Targumim and especially the Mishnah, Midrashim, Talmudim, and other sources are later and cannot as safely be used directly to illuminate the New Testament. And yet these sources are of value, not because they might have been read or otherwise known by the New Testament authors but because they illuminate how ancient texts from the Hebrew Bible were understood and appropriated by believers attached to the Jewish people and their Scriptures.

Neofiti, however, employs different terms. The servants are referred to as "boys" and Isaac as a "young man."¹⁷

Since Isaac is a *naʿar*, just as the servants who initially accompany Abraham and Isaac on their journey are *nĕʿārîm*, the early history of interpretation fills in the gap by speculating that Isaac, while youngish, is certainly a mature man in our terms and therefore no innocent victim, who mindlessly and passively goes along with whatever his abusive father intends to do to him.¹⁸

For Philo, Abraham was a priest with Isaac his sacrificial victim.¹⁹ This victim he described as "God's son," but as old enough to offer himself willingly, not even needing to be bound by his father.²⁰ It is not surprising, given Philo's influence on the early church, that Christian art often depicts Isaac as laying unbound on the altar.²¹

For Josephus, Isaac is 25 years old, the same age as his soldiers who, rather than give in to the Romans willingly, commit mass suicide, killing each other to avoid capture.²² Josephus, their fearless leader, who was to be the last to die, avoids suicide by claiming to have received a sudden revelation that power was passing from the Jews to Rome by divine will.²³ For Josephus at that moment at Jotapata in Galilee "drawing lots, each offered his naked throat to a brother-in-arms turned executioner. Once the executioner had struck, he in turn offered his own neck to another colleague."²⁴ Isaac has by this time, in this stream of Judaism, been transformed into a warrior-martyr who rushes to his sacrifice, both willingly and knowledgeably.²⁵ The mass suicide at Masada is explained in similar terms by Josephus.²⁶ The Maccabean martyrs had at least a victory over the Greeks as a prize for their martyrdom. Under the Romans, only divine approval and bodily resurrection was on offer.

In 4 Maccabees (c. 100 C.E.) Isaac is old enough to die as a young martyr, facing torture with astounding courage. Note especially the scriptural reference in the description of Eleazar as the fire was consuming him:

---

17. See the Comprehensive Aramaic Lexicon on *Targum Neofiti* on Gen 22:5 (On-line: http://cal1.cn.huc.edu). This lexical difference is noticed by Martin McNamara, *Targum Neofiti 1: Genesis* (Aramaic Bible 1A; Collegeville, MN: Liturgical Press, 1992), 117. Nevertheless, Flesher and Chilton translate the reference to Isaac as "young boy" in their rendering of this verse in *Targum Neofiti* (*The Targums*, 457).

18. I think Levenson, who misses this clue, exaggerates when he asserts, "Genesis 22 gives scant indication of his age" (*Inheriting Abraham*, 74).

19. Philo, *Abraham* 176, 197–98.

20. Philo, *Dreams* 1.173.

21. Flesher and Chilton, *The Targums*, 446.

22. Josephus, *A.J.* 1.227.

23. Ibid., 3.141–408.

24. Flesher and Chilton, *The Targums*, 446.

25. Josephus, *A.J.* 1.232.

26. Josephus *J.W.* 7.320–401.

> Most amazing, indeed, though he was an old man, his body no longer tense and firm, his muscles flabby, his sinews feeble, he became young again in spirit through reason; and by reason like that of Isaac he rendered the many-headed rack ineffective. O man of blessed age and of venerable gray hair and of law-abiding life, whom the faithful seal of death has perfected! (4 Macc 7:13–15)

Similarly, in 4 Macc 16:16–20, the mother of the soon-to-be martyrs exhorts her sons:

> Sons, noble is the contest to which you are called to bear witness for the nation. Fight zealously for our ancestral law. For it would be shameful if, while an aged man endures such agonies for the sake of religion, you young men were to be terrified by tortures. Remember that it is through God that you have had a share in the world and have enjoyed life, and therefore you ought to endure any suffering for the sake of God. For his sake also our father Abraham was zealous to sacrifice his son Isaac, the ancestor of our nation; and when Isaac saw his father's hand wielding a knife and descending upon him, he did not cower.

These words assume that the mother who speaks them, and presumably the author who records them, thought that Isaac was a fully mature, if young, man, able to overcome any fear and willingly yield himself to his father's knife. As the narrator in his own voice puts it, "Sympathy for her children did not sway the mother of the young men; she was of the same mind as Abraham."[27]

As the Jewish tradition develops and responds to the rise of Christian faith and the loss of the temple and the land of Palestine, there is further reflection on Isaac as an adult. Flesher and Chilton assert:

> the meaning of Genesis 22 undergoes a significant transformation from the time of the Maccabees in the second century BCE to the late rabbinic period about 600 CE, from a story about a young passive Isaac being sacrificed by Abraham to one in which Isaac becomes a willing, adult participant in his own slaughter. As part of a developing understanding of the role of martyrdom in early Judaism, in some accounts Isaac even appears to die and to be restored to life.[28]

But here Flesher and Chilton assume that Isaac in the original *Aqedah* was young and passive. As noted above, however, there is a clue in the Hebrew text that *Targum Onkelos* noticed but Flesher and Chilton missed. The alleged passivity of Isaac is an argument from silence. The developing understanding in later Jewish sources to which they refer, however, is germane. In *Genesis Rabbah* 55–56 (circa 600 C.E.), Isaac is now 37 and no longer a zealous martyr, but approaches his death in mournful humility. Tears fall from his eyes and he asks for Abraham to bind him fast, so that he will not struggle

---

27. 4 Macc. 14:20.
28. Flesher and Chilton, *The Targums*, 440–41.

and blemish his body before the sacrifice.[29] The number 37 seems to allude to the age of Isaac at the death of Sarah, the next event recorded in Genesis (Gen 23). The testing arose out of a dispute between Isaac and Ishmael, where the latter brags that his circumcision was superior because he was 13 and willingly accepted it, whereas Isaac's circumcision at eight days of age made it impossible for him to choose to be a part of the covenant. Isaac's willing submission to Abraham's knife in Gen 22 beats Ishmael at his own game of boasting. By the time of *Genesis Rabbah*, Isaac has, in some ways, surpassed Abraham as the real hero in the story.

Who Really Was Behind the Test?

With the development of and heightened interest in the doctrine of Satan, demons, and angels more generally, which we see among Jewish people beginning around 200 B.C.E., the question of ultimate and intermediate causes of evil things becomes a focal point for intense speculation. In the case of the *Aqedah*, this resulted in questioning whether God could be the immediate cause of a test, which called on Abraham to violate the law that God gave to Israel. In Jub 17:16–18, Abraham, not Isaac, is the focus of the story. The gap that Jubilees fills in is to explain how God could test Abraham to do such a thing. Like the righteous Job, Abraham is tested by Satan (Mastemah), who argues that Abraham loves his son more than God. It is Satan, not God, therefore, who initiates the test.

Jubilees may well be following the lead of the author of Chronicles, who reinterprets his source text in 2 Samuel. In 2 Sam 24:1, Yahweh, angry with Israel, commands David to number Israel and then hands downs judgment on the nation when David obeys. Referring to this incident, in 1 Chr 21:1 we read, "Then Satan stood up against Israel and provoked David to number Israel." The author of Chronicles may be explaining the intermediate cause, Satan, for David's taking the census, rather than the ultimate cause, Yahweh. In the same way, Jubilees, by introducing Satan into the *Aqedah*, may be attempting to explain the intermediate rather than the immediate cause.

Is Isaac a Martyr?

As noted above, Flesher and Chilton have documented a development in Jewish thinking about the *Aqedah* in which Isaac develops into a martyr. This begins in the second century B.C.E. in the books of 1 and 2 Maccabees. These early Maccabean works use the *Aqedah* as the foundation for a call to literal martyrdom, when faced with the alternatives of compromising faithfulness to the Torah and death at the hands of the Seleucid overlords.

In 1 Macc 2:52, the emphasis is on Abraham giving up his son to death at God's command as analogous to the way Mattathias encourages his sons to give themselves up to potential death. Just as Abraham was found faithful

---

29. Here *Genesis Rabbah* is dependent on the tradition found in the *Fragmentary Targum*. See Flesher and Chilton, *The Targums*, 460.

by passing the test and was considered righteous,[30] so his sons must zealously fight against anyone who would try to force them to disobey the Torah, even if it meant death. This counsel to martyrdom is developed even further in 2 Macc 6 and 7. According to 2 Macc 6:10, two women in Jerusalem who had circumcised their sons in defiance of the Seleucid's law, with their infant sons hanging from their breasts, were dragged around the city and thrown down from the city wall. In 2 Macc 7, a woman with seven adult sons encourages them all to martyrdom in the most sordid fashion rather than capitulate to disobeying the Torah in even the smallest of ways.

The Absence of Isaac

One of the text's great gaps is the failure to explain why it is that Abraham does not return to his young men with Isaac after the near sacrifice as he had promised. Traditional source criticism of the Pentateuch accounts for the failure of Isaac to return by suggesting that in the source underlying this part of the narrative (E) Isaac was in fact sacrificed and not substituted for with a ram.[31] The J additions are found in the angelic speech(es) and in the narrative, which recounts the provision of the ram that replaces Isaac. Interestingly, while the grounds for this reasoning are very different, some early Jewish sources suggest that Isaac was in fact sacrificed and, while still dead, went to study in Shem's heavenly academy. He is then later resurrected. Chilton explains:

> During the time he was dead, having died at his father's hand, it is said that Isaac studied in a heavenly academy, run by a supernatural figure named Shem (Noah's son), who is identified with Melchizedek, the mysterious figure who once gave Abraham a priestly blessing (Genesis 14:18–20). Isaac then returned to normal life when God raised him from the dead. Now the point of his age comes into clear focus, because he is of sufficient maturity to teach the wisdom that he learned in the heavenly academy.[32]

Summary

While many of the ways that ancient interpretation filled in the gaps of the *Aqedah* may strike us as fanciful and perhaps even silly at times, we also see genuine insight and plausible ways of relating the theology of the biblical text to other biblical themes and to the contemporary concerns of the Jewish people living in the shadow of great empires who were sometimes quite hostile to them. We also see that the New Testament's interpretation of the *Aqedah*, where God the father offers up his beloved son as a sin offering for all, anticipating his resurrection, and the son willingly offers up himself at Passover (Mark 14:12–26; 1 Cor 5:7), is part of the stream of

---

30. Here, Gen 15:6 ("Abraham believed in Yahweh, and it was accounted to him as righteousness") is related to his obedience in offering up Isaac in the *Aqedah*.
31. Richard Elliott Friedman, *The Bible with Sources Revealed: A New View into the Five Books of Moses* (San Francisco: HarperOne, 2003) 65.
32. Chilton, *Abraham's Curse*, 67.

Jewish interpretation and not something extraneous, imposed on the text from contexts foreign to the text. The *Fragmentary Targum* on Gen 22:10, although much later than the New Testament, could have been written by a Christian. At the moment of the near sacrifice, a voice from heaven says:

> Come, see two righteous unique ones in the midst of the world. One sacrifices and one is being sacrificed; the one who sacrifices does not hold back, and the one who is being sacrificed stretches out his neck.[33]

Engaging Modern and Contemporary Concerns about This Text

Immanuel Kant's reading of the *Aqedah* is a particularly egregious example of reading without empathy and without context.[34] If we had only read Kant and not the canonical biblical text, we would never imagine that child sacrifice was explicitly and repeatedly forbidden as one of the idolatrous Canaanite practices, which Israel must avoid on entrance into the promised land. Kant ignores this. For him, Abraham is a decontextualized everyman who is removed from his historical context and his tradition. Any moral person knows that one does not sacrifice children, and Abraham therefore is immoral in not distrusting the purportedly divine voice commanding him to do something inherently immoral. Ethics are universal and independent of historical context and the context of religious traditions. As Levenson notes:

> Everyman should surely know to avoid "butchering and burning" his good son. That the phrase "butchering and burning" may not do justice to the complex, if mystifying, dynamics of sacrifice in biblical Israel is another thought that Kant does not entertain. For him, sacrifice is simply killing. The all-important difference between the two acts in Israelite culture (and biblical terminology) quite eluded him. The effect of Kant's thinking is to remove the Aqedah from the realm of narrative and theology and to relocate it foursquare within the domain of ethics.... How could it ever be ethical to kill an innocent boy in cold blood?[35]

Kant is the father of many contemporary readings of the *Aqedah* in which Abraham is a horrendously abusive father. But his reading is a decontextualized one. Surprisingly, Søren Kierkegaard, in his classic work *Fear and Trembling*, gives the devil his due by accepting Kant's assertion that the command given to Abraham is immoral.[36] His response to this common ground, however, is very different from Kant's. He suggests that Abraham's

---

33. See Flesher and Chilton, *The Targums*, 460.
34. Immanuel Kant, "The Conflict of the Faculties," in *Religion and Rational Theology* (ed. and trans. A. W. Wood and G. di Giovanni; Cambridge: Cambridge University Press, 1996), 7:63 (p. 283).
35. Levenson, *Inheriting Abraham*, 107.
36. Søren Kierkegaard, *Fear and Trembling* (Garden City, NY: Doubleday Anchor, 1954) 41.

acceptance of the divine command is because of the teleological suspension of the ethical.

Chilton begins his absorbing book *Abraham's Curse* with the story of the murder of a young woman student of his on church property where he served as parish priest. Her eyes were, "still open and clear with apparent life, picked up the last rays of the sun."[37] He was reminded of the Midrashic text in which, just as he was about to be slaughtered, Isaac looked up to heaven and saw angels there, with Abraham seeing the reflection of the angels in Isaac's eyes. The murderer was a young man, whose not-guilty plea by reason of insanity was accepted, because he thought that the Afro-Caribbean god Ogun had commissioned the murder. Chilton's book serves as a potent reminder that texts such as Gen 22 have the potential to underwrite violence as divinely sanctioned and have in fact been used that way in the history of Christian, Jewish, and Islamic appropriations of the text.[38] We need to be ever vigilant to explain to the church, and especially those who would teach or preach in the name of Jesus Christ, that such appropriations are a fundamental misuse of those texts and must be soundly rejected by the church that bears the name of the lamb of God, who died a sacrificial death for the sins of all.[39]

But Chilton is representative of many contemporary interpreters in going beyond the rejection of such misappropriations to rejecting the text itself, as though such appropriations are legitimate ways of reading the *Aqedah*; as though the text itself, and not its misappropriations, is where a substantial portion of the blame is to be placed. It must be granted that, removed from its textual, historical, early interpretive, and canonical contexts, the *Aqedah* can and has been used to justify all manner of evil. Nevertheless, it is only within its textual, historical, early interpretive, and canonical contexts that this text has been accepted as authoritative. Those contexts do not support understanding this text as justification for God's people to inflict violence on the innocent. The tradition does support understanding the potential redemptive value of accepting violence in certain extreme circumstances inflicted by others on the people of God, whether as a martyr and/or as a form of sacrifice. But these are very different things. In a perverse sort of way, historical-critical approaches used independently of canonical context and the history of interpretation can enable readings that justify the people of God using violence on others. The canonical and interpretive contexts protect against these misuses in ways that historical-criticism by itself does not.

Sherwood seems to assume that "contemporary politics and ethics" can be grounded without a tradition, or on a secular tradition that is indepen-

---

37. Chilton, *Abraham's Curse*, 217–20.
38. Ibid., 171–95.
39. Siebert's sermon (*Disturbing Divine Behavior*, 217–20) attempts to do just this.

dent of religion and an historical-cultural context.⁴⁰ These pretensions may seem like common sense to many readers today, but they are ultimately naive. There is no canonical version of the *Aqedah* that justifies child sacrifice or child abuse. Sherwood's warnings about how such texts can be and have been abused into transcripts for action is helpful, whether or not her suspicion about the *Aqedah* being used to support the 9/11 bombers is accepted.

Conclusion

Levenson's rich treatment of the *Aqedah* shows how interconnected contemporary Orthodox Jews are to orthodox Christians. He notes:

> In the Aqedah, the alternative is indeed apostasy—in the form, however, not of defection to another god but of withholding the beloved son from the God who gave him, thus elevating the father's personal self-interest over obedience to the God to whom he owes not only Isaac but all his good fortune.⁴¹

Notice his use of the term *beloved*, which echoes the term used to refer to Jesus as the beloved son in the New Testament. On the other hand, Levenson's articulation of an orthodox Jewish understanding of sacrificial logic is distinctly different from the Christian understanding of Christ's sacrifice on the cross. But even in this area of theology there is still common ground between the Christian faith and Judaism. Levenson explains:

> In the paradoxical, sacrificial logic of which this text is the outstanding Jewish example, it is our ungrudging willingness to give that leads to gaining and retaining that which is most precious. It is in rising above self-interest that we secure that which a calculus of self-interest can never yield—or understand.⁴²

As an orthodox Jew, Levenson does not recognize the insight of the New Testament that, because Jesus is the divine Son of God, in offering up His beloved Son, God is the ultimate example of sacrificing self-interest to which Abraham points and that Jesus is the ultimate example of self-offering for others to which Isaac points. Levenson's empathetic reading of this text and the early interpretive tradition, and his resistance to modern and postmodern readings that cut themselves off from that tradition and lack empathy in reading the *Aqedah*, is encouraging to evangelical Christians. The New Testament's understanding of the *Aqedah* is well within the bounds of reasonable interpretation in an ancient context and flows from a rich tapestry of interpretation both within the Old Testament canon and in the Jewish literature that flows from it. It also encourages us to continue

---

40. Yvonne Sherwood, "Emily Arndt: A Tribute," in *Demanding Our Attention: The Hebrew Bible as a Source for Christian Ethics* (ed. Emily Arndt; Grand Rapids: Eerdmans, 2011) 85. See also idem, "Binding-Unbinding: Divided Responses of Judaism, Christianity, and Islam to the 'Sacrifice' of Abraham's Beloved Son," *JAAR* 72 (2004) 821–61.
41. Levenson, *Inheriting Abraham*, 81
42. Ibid., 85.

to engage in dialogue with Jewish interpreters, with whom we have far more in common than we often do with contemporary interpreters and whose familiarity with Jewish sources outside the New Testament often illuminates our own attempt at careful, empathetic, canonical reading of rich texts such as the *Aqedah*. Paul's words to the Romans, echoing the *Aqedah* and its interpretive tradition, remind us of how to read this text:

> He who did not spare his own Son but gave him up for us all, how will he not also with him graciously give us all things? (Rom 8:32 ESV).

CHAPTER 3

How Can We Bless Yhwh? Wrestling with Divine Violence in Deuteronomy

Daniel I. Block

According to the *World Report on Violence and Health*, violence involves "the intentional use of physical force or power, threatened or actual, against oneself, another person, or against a group or community, that either results in or has a high likelihood of resulting in injury, death, psychological harm, maldevelopment, or deprivation." By this definition, violence pervades the book of Deuteronomy. What is particularly troubling to many readers today is not so much the violence perpetrated by humans against humans, but the violence perpetrated by and commanded by God. Given modern "enlightened" sensitivities, this violence is difficult to accept. While many have tried to justify divine destructiveness and belligerence in the Hebrew Bible, my purpose in this essay is more modest; I would simply like to understand it as the book of Deuteronomy portrays it. I shall pursue this goal by asking several leading questions: (1) What forms does divine violence take? (2) Who are the objects of divine violence? And (3) what motivates divine violence?

At the outset, I recognize that my answers to these questions will be affected by how I read Deuteronomy and the provenance I assign to the book. In critical scholarship, it has become commonplace to stifle the divine voice in Deuteronomy and attribute the book's portrayal of Yhwh to misguided "deuteronomists," who, in the Persian period, sought to bolster Jewish identity in the face of external threats, or to mollify the image of God by interpreting divinely prescribed actions against the Canaanites and against their own people as metaphorical and hyperbolic rhetoric intent on preserving a pure religious community. With these approaches, many of the ethical problems raised by the policies prescribed in Deuteronomy evaporate. However, the theological problem remains inasmuch as Deuteronomy contains a considerable amount of divine speech and even more speech attributed to Moses, who purportedly spoke only as Yhwh commanded him to speak (e.g., 1:3; 4:1–2, 45; cf. 30:2). Even if the book represents an "abstract painting" rather than a "photograph" of Yhwh, and even if the book presents a late portrait retrojected to an earlier time, if this book was to be deemed canonical—which it was—it creates a troubling image of deity that many reject today. But this raises the question, in what sense can the book of Deuteronomy then be accepted as canonical and sacred Scripture?

If people's ethical conduct is to be inspired by the deities they serve (*imitatio dei*), eventually this image of Yhwh would prove ethically problematic for his people, unless they recognized their sacred texts to be fictional. But this seems unlikely. The writers of biblical texts did not think they were writing fiction, and ancient lay readers/hearers would certainly not have thought that was what they were reading/hearing.

The Forms of Divine Violence in Deuteronomy

In tabulating the forms of divine violence in Deuteronomy we note first that Deuteronomy not only attributes violence directly to God, but that he is also ultimately responsible for violent actions he commands others to execute. I shall examine these two categories separately.

The Forms of Direct Divine Violence

A quick survey of statements in which Yhwh is the subject of verbs of violence is revealing. Illustrative of the supreme acts of violence are instances in which Yhwh kills (9:28 [hypothetical]; 32:39), destroys (2:22; 31:4), exterminates (7:10; 8:20), and strikes (1:4; 28:22, 27, 28, 35). With respect to populations specifically, he cuts them off (12:29; 19:1), drives them out (33:27), expels them (6:19; 9:4), leads them off [into exile] (4:27; 28:37), dispossesses them [of their land] (4:38; 9:4), delivers one population/land into the hands of another (1:27; 20:13), scatters them (4:27; 28:64; 30:3), subdues them (9:3), intervenes [to punish] (5:9), and blots out persons' names from under heaven (9:14; 29:19[20]). Given the definition of "violence" above, here we note also Deuteronomy's emphasis on God intimidating and demoralizing people. The book has a remarkably full vocabulary of psychological and emotional violence: Yhwh performs "awesome deeds" (4:34; 26:8) and "terror" (32:25), causing "fright" (2:25), "dread" (2:25; 28:67), "trembling" (2:25; 28:65), "confusion" (7:23; 28:20), and "frustration" (28:20). Yhwh's determination to operate violently is reflected in 2:30, where Moses observes that just as Yhwh had hardened Pharaoh's heart to multiply the signs and wonders—all violent actions against Egypt (Exod 4:21; 7:3; 10:1; 14:4)—so "he stiffened Sihon's resolve and hardened his heart." This may be deemed a violent divine act, setting the stage for physical violence as Yhwh hands Sihon over to the Israelites and their execution of the principle of *ḥērem* in vv. 33–35. Two texts illustrate Yhwh's violence with particular poignancy: the covenant curses in chap. 28, most notably vv. 20–29, 35–37, and 59–66, and vv. 23–27 of chap. 32, which Deuteronomy casts as a sort of national anthem for the nation.

The Forms of Indirect Divine Violence

Indirect violence involves divinely mandated violent actions performed by a third party. In these instances Yhwh hands the instruments of violence into the hands of humans. The actions involved may be grouped into two categories: (1) the forms of violence listed above, that is, violence perpetrated against groups usually in conflict over land or in response to offenses of the population against the divine Suzerain; (2) forms of violence commanded by God but directed against individuals in the administration of justice and righteousness. With respect to the first, Yhwh charges Israel "to destroy" the Canaanites (7:24; cf. 33:27), "to exterminate" them (9:3) and their names from under heaven (7:24), "to dispossess" them (7:17; 9:1, 3; 11:23), to execute ḥērem on their population (3:2 [cf. 2:32–35]; 13:16[15]), and "to attack, defeat" (lit. "strike"; 2:33; 3:3; 7:2) with the sword (13:16[15]; 20:13). Israel's required disposition toward Canaanites is declared in 7:16, "Your eye must show no pity toward them." The second category is more extensive and as offensive to some modern readers as the first. In Deuteronomy we find general commands to execute offenders (13:6, 10[5, 9]; 17:6, 7; 21:22; 24:16) and specifically to execute by stoning (13:11[10]; 17:2–7; 21:18–21; 22:20–24), flogging (25:1–3; perhaps also 21:18; 22:18), and mutilation (25:11–12). If a man refuses to honor his deceased brother by marrying his widow, he is to be shamed publicly (25:7–10). Along with these actions, Moses warned Israelites not to be swayed by sentimentality or pity for offenders (19:11–13, 18–21; 25:11–12).

The Targets of Divine Violence in Deuteronomy

Non-Israelite Targets of Divine Violence

That the targets of much of Yhwh's violence in Deuteronomy are non-Israelites is not surprising. Much of the literature on divine violence in the First Testament has focused on the divine determination to wipe the Canaanites from the land Yhwh was handing over to Israel. However, this action, anticipated in Deuteronomy, would not represent the first expression of this disposition. In an earlier time south and east of the Dead Sea, Yhwh had "destroyed" the Emites, Zamzummites, and Horites and delivered their respective lands into the hands of the Moabites, Ammonites, and Edomites.

However, prior to the Israelites' arrival in the region, the primary targets of divine violence were Pharaoh and the Egyptians. Yhwh had personally invaded Egypt and terrified the Egyptians with daring acts, signs, wonders, war, a mighty hand, an outstretched arm, and great deeds of terror (4:34). In 11:2–4, Moses describes the climactic destructive act: "Remember . . . what Yhwh did to the Egyptian army, their horses and chariots, how he made the water of the Red Sea flow over them as they pursued you."

Closer to home, both in terms of time and location, Moses' audience remembers well the fate of Sihon and Og, the Amorite kings in the Transjordan. After the announcement in 1:4 that Yhwh had struck these kings (2:24–3:11), Moses summarizes the event. As Amorites, the peoples they represented were linked to the Canaanite tribes across the Jordan. But Moses paints an ambivalent picture of the Transjordanian Amorites and why they were in the crosshairs of the Israelites and Yhwh.

On the one hand, it appears that, in Moses' mind, originally they were not actual targets of divine violence. Reminiscent of the Israelite policy regarding the Edomites, Moabites, and Ammonites (2:1–23), the Israelites seem to have had no interest either in engaging them in battle or in claiming their territory. Because they stood between them and their actual destination on the other side of the Jordan, Moses had sent ambassadors to Sihon in Heshbon with overtures of peace, simply requesting permission to pass through their territory and promising not to threaten either the people or their claims to the land.

Moses' account of the event suggests Sihon and Og became targets of Israelite and divine violence only because they rebuffed the overture and marshaled their troops to block Israel's journey to the promised land. This disposition toward the Transjordanian Amorites is understandable, given explicit declarations that the Jordan River represented the eastern boundary of the promised land (Num 34:12) and Moses' own repeated references to crossing the Jordan into the land Yhwh is giving Israel as their grant (*naḥălâ*) in fulfillment of the promise to the ancestors.

On the other hand, Moses' report of Yhwh's involvement in these events suggests that the latter had Sihon and Og in his crosshairs from the outset. Before Moses offered peace to the Amorite king, Yhwh had charged the Israelites to engage Sihon in battle (cf. 2:9) and begin taking possession of the land, declaring that he had given Sihon and his land into their hands (2:24). This impression is reinforced by Moses' attribution of Sihon's rejection of the offer of peace to Yhwh, who "had hardened his disposition and stiffened his resolve" for the express purpose of delivering him into the Israelites' power (2:30). In the event, the Israelites executed the *ḥērem* policy on the population, while keeping the livestock and other booty (2:34–35).

In the defeat of the Transjordanian Amorites, we observe in microcosm the upcoming conflict with the dreaded Cisjordanian populations, who are a dominant target for Israelite violence in the remainder of the book. While the previous generation of Israelites had shrunk back in terror before their extraordinary physical size and fortifications (1:28–29), it is apparent that in the intervening 40 years their power had not diminished, nor had they become an easier target. Moses still characterizes them as "greater/more numerous and powerful" than Israel. However, the target of Israel's particularly violent *ḥērem* policy was strictly circumscribed. In chap. 20, where Moses instructs the Israelites on their conduct of hostilities with outsiders, he establishes distinct policies for "towns that are very far away" and "the towns of these nations nearby" (20:15). While conflicts with the former are to be avoided with overtures of peace, when these are rejected he limits lethal violence to adult males and precludes the slaughter of women and children. By contrast, conflicts with the latter are neither to be avoided nor delayed with offers of peace, but the entire human population is to be annihilated (20:10–17).

Deuteronomy also circumscribes the target ethnographically. In 7:1, Moses identifies seven people groups by name: Hittites, Girgashites, Amorites, Canaanites, Perizzites, Hivites, and Jebusites. Critical scholars' tendency to dismiss this list as fictional and the names as symbolic may resolve the human ethical problem of genocide, but it does not resolve the theological/theodical problem. The image of a deity purportedly commanding the elimination of whole populations remains. Our present concern is the boundary this list places on the extreme form of Israelite aggression. Moses later extends the policy to the Amalekites (25:17–19), but this would be the exception that proved the rule. He does not cast the resolution of the Amalekite problem as a part of the wars of conquest but projects it into the future when the Canaanites have been defeated and Yhwh had given them "rest" from all their enemies. The motivation for the addition of the Amalekites to the policy is quite distinct from the reason for eliminating the Canaanites.

According to 2:2–23, the Israelite stance toward Edomites, Moabites, and Ammonites was to be quite pacific, not only because they posed no hindrance to their occupation of the promised land, but specifically because they were ethnically related to the Israelites.

Furthermore, their title to their respective lands was as inviolable as Israel's would be to the land of Canaan, for Yhwh had given it to them as their possession (2:5, 9, 19). As for the peoples to the south and north of Canaan (Egyptians, Aramaeans, etc.), presumably they would fall into the category "distant" nations, but they are beyond the purview of Deuteronomy. The exclusion of Philistines from these lists is ethnographically and historically appropriate, because they were technically not Canaanites but latecomers to the Levant, who originated in the Aegean and did not appear in this region until the 12th century B.C.E.

Israelites as Targets of Divine Violence

Given scholars' preoccupation with the genocidal problem involving the Canaanites, many are surprised to learn that these are not the primary targets of divine violence in Deuteronomy. On the contrary, apart from targeting individual Israelites in the administration of justice, the Israelites as a whole appear as the object of Yhwh's fury more than twice as often as the Canaanites. These references are concentrated in chaps. 9 (in response to the apostasy involving the golden calf at Sinai), 28 (the covenant curses threatened in case of persistent future apostasy), and 32 (vv. 19–22, Israel's national anthem), but they are scattered throughout the book. In 1:27, faithless Israelites wrongly interpreted the exodus from Egypt as an act of divine violence against them motivated by hatred and with the goal of destroying them. In 4:3, Moses recalls Yhwh's judgment on idolaters at Baal-Peor. Summary threats of divine judgment for idolatry for which the covenant curses provide graphic explanation are scattered throughout his addresses.

These texts and this emphasis caution against isolating annihilation of the Canaanites as a distinctive ethical problem. Exploration of divine violence in Deuteronomy must take into account all these texts. We cannot understand the genocidal acts against the Canaanites without first considering the divine violence the book threatens against Yhwh's own people.

Regarding the internal administration of righteousness and justice, the targets of direct and indirect divine violence vary. The extreme form of punishment, execution, is to be applied to idolaters (5:9; 13:1–18; 17:2–7), false prophets who speak in Yhwh's name without his authorization or who speak in the name of another god (18:20), Israelites who do not comply with the divine verdict in otherwise insoluble cases (17:12–13), murderers, at the hands of the "blood-avenger (19:1–13), persistently rebellious children (21:18–21), a woman who proves not to have been a virgin at the time of her marriage (22:20–21), male and female adulterers, if the act occurs in a town and the woman is virgin pledged to be married (22:23–24), and male rapists, if the act occurs in the country and the woman is pledged to be married (22:25).

The Motivation for Divine Violence in Deuteronomy

Having identified the targets of divine violence in Deuteronomy, we may now explore Yhwh's motivation in these drastic measures. While the ancients viewed all of life with profoundly theological lenses, I shall divide the question into two parts: (1) divine violence in response to domestic and moral conduct and (2) divine violence in response to overtly religious conduct. The former category involves breaches in horizontal relationships, while the latter involves Israelites' vertical relationship with Yhwh. These are obviously not mutually exclusive, but this division is heuristically convenient.

The Motivation for Divine Violence in Response to Moral Offenses

Deut 16:20 declares the goal of all ethical conduct for the Israelites: "Righteousness, righteousness you shall pursue" (*ṣedeq ṣedeq tirdōp*). As used in Deuteronomy, *ṣedeq* refers to right behavior in accord with an established standard, in this instance the covenant stipulations as defined by Yhwh. However, Deut 32:4 includes this expression in the list of Yhwh's qualities: "The Rock, his action is perfect (*tāmîm*), and all his ways are just (*mišpāṭ*). A faithful God (*'ēl 'ĕmûnâ*), without deceit (*'ēn 'āvel*), righteous (*ṣaddîq*) and upright (*yāšār*) is he." The God portrayed in this book is anything but capricious, fickle, impetuous, self-indulgent, and forgetful. Whatever disposition modern readers may have toward Yhwh and his violence in Deuteronomy, the book itself understands both within the framework of divine perfection, justice, fidelity, integrity, righteousness, and consistency. These attributes govern both his own conduct and his disposition toward the conduct of human beings—created as his images—but especially toward Israel, whom Yhwh claimed as his own, his elect (7:6, 7; 10:15; 14:2), the objects of his redemption/deliverance from slavery and his covenant love, his adopted sons (14:1), his treasured people (7:6; 14:2; 26:18), and his holy people (7:6; 14:2, 21; 26:19; 28:9). Among other expressions of ethical expectation, he calls Israel to "walk in [all] his ways" (8:6; 10:12; 11:22; 19:9; 26:17; 28:9; 30:16). This magnificently ambiguous expression could mean either "to walk in the ways YHWH has commanded" (cf. 5:33; 13:6[5]), or to walk as YHWH walks. This ethical principle of *imitatio dei* is expressly enjoined in 10:17-19, which, after declaring that YHWH demonstrates covenant love toward the alien calls on the Israelites to do the same. If "righteousness" for YHWH meant that he kept the commitments to which he bound himself in his covenant relationship with Israel, this meant that Israel should do the same.

When we examine the types of Israelite behavior that provoked the "righteous" expression of YHWH's violence, we observe two broad categories of offenses: those that challenge the integrity of human relationships, especially within the family and the clan, and those that challenge the integrity of God's relationship with his people. Deuteronomy characterizes such breaches of the principle of "righteousness" as *tô'ēbâ*. The word derives from a root *tā'ab*, "to abhor, to reject as utterly disgusting." This is Moses' favored expression for all things idolatrous (cf. 12:31; 13:15[14]; 17:4; 32:16), but it is also used of taboo food (14:3), defective sacrifices (17:1), transvestite conduct (22:5), prostitution (23:18-19[17-18]), shaming one's wife by divorcing her for some physical issue and then remarrying her (24:4), and cheating in commercial actions (25:16). While the first three jeopardize the divine-human relationship, those that remain undermine the health of the home and the community. But they do more. Deuteronomy presupposes the divine stance toward abominable actions as expressed in Lev 18:19-30: abominable actions defile the land and compromise Israel's status as a "holy people," rendering them absolutely defiled and fundamentally degraded, a degradation that cannot be resolved ritually (see fig. 1). This interpretation is reinforced by Deuteronomy's frequent use of variations of the purgation formula: "and you shall purge the evil from your midst." [1] This formula is applied not only to idolatrous actions (13:6[5]; 17:7) and defiance of the divine determination in an otherwise insoluble legal case (17:12), but also to malicious witnesses (19:19), rebellious sons (21:21), a bride who is discovered not to have been a virgin at the time of her marriage (22:21), adultery by a man or woman (22:22), and kidnapping (24:7). While this purgation assumes the death penalty, the only procedure specified is stoning (17:5-7; 21:18-21; 22:20-21), presumably to avoid contamination of the executioners by direct contact with the criminal. [2]

---

1. The formula "to purge [exterminate] the evil from" appears in 13:6[5]; 17:7, 12; 19:13, 19; 21:9, 21; 22:21, 22, 24; 24:7. Cf. Judg 20:13; 2 Sam 4:11; 1 Kgs 4:10. Except for Deut 19:19, in Deuteronomy, all instances involve the death penalty.

2. Similarly, Cyril S. Rodd, *Glimpses of a Strange Land: Studies in Old Testament Ethics* (OTS; Edinburgh: T. & T. Clark, 2001) 12.

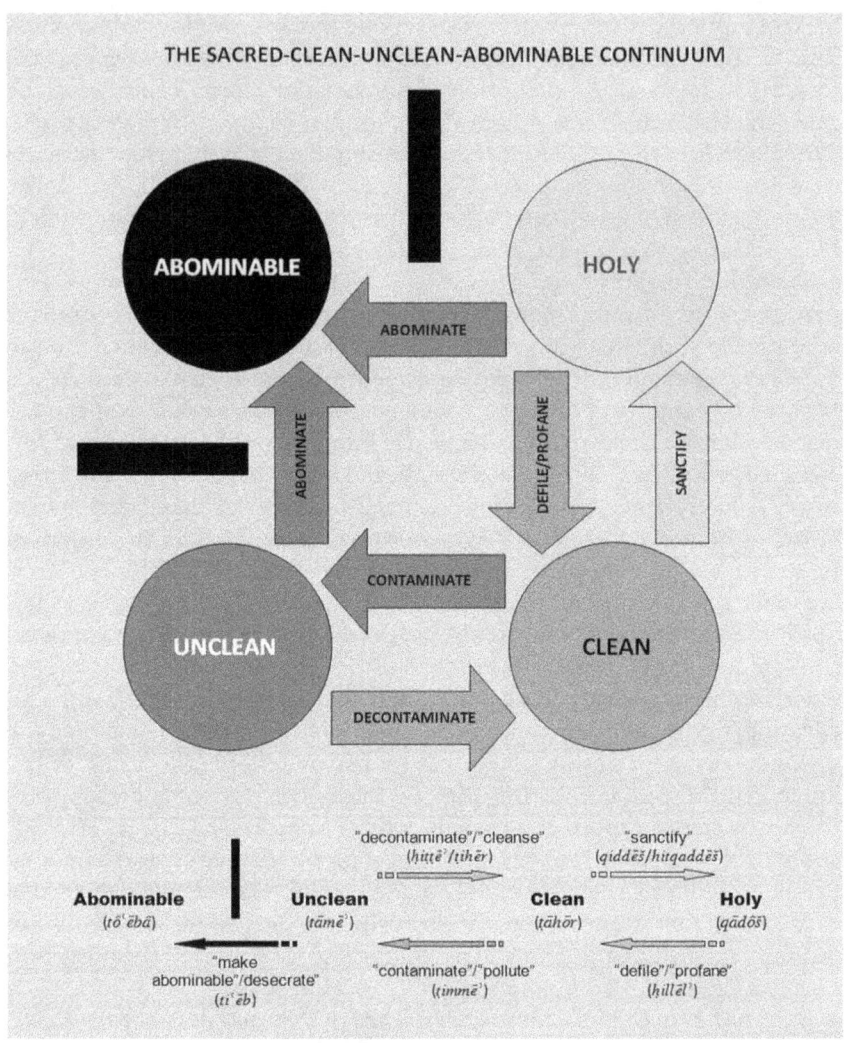

Figure. 1. Abominable actions defile the land and compromise Israel's status as a "holy people."

The purgation formula involves the verb *biʿēr* followed by the preposition *min*, "from," and the object of the preposition. In each instance of the formula the object from which contamination is to be purged is the community, identified specifically as "Israel" (17:12; 19:13; 22:22) or more generally as "your midst" (13:6[5]; 17:7; 19:19; 21:9; 21:21; 22:21, 24; 24:7). Significantly, the contaminant from which the community is to be purged is neither the criminal himself nor his victim, but the evil deed. This interpretation is reinforced by 19:13 and 21:9, which identify the contaminant as "blood," which functions metonymically for "bloodshed." The characterization of the blood as "innocent" in both cases demonstrates that there is nothing wrong with the blood itself. The issue here is not to wash the people of the blood of the victim, but to absolve them of the guilt of the crime. Until this expiatory action has been taken, culpability for the murder will hang over all the people. Caiaphas had it almost right when he said, "It is better for you that one man should die ... than that the whole nation should perish" (John 11:50).[3]

While all the purgation texts envision the decontamination of the community, in several the crimes affect the status of the third member of the covenantal triangle, namely, the land. According to 21:22–23, after executing a criminal[4] and impaling his body on a pole, the body is to be removed and buried before nightfall to avoid desecrating the ground. Although the verb differs, apparently failure to dispose of corpses properly had the same effect on the ground as crimes did on the people. Deut 24:1–4 is more explicit in declaring the effect of a moral act characterized as "an abomination before Yhwh" on the land. If a man defiled his wife by divorcing her for some physical problem,[5] and then remarried her, this would contaminate the land.[6]

These texts all assume the fundamental sanctity of people and land in covenant relationship with Yhwh. Unless readers grasp this notion, and the divine grace that underlies it they will not understand this motivation for divine violence. Through his redemptive and covenantal acts Yhwh has transformed an enslaved people into a holy people belonging to himself (7:6; 14:2; 21; 26:18).

However, the motivation behind divine violence in Deuteronomy is more complex than this. Several texts prescribe severe punishments as deterrents for others. It is tempting to link the violent response commanded by Yhwh in the face of criminal acts with the link between fear of Yhwh and obedience established already at Sinai (cf. 4:10; 5:29).[7] However, following the prescription of a specific punishment, the emphasis shifts from "awed trust" of Yhwh to fear of the consequences of one's action. Variations of the formula, "they shall hear and fear and avoid" particular actions occur four times: (1) in

---

3. Whereas Caiaphas had in mind the substitutionary death of an individual, in these cases the man dies for his own crime, but in the event lets the community be spared.

4. The opening clause of v. 22 is extremely dense: "Now if there is in a man a sin [calling for] a judgment of death." Cf. 15:21 and 19:11, the latter of which has the negative variant of this expression. The statement presupposes a process of careful investigation, leading to the conclusion that follows.

5. On this interpretation, see Block, *Deuteronomy* (NIVAC; Grand Rapids: Zondervan, 2012) 556–60.

6. This statement involves the relatively rare Hiphil form *heḥĕṭî'*, "to contaminate." In the Qal stem, the verb means "to miss the mark, to sin."

7. Hebrew *yārē'*, "to fear," is used frequently of reverent/trusting awe (6:2, 24; 10:12, 20; 14:23; 17:19; 31:12–13).

response to stoning those who promote idolatry (13:12[11]); (2) in response to the execution of a person who does not heed the divine verdict announced by the priest at the central sanctuary in an otherwise insoluble case (17:13); (3) in response to the punishment of a false witness (19:20); (4) in response to the stoning of a persistently rebellious son (21:21). Again the concern is a holy community, characterized by willing and grateful obedience to Yhwh. Lest Israel relax about this expectation, thrice Deuteronomy warns against letting sentimentality or personal feelings interfere with the administration with the "no pity formula" (13:9[8]; 19:13, 21).[8]

Although we have included divine violence in response to idolatry in passing in the preceding, this subject deserves separate attention, not because its primary concern is the well-being of the community, but because it strikes at the heart of the relationship between Israel and her God and at the heart of monotheistic convictions. Although we usually associate idolatry with worship involving physical images, either man-made of terrestrial materials[9] or the heavenly bodies (4:19; 17:3), and although Deuteronomy prohibits the manufacture of images as objects of worship (4:16, 23, 25; 5:8–9; 27:15), the real issue is the exclusive worship of Yhwh, a conviction embodied in the "First Principle of Covenant Relationship" (5:7–10) and the Shema (6:4–5).[10] To worship "other gods"[11] is to "abandon" (28:20; 31:16) and "despise" (31:20) Yhwh and to "break" his covenant (31:16, 20).

Israelite Yahwism was unique among ancient religions both in its repudiation of all other gods and in its demand for Israel's exclusive worship.[12] Yhwh's claim to Israel's total devotion is rooted not only in the nonexistence of other gods but especially in his gracious election, salvation, providential care, covenant, and call to mission. Yhwh's past acts on Israel's behalf are celebrated in the climax of Moses' first address (4:32–40), the

---

8. To these we must add 25:11–12, which commands cutting off the hand of a woman who has grabbed another man's genitals ("appendage of shame"), presumably intending to injure him so he cannot have children, which also strikes at the maintenance of the community's integrity. For a similar interpretation, see J. G. McConville, *Deuteronomy* (AOTC 5; Downers Grove, IL: InterVarsity, 2002) 371.

9. Designated as "images" (*pĕsîlîm*, 4:16, 23, 25; 5:8; 7:5, 25; 12:3; 27:15; *semel*, 4:16), "the work of human/a craftsman's hands" (4:28; 27:15), "cast metal image" (9:12, 16; 27:15), "other gods of wood and stone" (4:28; 28:36) and "silver and gold" (29:16[17]), "loathsome images (29:16[17]); and "feces" (29:16[17]).

10. On the significance of the Shema, see Daniel I. Block, "How Many Is God? An Investigation into the Meaning of Deuteronomy 6:4–5," *JETS* 47 (2004) 193–212. On the broader issue of monotheism in Deuteronomy, see N. MacDonald, *Deuteronomy and the Meaning of Monotheism* (Tübingen: Mohr Siebeck, 2003).

11. 5:7; 6:14; 7:4; 8:19; 11:16, 28; 13:3[2], 6–7, 14[13]; 17:3; 18:20; 28:14, 36, 64; 29:25[26]; 30:17; 31:18, 20.

12. See my *The Gods of the Nations: Studies in Ancient Near Eastern National Theology* (2nd ed.; ETSS; Eugene, OR: Wipf & Stock, 2013) 61–74; idem, "'No Other Gods': Bearing the Name of Yhwh in a Polytheistic World," in *The Gospel according to Moses: Theological and Ethical Reflections on the Book of Deuteronomy* (Eugene, OR: Cascade, 2012) 237–71.

"domestic catechism" (6:20–25), the "Little Creed" (26:1–11), and the Song of YHWH (32:1–14). For Israel to go after other gods is to trample underfoot the history of divine grace. Israel's mission is embodied in expressions such as "a holy people belonging to YHWH" (7:6; 14:2, 21; 26:19), "a treasured people" (7:6; 14:2; 26:18), and summarized in 26:19: "He will place you high above the nations . . . for [his] praise, fame, and glory," a mission that could be fulfilled only if the nation would be faithful to her covenant Lord and YHWH would respond with his blessing (28:1–14; cf. 4:5–8).[13] Because YHWH's agenda for the world depends on Israel's exclusive devotion, there is no room for compromise on this matter (12:1–4, 29–32), and those who would seek to deflect the people's devotion to other gods must be executed (13:2–18; 18:9–22). This is true of individuals who actually choose that course (7:25–26; 17:1–7; 29:13–20[14–21]), as well as the nation as a whole (6:14–15; 11:16–17; 28:15–68; 32:19–25). This violent response will never be understood if we extract it from the narrative of divine grace.

The Motivation for Divine Violence against the Canaanites

Recognizing the motivation for the divine response to idolatry, we may have arrived at the biblical explanation for the violence that Deuteronomy prescribes for Israel's treatment of the Canaanites and the other autochthonous tribes.[14] This is by all accounts the most difficult ethical question in the First Testament, and responses to the issue vary greatly. While Jews have rarely applied this policy,[15] regrettably European Christians have misappropriated this policy to justify all sorts of violent behavior, from the expulsion of Muslim Turks from the Holy Land to the annihilation of indigenous populations from the lands they were claiming as new homelands, most notably in the Americas and in Australia.[16] Others have rejected these

---

13. Although Moberly's metaphorical interpretation of the policy of ḥērem is problematic, his discussion of the relationship between the policy and Israel's election is excellent. See R. W. L. Moberly, *Old Testament Theology: Reading the Hebrew Bible as Christian Scripture* (Grand Rapids: Baker Academic, 2013) 41–74.

14. The primary texts addressing the problem are in 3:18–22; 4:37–38; 6:18–19; 7:1–11, 17–26; 8:20; 9:1–6; 11:23–25; 18:9–12; 31:3. Although technically not part of the conquest of the promised land, the defeat of the Transjordanian Amorite kings in 2:24–3:17 is portrayed as paradigmatic for the Cisjordanian campaign: as Commander in Chief, YHWH directs the campaign; YHWH fixes the disposition of the enemy; Israel engages the enemy in battle; Israel applies the policy of ḥērem; Israel allocates the land to their tribes.

15. For a warning to Israeli nationalists against using Scripture to justify violence against Palestinians and defend absolutist rights to the land, see Moshe Greenberg, "On the Political Use of the Bible in Modern Israel: An Engaged Critique," in *Pomegranates and Golden Bells: Studies in Biblical, Jewish, and Near Eastern Ritual, Law, and Literature in Honor of Jacob Milgrom* (ed. D. P. Wright, D. N. Freedman, and A. Hurvitz; Winona Lake, IN: Eisenbrauns, 1995) 461–71.

16. For examples of Puritan and Calvinist appropriation of these texts, see briefly John J. Collins, "The Zeal of Phinehas: The Bible and the Legitimation of Violence," *JBL* 122 (2003) 3–21, esp. pp. 13–14.

injunctions outright. The most radical response, represented by the early heretic Marcion, is to repudiate the entire First Testament because the violent God it portrays differs fundamentally from the gracious God of the New Testament, embodied in Christ.[17] More recently, Hector Avalos has argued that any depiction of God in the Bible as violent must be rejected as false, and any texts that portray him as such should be deleted.[18] Although Eric Seibert rejects the "Marcionite" label, the effect of his Christocentric hermeneutic is similar: when we encounter texts that portray God differently from Jesus Christ, we must declare, "This is not God," but is faulty ancient Israelite representation of the true God.[19] Mainstream First Testament scholars argue that while the policy of *ḥērem* as outlined in Deut 7 and 20 (as well as the conquest narratives in Joshua) appear to describe a ban of the past, they actually represent figurative if not utopian portrayals of a particular present, namely, Josiah's efforts to centralize worship in the sixth century.[20] Thomas Römer argues that these texts derive from the Persian era (5th century B.C.E.), when the loss of identity through contact with "others" threatened the "community in crisis."[21]

Others have tried to salvage the biblical texts by taking a more spiritual or theological approach. Origen allegorized the issue, suggesting that the policy as outlined in Deuteronomy and narrated in Joshua symbolized the conflicts that raged within a person's own soul, and that Christians should root out all vice and sinfulness from within.[22] While few scholars advocate Origen's particular approach, some find the impulse sound, using this as a base to develop a metaphorical interpretation of a policy in defense of monotheism, which is to be realized through the banning of intermarriage with all non-Israelites and the destruction of all pagan religious paraphernalia.[23] More generally, Douglas Earl finds the *ḥērem* policy to be a symbol of various notions:

---

17. On Marcion, see Adolf von Harnack, *Marcion: The Gospel of the Alien God* (trans. J. E. Steely and L. D. Bierma; Durham: Labyrinth, 1924; repr., 1990) 15–24.

18. See Hector Avalos, "The Letter Killeth: A Plea for Decanonizing Violent Texts," *JRCP* 1 (2007) n.p. [cited 19 January 2014]. On-line: http://religionconflictpeace.org/volume-1-issue-1-fall-2007/letter-killeth.

19. See Seibert, *Disturbing Divine Behavior*, 241; idem, *The Violence of Scripture: Overcoming the Old Testament's Troubling Legacy* (Minneapolis: Fortress, 2012).

20. Jerome F. D. Creach, *Violence in Scripture* (Int; Louisville, KY: Westminster John Knox, 2013) 104–12; Norbert Lohfink, "*ḥāram*," in *TDOT* 5:197.

21. Römer, *Dark God*, 87–91.

22. For representative excerpts of Origen's perspective on the Conquest narratives of Joshua, see John R. Franke, ed., *Joshua, Judges, Ruth, 1–2 Samuel* (ACCS 4; Downers Grove, IL: InterVarsity, 2005) 46–50.

23. Thus MacDonald, *Deuteronomy and the Meaning of Monotheism*, 108–23, building on the work of R. W. L. Moberly, "Toward an Interpretation of the Shema," in *Theological Exegesis: Essays in Honor of Brevard S. Childs* (ed. C. Seitz and K. Greene-McCreight; Grand Rapids: Eerdmans, 1999) 124–44; idem, *Old Testament Theology*, 41–74; Nicholas

separation from idolatry and exclusivist construction of identity (Deut); response to divine action in the world, and rethinking notions of the identity of God's people (Josh); comforting and encouraging oppressed Israel (Isa 34:2; Zech 14:31); and challenging complacent Israel (Josh 7; Jer 25:9).[24]

This interpretation is attractive, because it eliminates the historical and ethical problem of genocide. However, huge problems remain. Not only does it not resolve the offensive image of a violent God, but it also assumes an extremely sophisticated original readership/hearership. With few exceptions, those who heard the words of Deuteronomy read in worship[25] will have imagined a real Moses promulgating a real policy involving real people in a real historical past on behalf of a real God, YHWH the God of Israel. And even if they did not, but accepted its metaphorical quality, the image of God remains: What sort of God inspires such images of himself?

Scholars who follow these approaches assume that God would not and could not command this sort of violence; it is unbecoming not only of humans but especially of deity. This assumption raises serious questions: Have we not thereby cast God in images of our idealized selves? Have we imposed on the biblical texts interpretations that suit our preferred sensitivities? Theologian Stephen N. Williams has argued convincingly, that yes, God could have commanded the slaughter of the Canaanites, but no, he would never have done so glibly, arbitrarily, or capriciously. On the contrary, whether commanding the death of an individual, or the death of entire peoples, he would have done so with a heavy heart.[26] Although the Scriptures portray this violence as an appropriate response to revolt against the Creator, God treasures all that he has created, most of all human beings created especially to function as his images by governing the world on his behalf.[27] The Canaanites were not a subhuman species that could be annihilated without remorse. On the contrary, one of their members, plucked from the first city within the promised land to be destroyed (Rahab; Josh 6:15–25), became an ancestor not only of the Davidic royal line, but also of Jesus Christ, the Savior of humanity (Matt 1:5).

How then shall we interpret the policy of *ḥērem* as outlined in Deuteronomy? I am pessimistic that we will ever find a satisfying answer, but in

---

Wolterstorff, "Comments on 'What about the Canaanites?'" in *Divine Evil? The Moral Character of the God of Abraham* (ed. Michel Bergmann, Michael J. Murphy, and Michael C. Rea; Oxford: Oxford University Press, 2011) 283–88.

24. Douglas S. Earl, "Holy War and *ḥrm*: A Biblical Theology of *ḥrm*," in *Holy War in the Bible: Christian Morality and the Old Testament Problem* (ed. H. A. Thomas, J. Evans, and P. Copan; Downers Grove, IL: InterVarsity, 2013) 175.

25. Minimally, once every seven years at the Festival of Sukkoth (31:9–13).

26. Stephen N. Williams, "Could God Have Commanded the Slaughter of the Canaanites," *TynBul* 63 (2012) 161–78; idem, "Holy War and the New Atheism," in *Holy War in the Bible*, 312–31.

27. Gen 1:26–31 (cf. 2:15); Ps 8.

wrestling with the issue we need to keep in mind a series of considerations. In isolation none satisfies completely, but taken together they may provide a helpful perspective.

First, the Hebrew noun *ḥērem* derives from a verbal root *ḥāram/heḥĕrîm*, which means "to devote" something/someone completely to the deity, and thereby exclude it from human/common use.[28] As such, the lexeme shares a semantic field with *qādaš/qiddēš*, "to be holy"/"to consecrate."

Lev 27:21–29 uses both expressions of items/people devoted to Yhwh, declaring explicitly that "every devoted thing (*ḥērem*) is supremely holy (*qōdeš-qādāšîm*) to Yhwh" (v. 28). While the link between this text and the charge to "totally destroy" (*haḥărēm taḥărîm*) the Canaanites in Deut 7:2 are not obvious, that Joshua could declare Jericho and all its contents "devoted to Yhwh" (*ḥērem lyhvh*) and not to be touched by Israelites (Josh 6:17–20; cf. Mic 4:13), apparently lest they be contaminated by it (cf. Deut 7:25–26),[29] suggests this sacral nuance is retained in the Deuteronomic policy of *ḥērem* — as it is in the Moabite and Sabaean uses of the root.

Second, the Israelite policy of *ḥērem* was not a distinctly First Testament issue. The instance of the same word in the 9th century B.C.E. Mesha inscription indicates that similar policies were practiced in the first millennium by the Moabites:

> Then Kemoš said to me: "Go, seize Nebo from Israel!" So I went by night; and I fought against it from the break of dawn until noon; and I took it; and I put all to death: 7000 men and boys, and women and girls, and pregnant women, because I had dedicated (*ḥrm*) it to 'Aštar Kemoš. And I took from there the altar-hearths of Yhwh, and I dragged them before the Kemoš."[30]

The word, *ḥrm* also appears in a seventh-century B.C.E. Old South Arabian text, RÉS 3945:

> And he put its town to *ḥērem* . . . . . . and handed over DHSm and TBNY and DTNT [names of cities] to 'Almaqah, and to Saba.'[31]

---

28. For bibliography on lexical studies of *ḥrm*, see Earl, "Holy War and *ḥrm*," 154–55 n. 11.

29. Similarly J. S. Kaminsky, "Joshua 7: A Reassessment of the Israelite Conceptions of Corporate Punishment," in *The Pitcher Is Broken: Memorial Essays for Gösta W. Ahlström* (ed. S. W. Holloway and L. K. Handy; JSOTSup 190; Sheffield: Sheffield Academic Press, 1995) 331. Earl's rejection of this interpretation requires him to marginalize contrary evidence (Josh 6:19, 24) as "later priestly or post-priestly additions." See Earl, "Holy War and *ḥrm*," 157.

30. As translated by K. Lawson Younger Jr., "Some Recent Discussion on the *ḥērem*," in *Far from Minimal: Celebrating the Work and Influence of Philip R. Davies* (ed. D. Burns and J. W. Rogerson; London: T. & T. Clark, 2012) 514. For detailed discussion of this text, see P. D. Stern, *The Biblical* ḥērem: *A Window on Israel's Religious Experience* (BJS 211; Atlanta: Scholars Press, 1991) 19–56.

31. Text and translation adapted from Lauren A. D. Monroe, "Israelite, Moabite and Sabaean War-*ḥērem* Traditions and the Forging of National Identity: Reconsidering the Sabaean Text RES 3945 in Light of Biblical and Moabite Evidence," *VT* 57 (2007) 334–35.

Lauren Monroe has identified four key elements that this text shares with biblical and Moabite accounts: (1) *ḥērem* involves massive destruction and burning of the town; (2) a significant segment of the population is slaughtered and consecrated to the deity; (3) having been emptied, individual towns in the conquered territory are reoccupied by the victors; (4) to signify occupation of the territory by a new population and its deity, conquerors erect a cult installation.[32]

Third, as prescribed in Deuteronomy, Israel's policy of *ḥērem* was not a human convention, but a divinely ordered policy. Indeed, it is presented as conceived, commanded, executed, and brought to successful fulfillment by Yhwh.[33] Even though, for many modern readers, this is precisely the problem, within the conceptual world of the Scriptures this is a given. As the Creator of all things and all human beings, and as Sovereign over all, God can do anything he wants with anyone and be right in doing so (Gen 18:25). Although Yhwh was Israel's particular commander-in-chief, Deuteronomy presents him operating similarly on behalf of and against other nations as well. Earlier, he had destroyed the Horites in Seir and given their land to Edom (2:5, 12, 22), removed the Emmites from the land east of the Dead Sea and given it to the Moabites (2:9–11), and removed the Zamzummites from their territory east of the Jordan and given it to Ammonites (2:19–21). If Yhwh commands Israelites to eliminate Canaanites, he is perfectly within his rights to do so. He does not need to justify his actions or his commands (Jer 18:6–10). However, by itself this answer will not satisfy many, and certainly not the "new atheists."[34]

Fourth, Israel's policy of *ḥērem* directed at Canaanites was neither impulsive nor arbitrary but the culmination of an ancient plan. While this consideration does not remove the sting of the violence against a targeted race of people, readers of the Pentateuch have anticipated this since Gen 15:18–21, where Yhwh promised Abraham that after four centuries he would give their land over to Abraham's descendants. Yhwh's fidelity to this promise

---

32. Deut 11:29–32 and 27:1–26 prescribe that the last element should transpire as soon as the Israelites cross over into the land, prior to any battles. According to Josh 8:30–35, this actually happened after the destruction of Jericho and Ai. For brief discussion of this matter, see Daniel I. Block, "What Do These Stones Mean? The Riddle of Deuteronomy 27," *JETS* 56 (2013) 38–41. Some have suggested the Hittites had similar policies toward conquered territories. See G. F. Del Monte, "The Hittite *Ḥērem*," in *Babel und Bibel 2: Memoriae Igor M. Diakonof, Annual of Ancient Near Eastern, Old Testament, and Semitic Studies* (ed. L. Kogan; OC 8; Winona Lake, IN: Eisenbrauns, 2006) 21–45. However, Harry Hoffner cautions against making too much of the cited Hittite texts and against linking Hittite practices with the biblical *ḥērem* (in private communication, 1/21/2014).

33. So also Eugene H. Merrill, "The Case for Moderate Discontinuity," in *Show Them No Mercy: Four Views on God and Canaanite Genocide* (by C. S. Cowles et al.; Grand Rapids: Eerdmans, 1978) 80–81.

34. As represented by Evan Fales, "Comments on 'Canon and Conquest,'" in *Divine Evil*, 309–13. For discussion, see Williams, "'Holy War' and the New Atheism," 319–27.

underlies his call of Moses 40 years prior to the delivery of the addresses in Deuteronomy (Exod 3:8; 6:8), and through the defeat of Sihon and Og, the Cisjordanian nations were warned of the fate awaiting them. God's elimination of the Canaanites was a necessary step in the history of salvation.[35] In order for Israel to achieve the goals that God had in mind for them—that they might declare to the world his glory and grace—they needed a clean slate. This is a matter of ethical rather than ethnic cleansing. A holy people requires a holy land.

Fifth, the policy of *ḥērem* functions as a divinely ordained means of dealing with sin. The mandate to eliminate the Canaanites was driven by neither genocidal nor military considerations but by the eradication of evil and the prevention of evil from spreading to the new population. Although the Canaanites may not have been any more degenerate than other nations, this policy is rooted in the perception of the Canaanites as a wicked people, a characterization anticipated in Gen 15:16 ("the sin of the Amorites has not yet reached its full measure," NIV), and confirmed in Deuteronomy:

> 9:4: It is because of the wickedness of these nations that YHWH is dispossessing them before you.
>
> 18:12: because of these abhorrent practices (*ḥattô ʿēbōt*) that YHWH your God is dispossessing them before you.

Idolatry is isolated as a particularly pernicious Canaanite vice:

> When YHWH your God has cut off before you the nations whom you are about to invade to dispossess them, and when you have dispossessed them and are settled in their land, after they have been destroyed before you take care that you are not trapped into imitating them. Do not inquire about their gods, saying, "How did these nations worship their gods? I want to do the same myself." You must not worship YHWH your God the way they do, because for their gods they have done every abhorrent thing that YHWH hates (*kol-tôʿăbat yhwh ʾăšer śānēh*). They even burn their sons and their daughters in fire as sacrifices to their gods (12:29–31, my translation).

For Deuteronomy, these practices were worthy of judgment and presented a threat to the spiritual and ethical integrity of Israel, the holy people of YHWH (7:2–5). As Moses emphatically declared in 9:1–24, this did not mean that Israelites would receive the land as a reward for their own moral virtue or spiritual superiority; rather, it represents YHWH's strategy for preserving for himself a holy people.

Sixth, Israel's policy of *ḥērem* assumes a paradigmatic role both for Canaanites and Israelites. From a broadly biblical perspective, the Canaanites suffered a fate that ultimately faces all sinners: the judgment of God. The law of *ḥērem* involves but one of many ways by which YHWH executes judg-

---

35. Cf. Christopher J. H. Wright, *The God I Don't Understand: Reflections on Tough Questions of Faith* (Grand Rapids: Zondervan, 2008) 98.

ment on a sinful people. Later, in poetic verse, YHWH will catalog the resources available to him to accomplish this task when Israel is the targeted people (32:22–25). Within this list of agents, the sword, which serves metonymically for war, is exceptional because it alone involves the active participation of people in carrying out the plan of God.[36] The *ḥērem* ordinance represents a particular kind of war, but in its objectives, the extermination of the Canaanites is of a piece with God's actions against the human population as a whole in the great deluge (Gen 6–9), his call for the destruction of the Midianites (Num 31), his destruction of Judah (Ezek 4–24), and his eschatological defeat of the forces of evil in the book of Revelation. Insofar as the law of *ḥērem* was directed against a particular target, it depicts in microcosm the fate that awaits all who reject YHWH as God and Savior. The Scriptures are consistent in their message that evil and rebellion against YHWH yield death. Apart from the grace of God, this is the fate of all. The difference between the Canaanites subject to this law and the ultimate destiny of other sinful inhabitants of the world is that YHWH employed his people Israel as human agents to send them to their fate.

Seventh, Israel's policy of *ḥērem* was intentionally limited in its scope, both geographically and temporally. It applied only to the seven specific peoples listed in 7:1,[37] and apparently it would be terminated once the conquest of Canaan was complete. Deut 20:10–18 declares unequivocally that this was not to become the general policy governing Israel's relationships with the nations. When they would wage war against other "distant" nations, the Israelites' primary goal was to seek peace, and even when offers of peace were refused, to deal humanely with the innocent within the population. YHWH retained the right to extend the *ḥērem* to other peoples (e.g., Midianites, Amalekites), but the Israelites were not free to do so on their own. Philistines, Moabites, Ammonites, and Aramaeans were outside the scope of this policy.[38] And, contrary to the way Christians have used these texts, this policy provides no warrant for Christian violence against Jews and Muslims during the Crusades, the Puritans' campaigns against Catholics in Britain, or Europeans' claim to some sort of "manifest destiny" in their dispossession and slaughter of native North Americans.

Eighth, Israel's policy of *ḥērem* assumed a sense of corporate identity and corporate solidarity that is difficult for modern Westerners to understand. To us each individual is a separate entity and individual liberties and self-fulfillment is the highest ideal. According to the ancient Near Eastern ideal, however, one found one's significance and identity in relation to the

---

36. Cf. H. Eberhard von Waldow, "The Concept of War in the Old Testament," *HBT* 6 (1984) 34.

37. The number 7 does indeed symbolize the totality of Canaanite peoples, but Römer's rejection of this as a list of specific foreigners (*Dark God*, 88) is gratuitous.

38. This may account for David's apparent hesitation to engage the Philistines in 2 Sam 5:17–25.

community. When one member hurt, they all hurt; when one prospered, they all prospered. For this reason, the Decalogue warns fathers against defection to idolatry, lest Yhwh "visit the guilt of the fathers" on children "to the third and fourth [generation]."[39] In the ancient world, few would have objected on ethical grounds to the fact that children share the fate of their parents. Significantly, this principle applied not only to Canaanite targets of Israel's campaigns but also to the Israelites themselves (cf. Josh 7:6–26).

Ninth, if Israel's policy of *ḥērem* involves a comprehensive call for the extermination of the Canaanites, it also graciously opens the door for exceptions. Although Deuteronomy consistently portrays Canaanites as enemies of Israel, rather than potential "converts,"[40] the sparing of Rahab and her household demonstrates that Canaanites, who would acknowledge Yhwh and cast their lot with his people, would find grace and deliverance in him. Rahab's confession (Josh 2:8–11) acknowledges that her people had at least 40 years of advance warning. So complete was Rahab's incorporation into the community of faith that in the providence of God she became the ancestor of Jesus (Matt 1:5).

Tenth, Israel's policy of *ḥērem* plays no favorites. Although seven specific nations are targeted, Deuteronomy is emphatic that, if Israelites will act like Canaanites, abandon Yhwh, and serve other gods, they too will be subject to the same law—men, women, and children (7:25–26; 13:12–17). Deut 13:15–16 prescribes destruction for any Israelite town that defects in terms more severe and encompassing even than chap. 7 and 20:16–18 demand of Canaanite towns. Whereas 7:1–5, 25–26 had called for the utter destruction of the people and their cultic installations and artifacts, and 20:16–18 "any [person] that breathes," 13:15–16 specifies the inhabitants of that town, and all that is in it and its livestock. In fact, all its booty (cf. 20:14) shall be gathered in the open square and burnt completely to Yhwh.[41] With the

---

39. 5:7–11 (cf. Exod 20:3–6; 34:6–7). Rather than interpreting "to the third and fourth [generation]" linearly, the expression should be read horizontally, referring to the maximum number of generations that would make up a domestic unit. See further, Daniel I. Block, "Marriage and Family in Ancient Israel," in *Marriage and Family in the Biblical World* (ed. K. Campbell; Downers Grove, IL: InterVarsity, 2003) 35–40, 44.

40. So also Mark Fretz, "*Ḥerem* in the Old Testament," in *Essays on War and Peace: Bible and Early Church* (ed. W. M. Swartley; OP 9; Elkhart: Institute of Mennonite Studies, 1986) 15.

41. Accepting Earl's suggestion ("Holy War and *ḥrm*," 158) that *kālîl* be understood according to the common usage, "entirety, entirely, completely" (Exod 28:31; 39:22; Lev 6:15–16[22–23]; Num 4:6; Deut 13:17[16]e; Jdg 20:40; Isa 2:18; Lam 2:15; Ezek 16:14; 27:3; 28:12). Although the root *kll* is used in Punic inscriptions of a specific kind of sacrifice (see *DNWSI* 1:513), an explicitly sacrificial meaning in Hebrew requires an attendant cultic term: Deut 33:10, "They shall offer you incense to savor and whole-offerings (*kālîl*) on your altar"; 1 Sam 7:9, "Samuel took a nursing lamb and sacrificed it as a whole burnt offering (*'ôlâ kālîl*) to Yhwh"; Ps 51:21[19], "Then you will delight in righteous sacrifices, in burnt offerings and whole burnt offerings (*'ôlâ wĕkālîl*)." However, contra Earl, the

privilege of bearing labels like "chosen by YHWH," "holy people belonging to YHWH," YHWH's "treasured people," "sons of YHWH," and being the objects of his affection and redemption (7:6–8; 14:1–2, 21; 26:19), came the weighty responsibility of loving him and representing him well before a watching world. However, because the Israelites lost sight of their mission and went after other gods, in 734–22 B.C.E. the Northern Kingdom went the way of the Canaanites, and 586 B.C.E. the kingdom of Judah followed.

Conclusion

None of these answers to divinely mandated violence against the Canaanites will satisfy everyone, and none of them should be taken in isolation. In many ways, God's policy of *ḥērem* is inscrutable and incredible, and even distasteful. How could a God of mercy and grace call for the extermination of an entire population? Isaiah 55:8–9 reminds us that the ways of God are a mystery. In the end, modern readers may not like YHWH's policy of *ḥērem*, but the divine will is not determined by human sensitivities or values, and God is not bound by the definition of the *World Report on Violence and Health*. While for many this is precisely the problem, the challenge for us is not to forget the context in which we find this violence and the violence demanded in Israel's administration of justice.

Apart from faith and gratitude for YHWH's incomparably gracious acts of redemption, covenant, and provision of a homeland, Israel was indeed a nation like any other, and her migration from Egypt to the promised land was no different from the migration of the Philistines from Caphtor and the Arameans from Kir (Amos 9:7), and we could add, the prehistoric migration of Asians across the Bering Strait to the Americas; the relatively recent migration of Europeans to the Americas, southern Africa, and Australia; Russians beyond the Urals into the Far East; and the migration of Chinese throughout southeastern Asia. Sadly, such migrations have often involved the forceful uprooting and slaughter of indigenous of populations.

However, within the context of the Scriptures and the divine program of redemption for humanity, Israel was not a nation like all the rest. YHWH's covenant initiated with Abraham (Gen 15, 17), established with his descendants at Sinai (Exod 19–24), and confirmed with the generation poised to enter Canaan (Deuteronomy), had established her as his covenant people, his adopted sons, his treasured possession, and his holy nation—though not for their own sake. YHWH chose this people specially, redeemed them from slavery, and granted them the land of Canaan for the sake of the world. According to the biblical narrative, in the wake of Adam's sin all of humanity was condemned to the wrath of God. However, unwilling to abandon his creation, God graciously chose Israel to be his agents of mercy to a

---

construction *kālîl lyhwh*, "completely to YHWH," demands a sacral interpretation, even if this is not a sacrifice in the sense of a "whole burnt offering" (*'ôlâ*).

condemned world, to establish in Canaan a microcosm of the Eden that had been lost, and to display to all the world the divine glory and grace available to them (Deut 26:19).

Inasmuch as Yhwh had staked his reputation in the world on this people, the fulfillment of this universal mission depended not only on the continued judgment of evil, but also on displaying an alternative course. The divine focus from the outset was the world, but God's mission demanded an agent grateful for his mercy and pure in its religious devotion and ethic. Like the removal of cancerous growths, threats to Israel's fundamental spiritual health sometimes required radical surgery. However, even more than human surgeons, God does not impose these punishments callously or coldly; he does so with an extremely heavy heart. This does not mean we should be comfortable with divine violence, any more than we should passively accept misfortune and grief in our personal lives. The examples of Abraham (Gen 18), Moses (Exod 32, Num 14, Deut 9), and Amos (Amos 7) invite us to protest divine acts of violence and to question divine actions, but they do not authorize us to protest the divine agenda. Ultimately, their examples challenge us to accept the wisdom and righteousness of God. The challenge for us is that we treasure God's grace in our own lives and pray for him to extend his grace to others. Perhaps when they see what God has done for us, like Rahab outsiders will confess faith in our God.

Postscript

Having wrestled with the theme of divine violence in Deuteronomy, it strikes me that such a study should always be preceded by a study of divine grace in the book, not to evade or deny the painful reality, but to provide context for it.[42] Because Israel owed everything she had or was to Yhwh's gracious acts on her behalf—apart from which her ultimate fate was the same as the Canaanites—she should have gratefully accepted her role as a trophy of Yhwh's mercy, kept herself pure and unspotted from surrounding evils, and evoked the envy and admiration of the world, not because she was so great, but because she bore the name of Yhwh (28:9–10). His nearness to his people, his revelation of himself, and the righteousness of his will were without precedent or equal (4:5–8).[43]

---

42. Cf. Seitz's appeal ("Canon and Conquest," 292–308) to read the deuteronomic prescriptions and narrative accounts against the backdrop of divine grace. For a rejoinder, see Fales, "Comments on 'Canon and Conquest,'" 309–13.

43. I am grateful to Michelle Knight for her helpful responses to an earlier draft of this essay. Of course, any deficiencies in style and content are of my own making.

Chapter 4

Taking the Land by Force: Divine Violence in Joshua

HÉLÈNE M. DALLAIRE

Introduction

In Christian theology, the faces of God are manifold. On the one hand, God takes pity, expresses compassion, forgives sins, is slow to anger and great in mercy. On the other hand, God hates, punishes sins, fights military battles, puts individuals to death and brings judgment. In recent decades, scholars have sought to reconcile these various facets of God's character into a theology that expresses *univocality*, that is "a desire to identify a single, stable, divine character who remains fundamentally the same in every piece of biblical discourse."[1] But the task has been arduous and problematic because an exact description of God, based solely on the data found in Scripture, cannot be reconciled into a single and simple theology.

According to Terence Fretheim, Christian theology must consider the "two faces of God": (1) the "textual God" and (2) the "actual God." Fretheim describes the "textual God" as the God who is revealed within the pages of the Bible and portrayed by a people who lived in a specific historical and cultural context, and the "actual God" as the God who transcends those pages and allows the reader to encounter him personally "under the guidance of the Holy Spirit."[2] Eric Seibert notes that "one [the 'textual God'] is a literary representation; the other [the 'actual God'], a living reality."[3] He adds that, "any effort to use the Old Testament to know God as God really is requires us to distinguish between the *characterization* of God in Scripture [textual God] and the *character* of God in reality [actual God]."[4]

---

1. Timothy Beal, "The System and the Speaking Subject in the Hebrew Bible: Reading for Divine Abjection," *BibInt* 2 (1994) 171.
2. Terence Fretheim and Karlfried Froehlich, *The Bible as Word of God in a Postmodern Age* (Minneapolis: Fortress, 1998) 117.
3. Eric A. Seibert, *Disturbing Divine Behavior: Troubling Old Testament Images of God* (Minneapolis: Fortress, 2009) 170.
4. Seibert, *Disturbing Divine Behavior*, 170. Seibert adds that "anyone who spends even a little time with the Old Testament will quickly realize that God is portrayed in

Seibert contends that failure to distinguish between these two essentials has led to serious errors of interpretation and has resulted in unspeakable horrors and appalling acts of violence in the name of God (for example, the Crusades).[5] "Legitimizing wars and exterminating entire populations have, unfortunately, been constants throughout the history of Christianity."[6] These horrific events reveal a serious misrepresentation of the nature of the God of Abraham, Isaac, and Jacob, whose character is disclosed both through Scripture (the "textual God") and through personal encounter (the "actual God").

The portrayal of a seemingly bloodthirsty God, who commands the genocide of innocent people in the book of Joshua, is one of the most disturbing depictions of God in the whole of Scripture. In Daniel Hawk's words, "it antagonizes modern sensibilities."[7] War ideology and the slaughter of men,

---

many different ways. Often, these diverse portrayals do not stand in tension with one another but contribute to a multifaceted portrait of God. Yet there are times when one image stands in such contrast to another that the two seem mutually exclusive" (p. 172). Seibert points to examples where God changes his mind, while being depicted as unwavering in his decision making (e.g., 1 Sam 15:29; Jonah 3:10); God both punishes children for the sins of their forefathers and considers children innocent for the sins of their fathers (e.g., Exod 20:5; Ezek 18:20); God is gracious and merciful yet he hardens people's hearts (e.g., Exod 34:6; Num 11:1).

5. In "Joshua and the Crusades," Douglas S. Earl challenges the view of scholars who maintain that the book of Joshua served as a catalyst for the Crusades (in *Holy War in the Bible: Christian Morality and an Old Testament Problem* [ed. H. A. Thomas, J. Evans, and P. Copan; Downers Grove, IL: IVP Academic, 2013] 19–43). Earl's view is based on his examination of an anti-Jewish medieval work of the 13th century C.E. entitled *Bible Moralisée* (Codex 2554) in which connections between the book of Joshua and the Crusades are surprisingly absent. Earl concludes that during the time of the Crusades, "Joshua was read more in terms of the typology of the church than as a manifesto for conquest or crusades" and that "the books of Maccabees are quite appropriately taken as a paradigm for the Crusades while Joshua is not" ("Joshua and the Crusades," 25, 31). In his view, "the gospels played a far more prominent role in justifying the Crusades than the book of Joshua," because the crusaders "understood their actions not so much in terms of conquest, but of sacrificial love for their brethren in the Holy Land who were themselves suffering the results of conquest" (*The Joshua Delusion: Rethinking Genocide in the Bible* [Eugene, OR: Cascade, 2010] 7, 159 n. 14, respectively). For discussions from different perspectives on the relationship between the Crusades and the Old Testament, see, e.g., Daniel R. Heimbach, "Crusade in the Old Testament and Today," in *Holy War in the Bible*, 179–200; Roland Bainton, *Christian Attitudes toward War and Peace* (Nashville: Abingdon, 1960) 44–52; D. H. Green, *The Millstätter Exodus: A Crusading Epic* (Cambridge: Cambridge University Press, 1966) 207–8; Susan Niditch, *War in the Hebrew Bible: A Study in the Ethics of Violence* (New York: Oxford University Press, 1993) 4; Michael Prior, *The Bible and Colonialism: A Moral Critique* (Biblical Seminar 48; Sheffield: Sheffield Academic Press, 1997) 29–36; M. C. Gaposchkin, "Louis IX, Crusade and the Promise of Joshua in the Holy Land," *JMedHist* 34 (2008) 246, 273.

6. Thomas Römer, *Dark God: Cruelty, Sex, and Violence in the Old Testament* (trans. S. O'Neill; New York: Paulist, 2013) 71.

7. L. Daniel Hawk, *Joshua* (Berit Olam; Collegeville, MN: Liturgical Press, 2000) xii.

women and children have long troubled readers of the Bible. Recently, a friend wrote,

> I always begin on these "read-the-Bible-through-in-a-year" programs and do fine until I get to Joshua and Judges. Then I quit because of all the violence. Then I turn to the Gospels and am stumped once again by the need for blood in atonement/redemption. I want to return to my nice, clean, American, 21st-century Christian upbringing until I realize that, if I were a Christian woman in Nigeria or Nepal (or pick your place), the chances are great that I'd be dealing with sex-slavery, kidnapping, dying refugee children, and other violent horrors. Would I still believe that my Good Shepherd loves and pursues the one lost sheep or "blessed are those who mourn"?[8]

A close reading of the book of Joshua in its social and cultural context reveals that the book was never intended to advocate for divinely legitimated xenophobia, oppression, and violence. The "textual God" who commands the extermination of entire communities in Canaan, rains boulders on the heads of Israel's enemies, and leads fierce military battles cannot be equated to an "actual God," who would instruct believers in our modern age to annihilate people who hold a different worldview using the violent stratagems described in the book of Joshua. The thought of a brutal and inhumane God commanding the violent annihilation of a people is shocking to humanity, and the depiction of violence in Joshua, under the leadership of Yahweh, seems to support what we would identify today as "war crimes." Terminology such as "genocide" and "ethnic cleansing"—terms that evoke negative emotions—have been unnecessarily linked to the content of the book of Joshua.

Joshua: A Brief History of Interpretation

Over the last two millennia, interpretations of the book of Joshua have been wide-ranging. For the most part, early Church Fathers preserved an historical interpretation, while spiritualizing its message.[9] During the second century, Irenaeus sought to highlight the spiritual, nonliteral interpretation of the conquest narrative within the context of his apostolic tradition. During the 3rd century, Origen's reading of Joshua became the adopted standard interpretation until the Reformation.[10] Origen recognized the historical

---

8. Beverly McCoy, personal communication.

9. Earl asserts that in the writings of early Church Fathers (e.g., Origen, Augustine, Gregory of Nyssa), the book of Joshua was read not as a narrative of conquest and genocide but rather as an ideological myth replete with symbols "that invite emotional conviction and participation" (e.g., crossing the Jordan, the spy story, the deceit of the Gibeonites; *Reading Joshua as Christian Scripture* [Winona Lake, IN: Eisenbrauns, 2010] 17).

10. Creach notes that Origen interpreted the Deuteronomy 7 passage and the conquest of Canaan figuratively, with Joshua as a messianic figure pointing to Jesus (from the LXX name of Joshua appearing as *Iēsous*). Origen argues that, "Jericho (Josh. 6) is

and ethical difficulties of the text and pointed Christians toward the spiritual sense of the text—where he highlighted values and truth—rather than reflecting on its historical context.[11] For example, regarding Josh 10:20–26 (the violent treatment of the five Amorite kings), Origen states,

> if only my Lord Jesus the Son of God would grant that to me and order me to crush the spirit of fornication with my feet and trample upon the necks of the spirit of wrath and rage, to trample on the demon of avarice, to trample down boasting, to crush the spirit of arrogance with my feet, and, when I have done all these things, not to hang the most exalted of these exploits upon myself but upon his cross.... But if I deserve to act thus, I shall be blessed and what Jesus [Joshua] said to the ancients will also be said to me, "Go courageously and be strengthened; do not be afraid nor be awed by their appearance, because the Lord God has delivered all your enemies into your hands" [Josh 10:25]. If we understand these things spiritually and manage wards of this type spiritually and if we drive out all those spiritual iniquities from heaven, then we shall be able at last to receive from Jesus as a share of the inheritance even those places and kingdoms that are the kingdoms of heaven, bestowed by our Lord and Savior Jesus Christ.[12]

During the fourth century, Epiphanius justified the conquest of Canaan based on the claim that Noah had given the land to Shem and his descendants after the flood.[13] According to rabbinic interpretation, the violence of the book of Joshua was mitigated by the proposition that "Joshua must have offered terms of peace to his opponents before killing them as the last resort."[14] Another Jewish tradition "holds that the command to annihilate the enemy tribes was a one-time command that does not have validity beyond that one event."[15] Centuries later, Calvin returned to a more literal in-

---

a metaphor of the present age, to be overcome by the kingdom of God. The city of Ai (Josh. 7–8) represents the chaos of life and sin Jesus overcame on the cross. Most importantly, the order to place under ban all the residents of the land is not an injunction to kill other human beings. Rather, it is a figurative way of saying that the Christian must purge the self of all that would hinder pure devotion to God.... (Origen, *Homilies on Joshua*, 34)" (Jerome F. Creach, *Violence in Scripture* [Interpretation; Louisville, KY: Westminster John Knox, 2013] 102). Creach also notes that some early Jewish interpreters of Deut 7:1–5 did not adopt a literal interpretation of the passage. Early Jewish rabbis honed in on the expression "show them no mercy" (*lōʾ tĕḥānnēm*) and suggested that the verb did not come from *ḥnn*, "to show mercy," but rather from *ḥnh*, "to encamp." Consequently, the passage would mean that Israel should not provide living quarters for the Canaanites, thereby mitigating the offense of killing innocent people (ibid., 103).

11. Earl, *The Joshua Delusion*, 8.

12. Origen, *Homilies on Joshua* (FC 105; Washington, DC: Catholic University of America Press, 2002) 123–24 (from *Hom. Josh.* 12.3, trans. B. J. Bruce).

13. Ofri Ilany, "From Divine Commandment to Political Act: The Eighteenth-Century Polemic on the Extermination of the Canaanites," *Journal of the History of Ideas* 73 (2012) 448.

14. Rannfrid I. Thelle, "The Biblical Conquest Account and Its Modern Hermeneutical Challenges," *Studia theologica* 61 (2007) 73.

15. Ibid.

terpretation and stated that God unequivocally ordered the destruction of Canaanites and, because this "was his pleasure, it behooves us to acquiesce in his decision, without presuming to inquire why he was so severe."[16] Calvin noted that, because Israel was relentlessly attacked by its enemies—for example, the kings of Jerusalem, Hebron, Lachish, Jarmuth, Eglon, Hazor—it had the right to defend itself and to respond to its aggressors with just violence. This interpretation of the conquest narrative served as the basis for pervasive Christian geopolitical agendas of colonial expansion and cost countless innocent lives in the name of God, who would have never condoned this subjective agenda. Furthermore, the depiction of an immoral God in Joshua has led to questioning of the morality of the Bible as a whole.

According to Bill Templer, the book of Joshua "is the narrative of colonial conquest *par excellence*, the 'redeeming' of a 'devilish wilderness' and the subjugation and extermination of its 'heathen' inhabitants."[17] The Puritans who came to America between the 16th and the 19th century promoted this ideology and viewed themselves as the "New Israel," with their new land as a "Modern Canaan" to be conquered.[18] Puritan colonialism and genocides against Native Americans find their roots in the biblical conquest account of Joshua and in God's command to exterminate the Amalekites (Exod 17:16) and the Canaanites (Deut 7:16–26; 20:10–18). The Puritan national imagination led them to engage "in 'redemptive acts of violence' which promote[d] Anglo-American interests through displacement or destruction of the indigenous tribal cultures."[19] Templer notes that, "the first official war against Native Americans in North America, later described as a 'war of extinction,' was an archetype of *ur*-conflict in the conquest of the New Canaan."[20] The murder and burning of innocent men, women, and children was celebrated as an act of God, who laughed at his enemies, judged the heathen in the land, and made them a "fiery oven."[21] According to William Bradford, the 1637 Pequot massacre represented God's providence for his people in the conquest of the "New Canaan":

> Those that scraped the fire were slaine with the sword; some hewed to peeces, others rune throw with their rapiers, so as they were quickly dispatchte, and very few escapted. It was conceived they thus destroyed about 400 at this

---

16. John Calvin, *Commentaries on the Book of Joshua* (trans. H. Beveridge; Grand Rapids: Eerdmans, 1949) 157–58.
17. Bill Templer, "The Political Sacralization of Imperial Genocide: Contextualizing Timothy Dwight's *The Conquest of Canaan*," *Postcolonial Studies* 9 (2006) 380.
18. Templer, *art. cit.*, 362–63; Thelle, "The Biblical Conquest Account and Its Modern Hermeneutical Challenges," 74; Ilany, "From Divine Commandment to Political Act," 443–45.
19. Templer, "The Political Sacralization of Imperial Genocide," 368.
20. Ibid., 366.
21. Laura Elliff, "Cooking the History Books: The Thanksgiving Massacre," *Republic of Lakotah*. November 22, 2009. On-line: http://www.republicoflakotah.com/2009/cooking-the-history-books-the-thanksgiving-massacre/

time. It was a fearful sight to see them thus frying in the fyer, and the streams of blood quenching the same, and horrible was the stincke and sente there of, but the victory seemed a sweete sacrifice, and they gave the prayers thereof to God, who had wrought so wonderfully for them, thus to inclose their enemise in their hands, and give them so speedy a victory over so proud and insulting an enimie.[22]

John Mason, an English army captain who led attacks against Native Americans tribes in 1637, attributed the aforementioned holocaust to an act of God. In his attempt to justify the massacre, Mason wrote that God was involved in the event and had done great things for his people among the heathens who lived in the land.[23] This justification for the massacre is further confirmed in the writings of Captain Underhill, who recorded the bloodbath with these words: "It may be demanded, Why should you be so furious? Should not Christians have more mercy and compassion? Sometimes the Scripture declareth women and children must perish with their parents. Sometimes the case alters, but we will not dispute it now. We had sufficient light from the word of God for our proceedings."[24] In his study of the political-sacred imperial genocide of 1637, Templer writes:

> the conquest of Canaan's biblical narrative, the "Joshua mythologem", has provided the prime political-theological rationalization via scriptural narrative (the sacralization of politics) for the project of Western imperial and racist expansion, since 1500, into the peripheries and the divinely sanctioned subjugation and extermination of native peoples across the globe. Its ideology constitutes the dark ethnocentric underbelly of genocide in the foundation myths of the US Republic, the Spanish conquest of the Americas and Philippines, the white supremacist Afrikaner nation in South Africa.... It is the narrative "skeleton" in the closet of Western imperial conquest and its driving sacralized ideologies.[25]

During the two centuries that followed (18th and 19th centuries), many German conservative scholars defended the literal interpretation of the conquest narrative, while others distanced themselves from the traditional reading of Scripture. Conservatives such as Johann David Michaelis and Johann Gottfried Herder "formulated one of the earliest justifications for genocide on ethnic grounds. Once seen as an extraordinary outburst of divine violence, the Canaanite extermination was now normalized and naturalized, described as a probable and even necessary outcome of human nature."[26]

---

22. Ibid.
23. Ibid.
24. "The History," *Mystic Voices: The Story of the Pequot War*. On-line: http://www.pequotwar.com/history.html
25. Templer, "The Political Sacralization of Imperial Genocide," 380.
26. Ilany, "From Divine Command to Political Act," 461.

Joshua: Ideology

For some liberal scholars, Joshua is simply a legendary mythological figure, and consequently, genocide and ethnic cleansing in the book of Joshua are nonissues. The inclusion of the book of Joshua in the canon is justified by one or more of the following arguments:

First, King Josiah, who ruled in Judah during the seventh century B.C.E., needed to validate his territorial expansion policies in Canaan and his violent displacement of its inhabitants. In order to accomplish this, scribes of his day claimed that Israel had received the land directly from God through a divine promise made to their forefathers centuries earlier.[27] According to Richard Nelson, Joshua is a literary creation that serves as a prototype of King Josiah and serves to legitimize his actions during the seventh century. Nelson supports his view by highlighting some of the parallels between Joshua and Josiah: (1) both leaders were extremely loyal to the law of Moses (Josh 1:7; 2 Kgs 22:2); (2) both celebrated the Passover (Josh 5:10–12; 2 Kgs 23:21–23); (3) both sought to purge the land of foreign gods and establish the worship of Yahweh (Deut 7:1–5; 2 Kgs 23:4–20); and (4) both renewed publicly the covenant between Israel and Yahweh (Josh 8:30–35; 2 Kgs 23:2–3).[28] However, Nelson fails to take into account the numerous historical (for example, crossings, plagues, circumcision, Passover celebrations, theophanies), literary (for example, idiomatic expressions, divine commands, inclusios), and thematic (for example, leadership roles, divine missions, land promise) parallels that place Moses and Joshua in close proximity in time, centuries before Josiah's reign.[29]

Second, Israel needed to develop a sense of national identity that highlighted the polarized "us" vs. "them" ideology and justified the subjugation of the "Other"—in this case, the Canaanites—through oppression and conquest.[30] Failure of the "Other" to submit allowed for violent means of domination to be exercised by Israel.[31] Through the dehumanization of the Canaanites—making them powerless subordinates through fear, violence and intimidation—the Israelites could maintain their position of power and preserve their identity as subjugators. This line of argument can be

---

27. Seibert, *Disturbing Divine Behavior*, 141.
28. Richard D. Nelson, *The Historical Books* (IBT; Nashville: Abingdon, 1998) 89. For a fuller treatment, see idem, "Josiah in the Book of Joshua," *JBL* 100 (1981) 531–40; Creach, *Violence in Scripture*, 98–99; Römer, *Dark God*, 77–78; John Mansford Prior, "'Power' and 'the Other' in *Joshua*: The Brutal Birthing of a Group Identity," *Mission Studies* 23 (2006) 27.
29. Hélène Dallaire and Denise Morris, "Joshua and Israel's Exodus from the Desert Wilderness," in *Reverberations of the Exodus in Scripture* (ed. R. Michael Fox; Eugene, OR: Pickwick, 2014) 18–34.
30. Lori L. Rowlett, *Joshua and the Rhetoric of Violence: A New Historicist Analysis* (JSOTSup 226; Sheffield; Sheffield Academic Press, 1996) 29; idem, "Inclusion, Exclusion and Marginality in the Book of Joshua," *JSOT* 55 (1992) 15–23.
31. Rowlett, *Joshua and the Rhetoric of Violence*, 183.

refuted by the fact that Israel's identity ("us") had been distinctive from that of other nations ("the Other") for centuries since, (1) as early as the time of the Patriarchs (Gen 12:1–3), Abram's descendants were set apart from the rest of the nations of the world; (2) Israel's unique identity was marked by God, who called them a "chosen people" (Exod 19:5; Deut 7:6; 14:2; 26:18; Ps 135:4); (3) during their stay in Egypt, the Israelites did not assimilate into the Egyptian society but rather they lived in isolation in Goshen, away from the Egyptian population (Gen 45:10; 46:28–34); and (4) the law given to Moses at Mt. Sinai confirmed their unique status before God and further separated them from other nations (Deut 4:7–8). There was therefore no need for Israel to develop further a national identity neither during nor after her entry into Canaan.

Third, the conquest narrative served to inspire confidence in the Israelites in the face of powerful foes and the constant threat of attacks from surrounding nations, whose thirst for more land and greater wealth incited them to engage in military warfare.[32] Because Israel was a relatively small nation (Deut 7:7) strategically located between superpowers (such as Egypt, Assyria, and Babylon), the conquest narrative encouraged Israel to persevere in the face of the international giants who crisscrossed the land.

Fourth, it is argued that similarities between the language of Assyrian vassal treaties and the covenant language of Deuteronomy places the Deuteronomistic History in the 8th–7th century B.C.E.—that is, in Josiah's time period (cf. Deut 6:4–5 and 10:12 with "You shall love Assurbanipal... as yourself" in the 672 B.C.E. Treaty of Assarhaddon; "We will love Assurbanipal, king of Assyria, and hate his enemies.... We will neither establish nor seek another king or lord for ourselves" in the 650 B.C.E. Treaty of Assurbanipal).[33] As in ancient Near Eastern warfare rhetoric, Yahweh—the God of Israel—required absolute faithfulness from his subjects, beyond what was required by any Assyrian king. In both contexts, the leader is warlike and participates in the extermination of enemies. Based on this argument, Römer concludes that "the book of Joshua must therefore be understood primarily as a literary and ideological construction in which the invention of the conquest of the land serves the theological agenda of the Deuteronomists."[34] On the other hand, however, the language of the book of Joshua echoes reports of military campaigns that occurred in the second millennium B.C.E. (for example, Hittite, Hattusili I; Egyptian,

---

32. Ibid.; Nelson, *Joshua*, 18.

33. Römer, *Dark God*, 74–75. For additional examples of similarities between ANE warfare propaganda (e.g., Essarhaddon, Sargon II) and the book of Joshua, see Thomas Römer, "Joshua's Encounter with the Commander of Yhwh's Army (Josh 5:13–15): Literary Construction or Reflection or a Royal Ritual?" in *Warfare, Ritual, and Symbol in Biblical and Modern Contexts* (ed. B. E. Kelle, F. R. Ames; and J. L. Wright; Ancient Israel and Its Literature; Atlanta: Society of Biblical Literature, 2014) 50–51, 56–59.

34. Römer, "Joshua's Encounter," 51.

Merneptah).³⁵ Consequently, there is no need to date the account of the conquest of Canaan to the 8th or 7th century.

Fifth, and supposedly congruent with the emphases of Josiah's reign, the conquest narrative demonstrated that loyalty and obedience to Yahweh by those who followed the law of Moses were rewarded with blessings (Josh 1:7–8). This theory is validated by the account of Israel's obedience at Jericho, where Yahweh brought victory to Israel (Josh 6), and by the defeat of Israel at Ai and the subsequent destruction of Achan and his entire family (Josh 7) because of his disobedience. However, this argument is tenuous, because the book of Joshua includes several accounts of unpunished disloyalties by Israel (for example, the negotiation with the Canaanite woman [Josh 2]) and disobedience to his commands (for example, the covenant with Gibeonites [Josh 9]).

In addition, archaeological evidence (or the lack thereof) has led scholars to question the historical validity of the conquest narrative, theorizing that the presence of Israelites in the land can be explained by one or a combination of the following models: (1) protracted military conquest (my personal position); (2) peaceful infiltration; (3) peasant revolt; (4) collapse/abandonment model; (5) cyclic/nomadic interruption model; and (6) mixed multitudes.³⁶

On the literary level, doubts concerning the historical reliability of the conquest narrative in Joshua have arisen from apparent contradictory and hyperbolic statements found within the narrative. First, after reading that "everyone was destroyed by the sword" (11:11, 14),³⁷ that "the whole land was conquered" (11:16, 43), and that "none who breathed was left alive" (11:11, 14), we discover that the Israelites were "incapable of driving out" the Geshurites, the Maacathites, the Jebusites and the Canaanites from their land (13:13; 15:63; 16:10a; 17:12), and that "much land remained to be conquered" (13:1).³⁸ Second, the repetition of the phrase "all Israel" in the crossing of the Jordan (3:17), the stoning of Achan and his family (7:24), the reading of the law of Moses (8:33), the assault of the town of Ai (8:24), the defeat of the southern cities (10:29–43), and Joshua's final speech (23:2) stresses group identity rather than the literal inclusion of all Israelites.³⁹ Third, in Joshua 11—a summary of the conquest—hyperbolic language abounds. The word "all" (*kôl*) appears 24 times in 23 verses (especially vv. 10–23). Reflecting the

---

35. K. Lawson Younger Jr., *Ancient Conquest Accounts: A Study in Ancient Near Eastern and Biblical History Writing* (JSOTSup 98; Sheffield: JSOT Press, 1990) 122–23.
36. For a survey of views, see Ralph K. Hawkins, *How Israel Became a People* (Nashville: Abingdon, 2013) 29–48; Hélène M. Dallaire, "Joshua" in *The Expositor's Bible Commentary* (12 vols.; rev. ed.; Grand Rapids: Zondervan, 2012) 2:828–30.
37. Scripture quotations are from the ESV.
38. See also Judg 1:21, 29–31, 33, where the text confirms that the inhabitants of the land had not been completely driven out by Israel.
39. Siebert, *Disturbing Divine Behavior*, 142.

language of ancient Near Eastern annals of military campaigns, Joshua's victory is highlighted with hyperbolic and repetitive terminology. The summary in Josh 11 reflects the utopian and iterative encoded language found in Assyrian texts (for example, Annals of Tiglath-Pileser I), Hittite conquest accounts (for example, Annals of Hattusili I), and Egyptian campaign reports (for example, Merneptah Stela).[40] Because these Near Eastern military campaigns mentioned here are considered historical, there is no need to dismiss the historical validity of Joshua's campaigns in Canaan.

On the language of Joshua, Paul Copan notes that, "like his ancient Near Eastern contemporaries, Joshua used the language of conventional warfare rhetoric. This language sounds like bragging and exaggeration to our ears. . . . The language is typically . . . full of bravado, depicting total devastation."[41] Although the repetition of the Hebrew word for "all," "everyone," "no one," "completely" and "entirely" (*kôl*) in Josh 11 is hyperbolic and overemphasized, it is certainly fitting in summarizing the victories of Israel over the inhabitants of the land.[42] At the end of the conquest narrative, Joshua testifies that the Canaanites continued to live in the land and warns Israel to refrain from idolatry and Canaanite religious practices (23:12–13), thus confirming that the Israelites had not entirely subjugated the inhabitants of Canaan. Based on this textual evidence, we understand that the conquest of the land was partial at best—at least for the early years in Canaan—and that the rhetoric of the book of Joshua cannot always be interpreted literally. This said, these apparent literary inconsistencies should not lead readers to mythologize the

---

40. *Assyrian texts*: Younger, *Ancient Conquest Accounts*, 122–23; *Hittite conquest accounts*: ibid., 163; *Egyptian campaign reports*: ibid., 190–92. Younger highlights the repetition of what he calls "bombastic" syntagmas such as "never had the like been done" in Egyptian military accounts (p. 190). Paul Copan provides examples from annals of Egyptian Tuthmosis III and Ramses II, Merneptah son of Ramses II, Hittite king Mursilli II, Mesha king of Moab, and Sennacherib Assyrian king (*Is God a Moral Monster? Making Sense of the Old Testament God* [Grand Rapids: Baker, 2011] 171). See also Paul Copan and Matthew Flannagan, "The Ethics of 'Holy War' for Christian Morality and Theology," in *Holy War in the Bible: Christian Morality and an Old Testament Problem* (ed. H. A. Thomas, J. Evans, and P. Copan; Downers Grove, IL: IVP Academic, 2013) 215–39.

41. Copan, *Is God a Moral Monster?* 170–71; Thelle, "The Biblical Conquest Account and Its Modern Hermeneutical Challenges," 69–70.

42. Copan puts the historical nature of the Joshua campaigns in perspective, noting that unrecognized hyperbolic language

> has misled many Old Testament scholars in their assessments of the book of Joshua; some have concluded that the language of wholesale slaughter and total occupation—which didn't (from all other indications) actually take place—proves that these accounts are falsehoods. But ancient Near Eastern accounts readily used "utterly/completely destroy" and other obliteration language even when the event didn't literally happen that way.

(Copan, *Is God a Moral Monster?* 171; see also Paul Copan and Matthew Flannagan, "The Ethics of 'Holy War' for Christian Morality and Theology," in *Holy War in the Bible*, 215–39).

narrative in Joshua and question the historical validity of the text. The narrative must be interpreted through multiple lenses—literary, cultural, historical, archaeological, and contextual.

The Warrior God in Joshua

In the book of Joshua, Yahweh is depicted as a warlord, who orchestrates military strategies and participates actively in the conquest of the land (3:10; 5:13–15; 9:9–10; 23:3). Read in the context of the ancient Near East, where battles were won because the deity was on one's side and battles were lost as punishment from the god or goddess for offenses, the presence of Yahweh as divine warrior in the conquest narrative is reasonable.[43] Seibert, for whom the book of Joshua has been distorted and abused to legitimize violence, maintains that, "given the ubiquity of the divine warrior motif in the ancient world, Israel's description of Yahweh as a warrior is neither surprising or remarkable."[44] According to Römer, the ideological warfare rhetoric in the book of Joshua clearly depicts Yahweh "as a warrior-God who is the high chief of a people who are just as warlike as he is."[45] The theme of God as warrior is not unique to the book of Joshua. In Exodus, God destroys the Egyptians who are pursuing the Israelites as they attempt to flee the country (Exod 15:1–18).[46] Following their deliverance from bondage, the Israelites celebrate the miraculous event and sing the Songs of Moses, in which we find, "The Lord is a man of war" (Exod 15:3). This bold statement is the first explicit mention in Scripture of the warlike nature of the God of Abraham, Isaac, and Jacob. In Josh 10, God hurls large stone missiles on the enemies of Israel (10:11). In 2 Samuel, God defeats the Philistines in two separate battles, and David proclaims, "The Lord has broken through my enemies before me like a breaking flood" (5:20). In Ps 68, God is praised for scattering Israel's enemies and for blowing them away like smoke (68:1–2).

The theme of God as warrior finds its root in the concept of "holy war" or "Yahweh war."[47] Tremper Longman III and Daniel Reid note that, "in ancient Israel, all of life was religious, all of life was related to God. Warfare was no exception. Indeed, the biblical text is a witness to Israel's understanding

---

43. Seibert, *Disturbing Divine Behavior*, 171–72.

44. Ibid., 172.

45. Römer, *Dark God*, 76. For Römer, the conquest narrative is nonhistorical and an invention of the Deuteronomist (idem, "Joshua's Encounter," 51).

46. For a thorough study of Yahweh as divine warrior in the book of Exodus, see Charlie Trimm, "*Yhwh Fights for Them!" The Divine Warrior in the Exodus Narrative* (Gorgias Dissertations 58; Pistacaway: Gorgias, 2014).

47. Römer notes that the events of the book of Joshua should not be interpreted as "holy war," because in the traditional concept of "holy war" the people fight for their god, whereas in the Bible, God is the one who fights for his people (*Dark God*, 79). In *The Biblical Herem: A Window on Israel's Religious Experience* (Brown Judaic Studies 211; Atlanta: Scholars Press, 1991), Philip D. Stern echoes this view and notes that the label of "holy war" is a modern construct that does not reflect earlier interpretation (p. 218).

of God's pervasive role in its warfare."[48] Patrick Miller maintains that, "at the center of Israel's warfare was the unyielding conviction that victory was the result of a fusion of divine and human activity."[49] He notes that "the spoil and prisoners of war were holy and separated, even as the warriors who fought for Israel were holy."[50] Thelle states,

> biblical scholars have had a tendency to distinguish holy war as a specific category of war in the ancient world. More recently, however, scholars have realized that it is not correct to distinguish holy war from other types of war, and that all warfare must be considered holy in the ancient world. This applies as much to Israel as the rest of the Ancient Near East. The world view that understood gods as taking part in the events in the world and saw wars as wars between gods, was a view that the ancient Israelites shared with their neighbors and with the superpowers of that day.[51]

The topic of war appears in all but two books of the Hebrew Bible—Ruth and the Song of Songs. A glance at ancient Near Eastern literature reveals that the topic of war was ubiquitous and that gods regularly engaged in battle (for example, Baal defeats Yam in the Baal Epic, Ea and Marduk defeat Apsu and Tiamat in the Enuma Elish). In "Crusade in the Old Testament and Today," Heimbach summarizes von Rad's list of key elements that depict "holy war" in the Old Testament. Many of these features appear in the book of Joshua:[52]

1. God calls the people to battle with a trumpet call (*Josh* 6:8–9; Num 10:9; Judg 3:37; 6:34; 1 Sam 13:3–4)
2. Men are consecrated to God for battle (*Josh* 3:5)
3. Men are circumcised before the battle (*Josh* 5:5–8) and abstain from sexual intercourse (1 Sam 21:4–5; 2 Sam 11:11)
4. Weapons are consecrated to God before battle (1 Sam 21:5; 2 Sam 1:21)
5. The warriors make vows (*Josh* 1:10–18; Num 21:2; Judg 11:36; 1 Sam 14:24)
6. The army camp is ceremonially purified (*Josh* 5:2–9; Deut 23:9–14)
7. Israel brings sacrifices to God (1 Sam 7:9; 13:9–10, 12)
8. God gives directions and/or encourages the warriors with assurance of victory (*Josh* 1:6–9; 6:2–5; 8:1; Judg 20:13, 18; 1 Sam 7:9; 14:6–12)
9. God leads the army into battle (*Josh* 5:13–15; 6:2; 8:1; 10:8; Judg 4:14; 5:4; Deut 20:4; cf. Mesha Inscription line 14)
10. Little importance is placed on the quantity of ammunition, because God is the one who brings the victory, with Israel joining with him in battle (Judg 7:2–25; 1 Sam 14:6; 17:45, 47)

---

48. Tremper Longman III and Daniel G. Reid, *God Is a Warrior* (SOTBT; Grand Rapids: Zondervan, 1995) 32.

49. Patrick D. Miller Jr., *The Divine Warrior in Early Israel* (HSM 5; Cambridge, MA: Harvard University Press, 1973) 156.

50. Ibid., 157.

51. Thelle, "The Biblical Conquest Account and Its Modern Hermeneutical Challenges," 66.

52. Heimbach, "Crusade in the Old Testament and Today," 188–89.

11. God is the mighty Warrior who miraculously brings victory and gives strength to Israel for the battle (*Josh 10:14, 42; 23:10;* Exod 14:14; Deut 1:30; 1 Sam 14:23)
12. The Israelites are told to believe in God and not to fear their enemies (*Josh 8:1;* Exod 14:13–14; Deut 20:3)
13. The well-equipped enemies experience divine terror (*Josh 2:9, 11; 5:1; 10:1–2;* Exod 23:27; Deut 7:23; Judg 7:22–25; 1 Sam 14:15–23)
14. The spoil of warfare is subject to the "ban" (*ḥērem*) (*Josh 6:18; 8:26;* Deut 20:1–18; 1 Sam 15:3)
15. The dismissal of the army is announced officially (*Josh 22:1–6;* 2 Sam 20:1; 1 Kings 12:6)

Miller notes that, "because the war was sacral, a sphere of activity in which Israel's God was present, the camp and warriors had to be ritually purified (1 Sam 21:6; 2 Sam 11:11; Deut 23:13–15; Josh 3:5; 7:13)."[53] In Josh 5, before the conquest of Jericho, the men of war were circumcised and the community celebrated the Passover. Had the Israelites attacked Jericho without first performing these sacred rites, they would undoubtedly have been defeated. After the Passover celebration, Joshua encounters a heavenly visitor who identifies himself as "the commander of the army of the Lord," thereby confirming that God is ready to engage in battle on behalf of his people (Josh 5:13–15). Joshua's response to the messenger—his immediate posture of total submission and willingness to obey instructions given by God—reveals that he understood that a divinely ordained crusade "not only had to be authorized by God but also had to be led by God. The army of Israel was to follow God himself into battle. They were following his lead on his terms, not the other way around."[54] The presence of the ark of the covenant during the procession around Jericho confirms that military victory could only be guaranteed if God accompanied Israel on the battlefield (Josh 6:6–9).

The Rhetoric of Violence in Joshua:
The Ḥērem

One of the main concerns with the book of Joshua is the devotion of entire communities—men, women, and children—to complete destruction. The key term related to this practice—*ḥērem*—appears most frequently in Deuteronomy and Joshua, with the book of Joshua providing the most comprehensive description of this practice in the Old Testament.[55] Identifying the exact meaning of the term *ḥērem* is difficult for the following reasons:

---

53. Miller, *The Divine Warrior*, 157.
54. Heimbach, "Crusade in the Old Testament and Today," 197.
55. Major studies on the word *ḥērem* include W. L. Lyons, *A History of Modern Scholarship on the Biblical Word Herem: The Contributions of Walter C. Kaiser, Jr., Peter C. Craigie, and Tremper Longman, III* (Lewiston, NY: EdwinMellen, 2010); Stern, *The Biblical Herem*. For a brief history of scholarship on the *ḥērem*, see K. Lawson Younger Jr., "Some Recent Discussion on the Herem," in *Far From Minimal: Celebrating the Work and Influence of Philip*

(1) The semantic range of the term, as it appears in Scripture, is not clear (Is it a cultic term? Is it a warfare term? Is it both?).[56] (2) The exact origin of the practice cannot be determined from Scripture. (3) Comparative ancient Near Eastern evidence is limited, and wherever it is found, it belongs primarily to the realms of warfare and conquest (cf. Deut 7:1–5; 20:10–20). (4) The treatment of the *ḥērem* (spoil of war) is not consistent throughout the book of Joshua.[57] And (5) the application of the concept in the modern faith community raises major theological and ethical issues.[58]

The practice of *ḥērem* is not uniquely a biblical concept. In the Moabite (Mesha) inscription (9th century B.C.E.), the *ḥērem* (the spoil of war) is first consecrated to the deity before it is subjected to destruction (line 17). In a night battle against Israel, the Moabites claim to slay 7,000 men, boys, women, girls, and maidservants who had been devoted to destruction (*ḥrm*) for the god Chemosh (lines 15–16, 20). Modern scholars have proposed a number of meanings for the term *ḥērem*. Stern interprets the *ḥērem* of the book of Joshua as a way for God to deal with the chaos of the world and restore the moral order of the universe.[59] Susan Niditch follows two trajectories: (1) in the cultic sense, the *ḥērem* is a sacrifice devoted to God who determines its fate; (2) the *ḥērem* is God's justice against what is impure and can potentially damage God's relationship with Israel.[60] Creach notes that the *ḥērem* "serves as a metaphor for complete devotion to God. This way of interpreting the ban [*ḥērem*] was suggested by some of the earliest Jewish and Christian interpreters. It has largely been dismissed in the modern period."[61] Interpreted in its proper cultural and cultic context, "the ban [*ḥērem*] has become a symbol for religious fidelity, not a literal command to kill people."[62] Frédéric Gangloff interprets the *ḥērem* as "an instrument of cultic purification" through which a clear distinction is made between the clean (pure, monotheistic) and the unclean (impure, polytheistic).[63]

R. Davis (ed. D. Burns and J. W. Rogerson; LHB/OTS 484; New York: Bloomsbury T. & T. Clark, 2014) 505–22.

56. In his study of *ḥērem*, Stern notes that the following Hebrew roots appear in contexts where *ḥērem* is mentioned. These provide an "incomplete" matrix to understand the semantic range of the term *ḥērem*: *y-r-š*, "to inherit, dispossess"; *h-r-g*, "to kill"; *g-r-š*, "to separate"; *l-ḥ-m*, "to fight"; *ʾ-ḥ-z* "to grasp"; and *y-š-b* "to dwell" (*The Biblical Ḥerem*, 226).

57. In some cases, everything is destroyed and all living beings are killed; in other cases, human spoil is killed, and animals are kept alive and used by the Israelite community.

58. Younger, "Some Recent Discussion on the Herem," 505.

59. Stern, *The Biblical Ḥerem*, 220–26.

60. Niditch, *War in the Hebrew Bible*, 193.

61. Creach, *Violence in Scripture*, 99.

62. Ibid, 105. See R. W. L. Moberly, "Toward an Interpretation of the Shema," in *Theological Exegesis: Essays in Honor of Brevard S. Childs* (ed. C. Seitz and K. Greene-McCreight; Grand Rapids: Eerdmans, 1999) 135.

63. Frédéric Gangloff, "Joshua 6: Holy War of Extermination by Divine Command (Herem)?" *TRev* 25 (2004) 18, 20. See Koert van Bekkum, *From Conquest to Coexistence: Ide-*

In Num 21:1–3, we find that the practice of the *ḥērem* was not always initiated by God. In this passage, where "the ban was imposed as a vow meant to gain God's help in battle,"[64] the practice is initiated by Israel. Israel makes a conditional promise to "utterly destroy" (*wĕhaḥăramtî*) the enemies, *if* God gives her the victory in battle against the Canaanites. In this case, the destruction of enemies is proposed by Israel and will be fulfilled only *if* God gives Israel favor in the battle. The book of Joshua indicates that the *ḥērem* was not only reserved for the enemies of Israel. The Israelites who mishandled the *ḥērem* spoil of war could be destroyed (for example, Achan in Josh 7).

In Deut 7, the *ḥērem* is justified by the need to annihilate those who could cause Israel to turn away from God. In this case, the rhetoric is primarily cultic. The Israelites are to make no "covenant" with their enemies, and refrain from intermarrying with them, lest their enemies incite them to serve "other gods," something that was strictly forbidden by the law (Exod 20:3–5; 23:20–33; Deut 5:7–9):

> When the LORD your God brings you into the land that you are entering to take possession of it, and clears away many nations before you, the Hittites, the Girgashites, the Amorites, the Canaanites, the Perizzites, the Hivites, and the Jebusites, seven nations more numerous and mightier than you, and when the LORD your God gives them over to you, and you defeat them, then you must devote them to complete destruction [*haḥărēm taḥărîm*]. You shall make no covenant with them and show no mercy to them. ³ You shall not intermarry with them, giving your daughters to their sons or taking their daughters for your sons, ⁴ for they would turn away your sons from following me, to serve other gods. Then the anger of the LORD would be kindled against you, and he would destroy you quickly. ⁵ But thus shall you deal with them: you shall break down their altars and dash in pieces their pillars and chop down their *Asherim* and burn their carved images with fire. (Deut 7:1–5)

In Deut 7, where the Canaanites are depicted as morally, ethically, and spiritually deficient,[65] the text seems to imply that God initiates and ordains the unequivocal annihilation of the enemy—a sort of ethnic cleansing. The Israelites are instructed "to utterly destroy" the Canaanites once and for all (*haḥărēm taḥărîm*), to break down their altars, dash in pieces their pillars, chop down their *Asherim* and burn their carved images (Deut 7:2, 5; 34:13; Num 33:52). In other passages, however, the practice of destroying enemies (*ḥērem*) and/or their belongings is less dramatic and less austere. In Exod 23, God promises "to drive out" (*'ăgārěšennû*, not the verb *ḥrm*) the Amorites, Hittites, Perizzites, Canaanites, Hivites, and Jebusites from the land not

---

ology and Antiquarian Intent in the Historiography of Israel's Settlement in Canaan (Leiden: Brill, 2011) 298–304.

64. Creach, *Violence in Scripture*, 100

65. The Reformer Calvin argued "that the Canaanites were rightly the object of God's wrath because they were so depraved" (Creach, *Joshua*, 41).

"in one year," but rather, "little by little . . . until you have increased and possess the land" (Exod 23:29–30; cf. Deut 7:22). Copan notes that "driving out or dispossessing is different from wiping out or destroying. Expulsion is in view, not annihilation. . . . And upon examination, the driving out references are considerably more numerous than the destroying and annihilating ones."[66]

In Deut 20:16–18, the *ḥērem* is mentioned in the context of the laws of warfare.[67] Outside Canaan, Israel could negotiate peace agreements with her enemy, but within Canaan—the land given to Israel by Yahweh—the enemy was to be annihilated, and nothing that breathes was to be spared. Because warfare in Israel was theological, the text echoes Deut 7 and highlights the risk of apostasy in Israel as a reason for the total destruction (*ḥērem*) of the enemy. The Canaanites were a danger to the welfare of the Israelite community in that they could draw them away from God and draw them into their evil practices. This scenario was sufficient to warrant annihilation.

> But in the cities of these peoples that the LORD your God is giving you for an inheritance, you shall save alive nothing that breathes, but you shall devote them to complete destruction [*haḥărēm taḥărîm*], the Hittites and the Amorites, the Canaanites and the Perizzites, the Hivites and the Jebusites, as the LORD your God has commanded, that they may not teach you to do according to all their abominable practices that they have done for their gods, and so you sin against the LORD your God. (Deut 20:16–18)

Early Jewish interpretations of the *ḥērem* in Deuteronomy vary. In his study of the *ḥērem*, Ishai Rosen-Zvi discusses two major views in Tannaitic Literature regarding the biblical *ḥērem*.[68] First, in Mishnah *Avodah Zarah* 3:3–4, the prescription to destroy what is considered *ḥērem* is mostly replaced by a command to stay away from idols and receive no benefit from them or enjoy them.[69] This mitigated view of the *ḥērem* allowed for the ongoing presence of the Canaanites in the promised land, as long as Israel abstained from engaging in any of the idolatrous practices of the Canaanites. Second, in the homilies of *Sifre Deuteronomy* 60 (Rabbi Akiva) and *Mekhilta Deuteronomy* (Rabbi Ishmael), the obligation to destroy completely any idol or individual involved in idolatry is preserved.[70] The *Mekhilta* on Deut 12:3—the strictest of the two views—highlights the need for the annihilation, obliteration,

---

66. Copan, *Is God a Moral Monster?*, 181.
67. Van Bekkum, *From Conquest to* Coexistence, 312–19.
68. Tannaitic literature was written by rabbis around 10–220 C.E. and includes the Mishnah, Baraita and Tosefta, and Tannaitic Midrashim.
69. Ishay Rosen-Zvi, "Reading *ḥerem*: Destruction of Idolatry in Tannaitic Literature" in *The Gift of Land and the Fate of the Canaanites in Jewish Thought* (ed. K. Berthelot, J. E. David; and M. Hirshman; Oxford: Oxford University Press, 2014) 51–53.
70. Ibid., 53–54.

burning, destruction, and removal from the world of all idols and altars dedicated to the idols.[71] In *Sifre Deuteronomy*, the prohibition is less severe. Only the *asherah* trees are to be destroyed and/or burned. Rosen-Zvi notes that, "while the *Sifre* follows here the Deuteronomistic ideology that limits the need to destroy idolatry to the Holy Land, the *Mekhilta* knows only of political restrictions but does not know of limitations in principle to the destruction imperative."[72]

Medieval Jewish interpretation of the *ḥērem* relied heavily on rabbinic teachings and the exegetical responses of sages. Maimonides (1135–1204) considered war against the seven nations (Hittites, Amorites, Canaanites, Perizzites, Hivites, Jebusites, Amalekites) "obligatory war" (*milḥemet mitzvah*), a method necessary for Israel's survival during the conquest of the land. He noted that the injunction was binding for all times, throughout all generations, as long as descendants of Amalek existed and promoted their morally corrupt ideology.[73] Maimonides offered two innovative ideas for interpreting the Deuteronomy texts: (1) Israel was required to offer to the seven nations the opportunity to submit to her authority; and (2) a peace treaty could only be ratified if the nations agreed "to abide by the seven Noahide laws and to pay a tax to the Israelite authorities as a sign of their suzerainty."[74] Refusal to accept these terms meant certain death—complete annihilation, *ḥērem*—for Israel's enemies. For Maimonides, war against the seven nations meant the eradication of idolatry and moral corruption, and consequently, a clearing of the path for the propagation of truth. Rashi (1040–1105) understood the *ḥērem* as speaking of an "optional war," with the offer of peace for far away nations only. As for the seven nations, he advocated for complete annihilation and refused to accept the repentance of its members.[75]

Nachmanides (aka Ramban, 1194–1270) deviated from Rashi and Maimonides, and taught that only men were to be killed, both in "obligatory" and "optional" wars. Women and children were to be spared in all situations.[76] Israel was to demand tribute and service, and the abstinence from worship of idols. Nachmanides supported his view by pointing to Solomon, who enslaved the Canaanites rather than eradicating them (1 Kgs 9:20–22).[77] Bahya ben Asher (1255–1340), a follower of Nachmanides, offered a more moderate explanation and sought to mitigate the extreme interpretation of

---

71. Ibid., 54.
72. Ibid., 57.
73. Menachem Kellner, "And Yet, the Texts Remain: The Problem of the Command to Destroy the Canaanites," in *The Gift of the Land and the Fate of the Canaanites in Jewish Thought* (ed. Katell Berthelot, Joseph E David, Marc G Hirshman; Oxford: Oxford University Press, 2014) 155–56, 59.
74. Ibid., 157.
75. Ibid., 161, 163.
76. Ibid.
77. Ibid., 162, 164.

the *ḥērem* by stating that peace was to be offered to all whom Israel encountered before engaging in war with anyone. In the case of the seven nations, refusal to accept the peace offer resulted in the annihilation of its entire population—men, women and children.[78] Additional rabbinic sages (for example, Gersonides, Abravanel) noted that Joshua would in all likelihood provide the peace option to everyone before engaging in war with them (for example, he made peace with the Gibeonites), but because all cities except Gibeon refused the offer of peace, their men engaged Israel in battle and suffered great loss. Their willingness to make peace with Israel would have spared them loss and would have allowed them to continue living in the land, in the midst of Israel. For centuries, Jewish sages attempted to answer the religious and moral problems of the biblical passages, but the difficulties of the text still remain.

Much of the language of the Bible is directed toward two extremes (for example, the righteous vs. the wicked; the holy vs. the unholy; the pure vs. the impure). In the worldview of Israel, life was sorted into "categories akin to those of purity and impurity, sacred and profane, or that which is for humans and that which is beyond, exempt, outside."[79] Israel was to remain holy in a world where temple prostitution, bestiality, homosexuality, and child sacrifice were practiced openly (for example, Lev 18:20–30). Israel was to emulate her holy and righteous God in a context, where foreign nations imitated the morals of their unholy gods.

Copan notes that, "in the case of the Canaanites, the Canaanites' moral apples didn't fall far from the tree of their pantheon of immoral gods and goddesses. So if the Canaanite deities engaged in incest, then it's not surprising that incest wasn't treated as a serious moral wrong among the Canaanite people."[80] He adds, "the sexual acts of the gods and goddesses were imitated by the Canaanites as a kind of magical act: the more sex on the Canaanite high places, the more this would stimulate the fertility for Baal to have sex with his consort, Anath, which meant more semen (rain) produced to water the earth."[81] If this was in fact a practice among the Canaanites in the Land—a view now challenged by many scholars—such a scenario in Canaan would have been risky for Israel, whose spiritual stamina had often showed weakness and susceptibility.

---

78. Ibid., 165–66.
79. Thelle, "The Biblical Conquest Account and Its Modern Hermeneutical Challenges," 65.
80. Copan, *Is God a Moral Monster?*, 159.
81. Ibid. This view has been disputed by many scholars who point to the lack of textual evidence for such "sacred" sexual perversions in Canaan. See John B. Burns, "*Qadesh* and *qedesha*: Did They Live Off Immoral Earnings?" *Proceedings* 15 (1995) 157–68; Stephanie L. Budin, *The Myth of Sacred Prostitution in Antiquity* (Cambridge: Cambridge University Press, 2008); JoAnn Hackett, "Can a Sexist Model Liberate Us: Ancient Near Eastern 'Fertility' Goddesses," *JFSR* 5 (1989) 65–76.

The story of Rahab and the spies (Josh 2), where Israel first encounters the inhabitants of the land, provides an important truth regarding the possibility of redemption for the Canaanites. During her first encounter with the two Israelite spies, Rahab makes a clear proclamation of faith in the God of Abraham, Isaac, and Jacob. After revealing her knowledge of Israelite history, she states,

> I know that the LORD has given you the land, and that the fear of you has fallen upon us, and that all the inhabitants of the land melt away before you. For we have heard how the LORD dried up the water of the Red Sea before you when you came out of Egypt, and what you did to the two kings of the Amorites who were beyond the Jordan, to Sihon and Og, whom you devoted to destruction. And as soon as we heard it, our hearts melted, and there was no spirit left in any man because of you, *for the* LORD *your God, he is God in the heavens above and on the earth beneath*. (Josh 2:9–11, emphasis added)

Rahab lived in a strategic location in Jericho, close to the gate of the city, in a place where travelers stopped in for lodging (and other services). From her visitors and clients, she had heard about the fame of Israel's God, the way he had delivered miraculously the Israelites out of Egypt, and how he had given them victory in battle against the Amorite kings. Her faith in Canaanite gods was challenged by the truths she heard about the God of Israel, and consequently, she decided to abandon her gods and to join the worshipers of the God of heaven and earth. In light of what is said in Deut 7 and 20, Rahab should have been killed, because she was a Canaanite. If Deut 7 and 20 are to be taken literally, she was extremely wicked and a danger to the Israelites. Rahab and her family should have been annihilated, but faith in the living God prevailed, and life was granted to Rahab, whose heart was turned toward the God of Abraham, Isaac, and Jacob. According to Copan, the Rahab story proves "that other Canaanites could potentially have been rescued as well."[82] The Rahab narrative shows us that God will have mercy on all who turn to him in faith and that not all who lived in Canaan were subject to the *ḥērem*.

In a recent article, Richard Hess challenges the view that all Canaanites were considered "utterly wicked."[83] He presents a picture of positive

---

82. Ibid, 163.

83. In the mid-1950s, scholars began to challenge the view that Canaanites practiced child sacrifice. After a thorough examination of Ugaritic literature, W. F. Albright concluded that, "the extent to which human sacrifice was practiced among the Canaanites has not been clarified by the discoveries at Ugarit, which nowhere appear to mention it at all" (*Archaeology and the Religion of Israel* [3rd ed.; Baltimore: Johns Hopkins University Press, 1953] 92–93). For a summary of views on the controversial religious practices of the Canaanites, see Y. Kauffman, *The Religion of Israel: From Its Beginnings to the Babylonian Exile* (trans. Moshe Greenberg; New York: Shocken, 1972); G. E. Wright, *The Old Testament Against Its Environment* (London: SCM, 1950); F. M. Cross, *Canaanite Myth and Hebrew Epic* (Cambridge: Harvard University Press, 1973); N. K. Gottwald, *The Tribes of Yahweh*

Canaanite ethics that is based both on biblical records and on extrabiblical evidence found in West Semitic letters, myths, legal, economic texts and wisdom literature primarily from Mari, Emar, Ugarit, Alalakh and Assyria.[84] Hess first addresses four views whose unconvincing conclusions are based solely on the biblical text: first is the antiquated dichotomy of Israel's moral religion and the Canaanites' depraved religion, a view that Hess notes as "thoroughly critiqued and largely rejected in serious studies in the field."[85] Second is the view that the language of "wickedness" as related to the Canaanites justifies Israel's aggressive behavior, while she is in the process of developing her national identity.[86] Third is the view of the "new atheists," who exonerate the Canaanites from any wrongdoing and blame the intolerant and prejudiced Israelites for the violent and bloody assaults on the inhabitants of the land.[87] The fourth view—the most useful of the four views—recognizes the Canaanites as "the Other," who require face-to-face encounters with their neighbors in order "to use these experiences as a basis for forging ethical decisions for justice among oppressed humans in the world."[88] By surveying the West Semitic corpus of literature, Hess shows that the behavior of the Western Semites exhibited a high level of familial, social, and communal ethics in marriage, raising children, adoptions, legal matters, cultic practices, the treatment of foreigners, and the expression of justice. Hess allows for the rehumanization of the Canaanites. He advocates for a mitigated view of their perceived dreadful state and concludes that,

> much like other peoples of their own time and not unlike peoples of every age, the Canaanites were not uniformly wicked or righteous by any moral standard. The Bible attests that their wickedness reached a point that called for judgment when Israel appeared on the scene (Gen 15:16, Deut 9:4–5). Throughout

---

(Maryknoll, NY: Orbis, 1979); and D. R. Hillers, "Analyzing the Abominable: Our Understanding of Canaanite Religion," *JQR* 75 (1985) 259–68.

84. Richard S. Hess, "'Because of the Wickedness of These Nations' (Deut 9:4–5): The Canaanites—Ethical or Not?" in *For Our Good Always: Studies on the Message and Influence of Deuteronomy in Honor of Daniel I. Block* (ed. J. S. DeRouchie, J. Gile; and K .J. Turner; Winona Lake, IN: Eisenbrauns, 2013) 17–37.

85. Hess notes that ethicists such as Christopher Wright and Paul Copan hold to this view in order to explain the destruction of the Canaanites by the Israelites (ibid., 20). Hillers notes that "Jews and Christians who pay allegiance to the Biblical view of ancient history will be strongly inclined to cast the Canaanites in the role of villains" ("Analyzing the Abominable," 254).

86. According to Hess, Native American Robert Allen Warrior, Robert Oden, and Randall Bailey hold this position (Hess, "'Because of the Wickedness of These Nations,'" 21).

87. Hess names Richard Dawkins and Christopher Hitchens as the main proponents of this view (ibid., 21–22).

88. Ibid., 22. Hess points to Cheryl Anderson and Frank Yamada, who followed in the footsteps of philosopher Emmanuel Levinas.

their history, however, Canaanites included those with a higher level or [sic] morality as well as those similar to the ones described in Deuteronomy.[89]

Hess adds an important human dimension to the characterization of the Canaanites—they were not "uniformly wicked." Hess does not deny the malevolence of the inhabitants of Canaan, but rather, in his representation of the Canaanites, he seeks to present a balanced perspective between the view of those who advocate that "all" Canaanites were completely degenerate and the position of the new atheists who speak of the "Canaanites as innocent and good-natured people upon whom Israel and its malevolent deity preyed."[90]

I agree with Hess's premise that Canaanites were not "all" evil to the core. It is possible that a segment of the inhabitants of Canaan—especially the leaders—developed abhorrent practices that colored their reputation as ruthless people.[91] Copan notes that the Canaanites did not win "the immorality contest for worst-behaved peoples in all the ancient Near East. That said, the evidence for profound moral corruption was abundant. God considered them ripe for divine judgment."[92] Scripture suggests that a decline in the morality of the Canaanites occurred over an extended period of time. In Gen 15:16, at the time of the ratification of the Abrahamic covenant, the presence of the Canaanites in the land (Gen 12:6; 13:7) was less threatening than centuries later, when their reputation was known through the lens of their wicked practices (sexual perversions, sacrificing of children in fire, sorcery [Deut 18:10], etc.).

Conclusion

Over the centuries, based on the narrative of the book of Joshua, the Israelites and their God have been depicted as ruthless xenophobes and cold-blooded warmongers. However, after a review of the rhetoric of the book, of its warfare literary conventions and of its ancient Near Eastern parallels, we can assert that the book of Joshua—though historical in nature—does not provide an exact description of the events that occurred when Israel entered Canaan. A literal interpretation of the book is certainly problematic. The narrative must be interpreted in light of the entire counsel of Scripture. Because God told Abraham (Gen 12:1–3) that, through him, all the families of the earth would be blessed (including the Canaanites), how could God instruct his people to kill all Canaanites or anyone else indiscriminately? A

---

89. Ibid., 37.
90. Ibid., 17.
91. This phenomenon is evident is modern societies where pockets of violent radicals color the reputation of the society from which they come (e.g., ISIS and Hamas in the Middle East, Boko Haram in Nigeria, MNLF and MILF in the Philippines). The areas controlled by such groups are usually depicted as unsafe and unfriendly to those who disagree with their views.
92. Copan, *Is God a Moral Monster?* 160.

literal interpretation of the conquest narrative that includes the annihilation of all foreigners in the land corresponds neither to the greater mission of God for the world nor to the true character of the God of heaven and earth as revealed in the full extent of the Bible. The conquest narrative also must be understood in its ancient Near Eastern context, in a world where warfare was theological. Its theology and significance must consider the connections between the biblical account and the extrabiblical evidence (Mesha Inscription, ancient Near Eastern military annals, etc.). The *ḥērem* mentioned throughout the book of Joshua can only be understood and appreciated in this context.

In reality, the Israelites were far from being a band of relentless barbarians who were marching forward confidently aiming to destroy everyone and everything on their path under the leadership of their God. The events narrated at the beginning of the book of Joshua—the conquest of Jericho and Ai, the cultic rituals at Shechem, the covenant with the Gibeonites—portray Israel as a semiorganized group of people who were feared by the inhabitants of the land, not because of who they were but because their God was mightier than the gods of the surrounding nations (Josh 2:9, 11; 5:1; etc.). In Joshua and in other books of the Old Testament, the Israelites lived more often on the defensive than on the offensive, shielding themselves from attackers (Amalekites, Exod 17:8; the Amorite King Sihon, Num 21:21–32, Deut 2:26–30; Og, king of Bashan, Num 21:33, Deut 3:1; kings of the north, Josh 11; etc.) and rescuing others from aggressors (e.g., Israelites from the king of Arad, Num 21:1; the Gibeonites from the kings of Judah, Josh 10). Israel's need to defend herself against the aggression of the Canaanites places her in a better light morally and ethically as her defensive position was necessary for her survival. The book of Joshua should therefore not be read as an exact description of the events but rather as historical national literature in which the accounts reflect the literary traditions of the day, the rhetoric of military records, and the theological language of Israel.

On the practical level, Kah-Jin Jeffrey Kuan reminds us of the importance of looking at ourselves in our treatment of "the Other," to address current political conflicts with nonviolent means wherever possible and to take seriously our responsibility to bring peace to this earth before blaming the evils of the world on those whose worldview, behavior, and cultic practices differ from our own. He states, "As a mirror of our human affinities with violence and war, the book of Joshua may serve today, with two wars still being waged, to remind the people of faith their own complicity in perpetuating ideologies that foster violence, whether they are of ethnic, religious or political nature. May it obligate us to work ethically for the liberation of all of God's people."[93]

---

93. Kah-Jin Jeffrey Kuan, "Biblical Interpretation and the Rhetoric of Violence and War," *AJT* 23 (2009) 202. The "two wars" noted in this quotation refer to U.S. military involvement in Afghanistan and Iraq.

In conclusion, the narrative of the book of Joshua provides only a partial depiction of the God of Abraham, Isaac, and Jacob, who fulfilled his promise of a promised land to Israel, who participated in battle on behalf of his chosen people and who performed the miracles necessary for Israel to establish herself as a nation in the land of Canaan—the place God had chosen for her. As mentioned in the introduction of this chapter, God cannot be understood solely through the narrative of Scripture. The "actual God" who transcends the pages of Scripture must be encountered personally in order for one to think responsibly and rightly about God, and develop a sound theology.

Chapter 5

Cries of the Oppressed: Prayer and Violence in the Psalms

David G. Firth

Contexts for Violence

Readers of the Psalms are often surprised to discover the extent to which violence is expressed within them. This violence is generally expressed in three contexts. First, it can be expressed within a narrative context where a psalmist describes experiencing violence from others. This violence can affect either the individual or the community as a whole, though often enough of these descriptions move across this division. This violence can be seen to operate at three levels. First, the psalmist can describe physical violence. We see an example of this in Ps 74:4–8, where the psalmist describes the activities of those who attacked the sanctuary, perhaps the Babylonians under Nebuchadnezzar, destroying its features and also burning other meeting places. Second, violence can also be experienced at the structural level, when the basic order of society itself is removed. For example, in Ps 94:3–7 the psalmist describes the activities of the powerful who crush the poor. There is clearly physical violence in these activities, but the concern of the psalmist is with the fact that the structure of society itself has been attacked, and it is this issue that Yahweh is called to address. Third, violence can be primarily psychological, expressed in threatening behavior and words. For instance, in Ps 3 the psalmist describes the activity of numerous foes who attack the poet, but who primarily do so through their words. They have not, to this point, physically assaulted the psalmist, but the threat that lies behind their words is still experienced as violence. These three levels are not absolutely discrete, and each will merge into the others, but it is worth noting that one of them will generally dominate in any given psalm.[1] Perhaps more importantly, it shows that one does not need to experience physical assault to have experienced violence. Violence is inclusive of all experiences of life, and anything that by threat or excess

---

[1]. On this distinction, see further David G. Firth, *Surrendering Retribution in the Psalms: Responses to Violence in the Individual Complaints* (PBM; Milton Keynes: Paternoster, 2005) 5–6.

force damages an individual or community's ability to live before God can be narrated within the psalms as the experience of violence. However, it is not generally the case that readers today find the narration of experienced violence troubling in itself. After all, we live in a world where violence is frequently experienced, so we would be surprised if the psalmists did not describe this, and of course the psalms claim that violence of this sort is illegitimate and should therefore be rejected. Indeed, it is (in part at least) the simple fact that Psalms describes a world with experiences similar to our own that makes them accessible to us for our own prayer.

A second context can be described as legitimated enforcement. This refers to psalms that describe or anticipate violence as something necessary to restore order and typically appears in psalms that describe the activities of Israel's king, though it might also refer to points when Yahweh is expected to act directly in restoring justice. From the perspective of Psalms, the king acts on Yahweh's behalf to ensure justice and righteousness, so the king's and Yahweh's actions often merge. This is seen in Ps 2:9 in the picture of the king breaking the kings who oppose Yahweh and his anointed with an iron rod, though the goal is that the nations should submit themselves to Yahweh through this king. However, a number of text-critical issues make the interpretation of this psalm less than clear,[2] so a better example might be seen in Ps 72:12–14 where part of the king's role as the bringer of God's justice and righteousness is to deliver the poor and needy from oppression and violence. This suggests that the king's role is to counter the sort of violence that is typically narrated in the complaint psalms. Although Ps 72 does not describe the activities that would ensure this deliverance of the needy, we probably see the king achieving this in Ps 101:8,[3] when the psalmist vows to destroy the wicked, cutting off those who do evil. Becaue the psalmist earlier repudiated slanderers (v. 5), we can see that the evildoers whom the king will oppose are those who enact all the levels of violence we noted above. No human but the king can act in this way, because the king alone has the task of working to bring God's justice to the community. Because this is a specific function of the king in his role under Yahweh, we can suggest that this violence is legitimated. At other points, such as Ps 94:2–7, the hope is that Yahweh will act directly to restore justice as an expression of his reign. Whether through the king or through Yahweh's direct action, this context

---

2. A revocalization of v. 9 would lead to a translation of "you shall rule them with a rod of iron" (ESV margin), while vv. 11–12 pose a host of issues. See John Goldingay, *Psalms* (BCOTWP; Grand Rapids: Baker Academic, 2006) 1:101–3; and Allen P. Ross, *A Commentary on the Psalms* (KEL; Grand Rapids: Kregel, 2011) 1:208–13 for contrasting approaches.

3. Unlike Psalms 2 or 72, Psalm 101 never directly refers to the king. However, the nature of the tasks described within the psalm makes the royal interpretation the most probable. For a recent exploration of the issues, see Frank-Lothar Hossfeld and Eric Zenger, *Psalms 3: A Commentary on Psalms 101–150* (trans. L. M. Maloney; Hermeneia; Minneapolis: Fortress, 2011) 11–17.

for violence has not proved especially troubling for recent readers of the Psalms, perhaps because from the perspective of Psalms this violence is limited to what is immediately necessary to restore justice and righteousness.

It is the third context that has proved most troubling for modern readers of the Psalms. Where the first narrates violence that has been experienced, and the second tends to describe what is needed to restore equity, the third appears when psalmists pray that Yahweh will enact some form of violence against an enemy of some sort. These prayers are known as imprecations. There is no doubt that the imprecatory psalms continue to pose a theological problem for contemporary Christian practice, as is evident from the fact that many lectionaries and reading systems for the psalms omit the majority of them. There is, indeed, something that many find unpleasant about these texts, even when they are otherwise perfectly orthodox defenders of the authority of the Old Testament. Prayers for vengeance against enemies, including some significant wishes for violence against them, do not sit well with contemporary practice. Accordingly, the rest of this chapter will focus on these psalms.

A good example of this can be seen in the treatment of Ps 137, perhaps the imprecation that most obviously troubles modern readers, offered by John Bright.[4] Bright is concerned throughout his book to emphasize the fact that the Old Testament is authentically Christian Scripture and that, properly approached and understood, it continues to provide texts that can be proclaimed to our congregations. Bright, it must be said, does not accept the practice of his Presbyterian tradition of omitting the final three verses, which otherwise creates the impression of a psalm that might in some sense be considered exemplary. He rightly insists that we need to hear the whole of Scripture rather than an expurgated portion that we find more immediately edifying. Bright is also clear that we cannot ask what lessons we might learn from this text but must rather focus instead on the psalmist. When we do this, he suggests that we encounter someone who had lived in the exile and who on return was still driven by the savagery of that experience and who, though someone who loves God, offers a prayer that is sub-Christian. Finally, Bright argues that we must bring this person, with both his love and hate, to Christ. As he is baptized into Christ, the passion with which he speaks can then be properly directed.

In many ways, there is much to admire in Bright's argument, but it is finally deficient, because it relocates authority away from the text of Scripture itself and onto the person who prays. As such, the psalm becomes a warning of what can go wrong when our passion is not surrendered to Christ, rather than a text with something to say in itself. Although it is right to want to bring this person to Christ because that is where we all ultimately must go, it is a devaluation of the text to treat it in this way, because it places authority in the wrong place. In terms of hermeneutical theory, it is concerned

---

4. John Bright, *The Authority of the Old Testament* (Nashville: Abingdon, 1967) 234–41.

with (and locates its authority in) the world behind the text rather than the text itself. Rather, appropriate consideration of these psalms has to consider them as texts in their own right and then also reflect on their function in the book of Psalms. When we do this, we can see these psalms functioning in ways where they do indeed have something to say as they are and not through our critique of their authors, even though we will still need to consider them in terms of their place within the whole of Scripture.[5]

Which Psalms Are Imprecatory?

Apart from these concerns, we cannot ignore the fact that imprecation is something that is woven into many of the psalms; so it is not simply the case that Ps 137 is in some sense unusual. Imprecation appears in a number of psalms, though deciding exactly which are imprecatory is actually rather complex, and depending on certain exegetical conclusions between 18[6] and 39 psalms have sometimes been said to contain at least one verse of imprecation, though not all are probable. The most detailed examination of which psalms are imprecatory is offered by Luc, who argues that we can identify an imprecation only when there is either a jussive or imperative in which the psalmist expresses either a wish for vengeance against an enemy or requests one directly. On this basis, Luc proposes that there are 28 imprecatory psalms,[7] though one might vary this on the basis of some text critical points. However, his form-critical approach does not take into account the possibility of the precative perfect in Hebrew, consideration of which could add a further five psalms to the list.[8] Of course, because the jussive is not directly marked in all Hebrew verb stems, one might also reduce the list.[9]

---

5. For an exploration of ways in which such psalms function as Scripture, see Kit Barker, *Imprecation as Divine Discourse: Speech Act Theory, Dual Authorship and Theological Interpretation* (Th.D. diss., Australian College of Theology, 2013). Barker deploys a sophisticated hermeneutic that draws especially on the models of speech-act theory developed by Kevin Vanhoozer and Nicholas Wolterstorff. Nancy L. deClaissé-Walford, "The Theology of the Imprecatory Psalms," in *Soundings in the Theology of the Psalms: Perspectives and Methods in Contemporary Scholarship* (ed. R. A. Jacobson; Minneapolis: Fortress, 2011) 80–83, also points to canonical reasons for the abiding place of these psalms.

6. A minimal list is Psalms 5, 6, 11, 12, 35, 37, 40, 52, 54, 56, 58, 69, 79, 83, 109, 137, 139, and 143.

7. Alex Luc, "Interpreting the Curses in the Psalms," *JETS* 42 (1999) 396. He later lists (p. 410) the imprecations as 5:10; 7:13; 9:19–20; 10:15; 12:3; 28:4; 31:17–18; 35:4–8, 26; 40:14–15; 54:5; 55:15; 58:6–7; 59:11–12; 68:1–2; 69:22–28; 70:2–3; 71:13; 79:6, 12; 83:13–17; 104:35; 109:6–20; 119:78; 129:5–8; 137:7–9; 139:19–22; 140:9–11; 141:10; 143:12. All references are to English versification.

8. I would add Psalms 3, 6, 37, 63, and 64, as well as some additional verses, to the psalms Luc identified already. See the listing in Willem A. van Gemeren, "Psalms," in *The Expositor's Bible Commentary* (ed. T. Longman III and D. E. Garland; rev. ed.; Grand Rapids: Zondervan, 2008) 5: 955.

9. For instance, the ESV translates Ps 68:1–2 as imperfect rather than jussive.

This is not the place to argue in detail for the texts that one should include in the list of imprecatory psalms. What is clear is that, even on the minimal listing, more than 10 percent of all psalms contain at least some element of imprecation, and this could reasonably rise to cover about 20 percent of the Psalter as a whole. The point that arises from this is that it is not enough for us simply to find some strategy for surviving Pss 109 and 137, which are generally recogniszd as the most severe of the genre. Prayers and wishes for imprecation are an integral component of a significant portion of the Psalms. What is perhaps most surprising is that, although the majority of the imprecations appear in psalms of complaint, this is not always the case—the imprecation in Ps 119:78 appears in what is otherwise considered a Torah (or perhaps wisdom) psalm. Moreover, the idea of vengeance is not limited to the imprecatory psalms alone, as the idea that Yahweh is a God of vengeance is included in a number of psalms that are not strictly imprecatory in Luc's model.[10] Given the frequency with which the Psalms mentions the enemies, perhaps we ought not be surprised. After all, after God and the psalmist, the enemies are the most frequently mentioned character in the book of Psalms. The psalmists lived in a world that was frequently violent and harsh, one where armies were willing to invade and destroy and adversaries were prepared to seize assets through a range of devious means. It was a world of continuous threat and counter-threat, and in that world these psalms acted as models of prayer.

A Hermeneutic for the Imprecatory Psalms

Because imprecation is an element that occurs across such a wide range of psalms, it is therefore clear that we need to develop a hermeneutic for dealing with these texts. This sort of hermeneutic is specifically Christian in its orientation, because it needs to take into account the whole of Scripture, though it would still keep its primary focus on the texts themselves. This also recognizes the fact that these psalms pose a specific problem for Christian theology in light of Jesus' comments to love one's enemies in Matt 5:43–48, though in fact the problems themselves are not exclusively Christian.[11] The wider political contexts in which we now operate make many people sensitive to these texts,[12] which would perhaps mean that they would pose a problem irrespective of Christian convictions about the Sermon on the Mount.

What would this sort of hermeneutic look like? Because each psalm appears within an immediate literary context, we can suggest that we begin

---

10. E.g., Psalms 1, 2, 94, 149. See Erich Zenger, *A God of Vengeance: Understanding the Psalms of Divine Wrath* (Louisville, KY: Westminster John Knox, 1996) 1–13.

11. Cf. idem, *God of Vengeance*, 2, 13–23.

12. Although Richard Dawkins (*The God Delusion* [London: Bantam, 2006] 237–50) does not comment on Psalms in his treatment of what's wrong with the Old Testament, the imprecatory psalms are certainly typical of the texts he does consider.

by recognizing that the *book* of Psalms has a canonical function, and that the function is determined by its final shape.[13] That the book grew over a period seems undeniable. There are five books within the Psalter, and the headings to various collections (such as the Songs of the Ascents) makes clear that they belonged together in some way even before their respective books were put together.[14] In addition, of course, we have certain repetitions across the Psalms, so that Ps 14 = Ps 53, Ps 40:13–17 = Ps 70, and Ps 108 = Pss 57:7–11 + 60:5–12. The book of Psalms is a collection of collections, and yet in spite of this it appears to have of its own integrity by which it builds from the double introduction in Pss 1–2 through to the concluding hallelujah of Pss 146–150. Within this context, the introduction is of particular importance, for Ps 1 encourages the righteous to live a life that is centered on knowing the Torah of Yahweh, which is probably meant to cover the totality of the instruction that Yahweh has given and not just the Pentateuch.[15] But this is also placed within an eschatological framework by Ps 2, which continues to celebrate kings of the line of David, even though when the Psalter was finally redacted there was no such king. However, as noted above, a key role of the king was to overcome the enemies of the people, as is clear from Ps 2:9 and celebrated in texts such as Ps 18:42.[16] The role of the king was to execute Yahweh's justice, though this came to be seen in an eschatological light in the whole of the Psalter, and finally something that Yahweh would ultimately do through the whole of his people (Ps 149:4–9).

The key element that arises from this in reading the imprecatory psalms is that they have to be understood against the background of Scripture as a whole. But they also need to be interpreted within a framework in which there is the hope of Yahweh's justice, justice which might be manifested within normal historical circumstances or which might also be experienced eschatologically. Reading these psalms against the background of Scripture as a whole must first examine the background within the Old Testament, because this provides the immediate setting against which the book of Psalms understands these imprecations. But a Christian reading will also need to come to the New Testament, though not before we have under-

---

13. See Eric Zenger, "Psalmenexegese *und* Psalterexegese: Eine Forschungsckizze," in *The Composition of the Book of Psalms* (ed. E. Zenger; BETL 238; Leuven: Peeters, 2010) 17–66; and Beat Weber, "Von der Psaltergenese zur Psaltertheologie: der nächste Schritt der Psalterexegese?! Einige grundsätzliche Überlegungen zum Psalter als Buch und Kanonteil," in ibid., 733–44.

14. For an exploration of one way the book may have come together, see Klaus Seybold, "The Psalter as a Book," in *Jewish and Christian Approaches to the Psalms: Conflict and Convergence* (ed. S. Gillingham; Oxford: Oxford University Press, 2013) 168–81.

15. Similarly, Goldingay, *Psalms*, 1:80–81.

16. Because we are concerned with final form, issues such as the proposed *Fortschreibung* in 18:21–32, 44a need not be considered. For more, see Klaus-Peter Adam, *Der Königliche Held: Die Entsprechung von kämpfendem Gott und kämpfendem Köning in Psalm 18* (WMANT 91; Neukirchen-Vluyn: Neukirchner Verlag, 2001) 128–44.

stood them adequately in their Old Testament setting. What we will see is that many of them will be less a problem for us when understood in this way than might at first sight seem to be the case, though problems will still exist. Nevertheless, a Christian reading must still wrestle with the fact that calls for violence against our enemies sits awkwardly with Jesus' teaching in Matt 5:43-48. That said, the New Testament is not lacking in both imprecatory prayers or prayers that reflect an understanding of vengeance, such as 1 Cor 16:22; 2 Tim 4:14; Rev 11:17-18, 15:2-4, 16:5-7, and 18:1-8, while a passage such as 1 Thess 4:6 insists that Yahweh is an avenger.[17] Moreover, even if we stayed only in Matthew's gospel, we would still have to consider Jesus' woes on the scribes and Pharisees in Matt 23:1-36, which, if not strictly imprecatory, are not far from it. Furthermore, the cursing of the fig tree is certainly imprecatory, and even more so if it is symbolic of judgment on the temple. What arises from these wider texts in the New Testament is that they still expect God's justice to be demonstrated.[18] Expressing love for someone in New Testament terms does not necessarily mean that one sets aside the call for justice, and the one thing that binds the imprecatory psalms together is the call for justice. Setting the New Testament against the Old in this context may thus be a facile exercise.

Operating this way is not intended to suggest that there is a one-size-fits-all approach to the imprecatory psalms, whereby an appeal to one feature such as covenant or prophetic judgement[19] will suffice. Rather, within the larger framework of the cry for justice one must examine each in its own right, though certain common themes do emerge from this.[20] In particular, we will see that the imprecatory psalms are marked by an act of surrender, in which the right to retribution is left to Yahweh. Whether this happens in normal history or eschatologically is not something that can now be resolved, because the book of Psalms allows these elements to engage with one another in a form of realised eschatology centered on Yahweh's reign through his king. What matters, though, is that justice belongs finally to Yahweh. In addition, in the case of the individuals who pray, the requested vengeance is controlled by either the law of exact retribution (*lex talionis*) in

---

17. Cf. Eric Peels, *Shadow Sides: God in the Old Testament* (Carlisle: Paternoster, 2003) 100-104.

18. As such, Joel M. LeMon ("Saying Amen to Violent Psalms: Patterns of Prayer, Belief and Action in the Psalter," in *Soundings in the Theology of the Psalms: Perspectives and Methods in Contemporary Scholarship* [ed. R. A. Jacobson; Minneapolis: Fortress, 2011] 98-100) is right to reject the sort of supersessionist reading that makes the imprecations part of a religion that Christians have now left behind.

19. *Covenant*: J. Carl Laney, "A Fresh Look at the Imprecatory Psalms," *BSac* 138 (1981) 40-43. *Prophetic judgment*: Luc, "Interpreting," 400-407.

20. So also John N. Day, "The Imprecatory Psalms and Christian Ethics," *BSac* 159 (2002) 166-86, though without accepting all his conclusions. This is developed more fully in his *The Imprecatory Psalms and Christian Ethics* (Th.D. diss., Dallas Theological Seminary, 2001).

general or the law of false accusation (Deut 19:15-21) in particular, though the latter does include the *lex talionis* as an element within it. In the case of the communal psalms, the vengeance requested is shaped by the concerns of covenant, especially in terms of the covenant curses, though they may also draw on a wider range of texts, especially prophetic judgment speeches.

Individual Imprecatory Psalms

Because the psalms of the individual take a slightly different path to those of the community, it will be worthwhile to examine them separately. It should be pointed out that none of the generally recognised royal psalms employs an imprecation, although this is not the case in every listing of royal psalms. In particular, we can look at two subgroups that are representative of the wider concerns of the individual imprecations: prayers of the accused and prayers of the sick. For reasons of space, we will look only at one psalm in each group, but because they include the most significant imprecations within the psalter, they are representative not only of the wider issues but also of the most significant examples of them.

A Prayer of the Accused: Psalm 109

A number of the imprecatory psalms of the individual fall into the category of the prayers of the accused. This group of psalms was first noted by H. H. Schmidt, who proposed that Pss 3; 4; 5; 7; 11; 13; 17; 26; 27; 31:1-9; 55:1-19; 56; 57; 59; 94:16-23; 109; 139; 140; and 142 fell into this category.[21] According to Schmidt, they were prayers for use in an institution in which those accused of serious crimes presented their cases in the temple. This proposal draws on the fact that Deut 17:8-13 sees the temple as the final place of appeal for difficult criminal cases. Schmidt's work was taken up and developed by Beyerlin, who refined his institutional approach, and modified by Delekat, who essentially saw these prayers as related to someone seeking asylum in the temple.[22] Neither of these scholars accepted exactly the same listing as Schmidt, and Beyerlin made the important point that not all psalms that might reflect a setting of accusation were necessarily to be understood in terms of the institution. Certainly, Schmidt lacked firm criteria by which to identify these psalms, and many of the psalms he suggests lack clear evidence of belonging to this group. But because certain psalms include elements such as an appeal to be judged or tested or include affirmations of innocence; we can be reasonably confident that some psalms were used this way. The clearest examples are probably Pss 7, 17, 26, 109 and 139.

---

21. H. H. Schmidt, *Das Gebet der Angeklagten im Alten Testament* (Giessen: Alfred Töpelmann, 1928).

22. Walter Beyerlin, *Die Rettung der Bedrängten in den Feindpsalmen der Einzelnen auf institutionelle Zusammenhänge untersucht* (FRLANT 99; Göttingen: Vandenhoeck & Ruprecht, 1970); Leinhard Delekat, *Asylie und Schutzorakel am Zionheiligtum: Eine Untersuchung zu den privaten Feindpsalmen* (Leiden: Brill, 1967).

However, the canonical form of the book of Psalms has removed any rubrics that might have been used, so that an attempt to trace a liturgy for the accused is probably doomed from the outset.[23] Of more importance is the fact that these psalms model an attitude in which the right to retributive violence is surrendered to Yahweh in terms of the *lex talionis* and law of false accusation. The key theme is thus the ways in which these psalms instruct through a dialogue with the rest of the psalms and also with Scripture more generally.[24]

We can consider Ps 109[25] as the obvious example here, because its imprecation in vv. 6–19 is without doubt the longest and most detailed of all. It is, perhaps, worth noting at this point that the apostles quote from this passage (along with Ps 69) in terms of Judas following his betrayal of Jesus in Acts 1:20. However, it is arguable that in both of these cases the quotation is by way of analogy rather than suggesting that the psalms concerned were only ever related to Judas.

The content of the psalm is not difficult to analyse. In vv. 1–5, the psalmist describes the violence that is felt while the wicked surround him and make accusations. The use of the root *śṭn* indicates that we are dealing with legal accusations, and this theme is certainly taken up in vv. 6–19, which comprises the imprecation. However, there is an important shift at v. 6 where we move from a group of enemies to an individual.[26] Because of this, some interpreters have wanted to argue that these verses represent a quotation by the accused of what was being argued by the enemies, and the NRSV goes so far as to insert "They say" at the start of this section. However, it is doubtful that this sort of interpretation can stand, despite the fact that Hebrew does not use quotation marks.[27] As such, the best approach is to regard this long imprecation as the psalmist's own wish, one that is generalized in v. 20 to all the enemies and not just the one singled out here.

It is clear that this is a severe imprecation, though it is one that is based on the guilt of the enemy being revealed. From this, vv. 7–11 then describe the almost inevitable outcome for the family of a criminal convicted of a

---

23. Firth, *Surrendering Retribution in the Psalms*, 18, contra K. van der Toorn, "Ordeal Procedures in the Psalms and the Passover Meal," *VT* 38 (1988) 430.

24. For a treatment of the ways in which Psalms offers instruction, see my "The Teaching of the Psalms," in *Interpreting the Psalms* (ed. P. S. Johnston and D. G. Firth; Leicester: Apollos, 2005) 159–74.

25. For a fuller discussion, see idem, *Surrendering Retribution*, 36–42.

26. The singular noun here could be distributive, that is, applying to each enemy facing the psalmist, but the imprecation is so specific it seems best to understand it as referring to a particular individual, perhaps the ringleader of those who have accused the psalmist.

27. See the criticisms in J. Clinton McCann, *A Theological Introduction to the Book of Psalms: The Psalms as Torah* (Nashville: Abingdon, 1993) 113, though his view seems to have shifted somewhat in idem, "Psalms," in *The New Interpreter's Bible* (ed. L. E. Keck; Nashville: Abingdon, 1996) 4:1125, though without abandoning this view.

capital offense. That the enemy should be convicted in this way is made clear from vv. 12–18, in which various crimes are listed, in particular that he pursued the poor and weak to death. That is to say, the enemy has acted in this way, and the accusations made against the psalmist are thus to be understood in similar terms. What is requested therefore is an expression of justice linked to the outcome that would have applied had the psalmist been convicted, which is in effect an application of the *lex talionis*. However, in this case it is also a specific application of the law of false accusation in Deut 19:16–19, which stipulates that someone who maliciously accuses another should receive the penalty that applies to the crime in question.

The poet's personal desire is to experience Yahweh's *ḥesed* once again and to know the security that comes from it. But that the psalmist has no intention of enacting this violence personally seems clear from vv. 26–29. It is clear here that the resolution of the problem lies with Yahweh alone and that Yahweh is the one who must bring about justice. Within the larger context of the prayers of the accused, we can see a pattern that emerges in imprecations in which this act of surrender is central. Justice is something that only Yahweh can bring about, and it must be left to him. When that justice will be resolved is a different matter, and the psalms provide no answer on this point. But the imprecation is the end point. Once the matter has been raised, with all its anger and hurt, it is submitted to Yahweh and remains there.

A Prayer of the Sick: Psalm 69

Although a number of psalms can be said to be associated with sickness, the history of Psalms' research on this point is rather mixed. Early on, Gunkel[28] assigned virtually all the complaint psalms to a situation of illness, and though this was initially followed by Mowinckel, it was totally rejected by Birkeland,[29] who argued that enemies in the psalms were always foreign powers and therefore illness as a problem was ruled out in principle. This sort of conclusion seems forced, and even Mowinckel, whose later work was influenced by Birkeland, concluded that he had gone too far.[30] Both Gunkel and Birkeland undoubtedly went too far because of their desire to have a consistent identity for the enemies, and once we accept a diverse range of enemies, then *a priori* conclusions about illness are ruled out. Rather, we need to note psalms that have features that would point to illness, not least the description of symptoms. This is not to say that we have psalms that are

---

28. Herman Gunkel, *The Psalms: A Form Critical Introduction* (Philadelphia: Fortress Press, 1967) 20.

29. Harris Birkeland, *The Evildoers in the Book of Psalms* (Oslo: Jaco Dybwad, 1955) 41ff. In his earlier *Die Feinde des Individuums in der israelitischen Psalmenliteratur* (Oslo: Grøhndahl, 1933) he had expressed himself more circumspectly, but his final conclusion that the enemies were always national figures drove his argument.

30. Sigmund Mowinckel, *The Psalms in Israel's Worship* (Oxford: Blackwell, 1962) 2:1ff, esp. 2:2 n. 2.

only about illness, but in some cases it is a dominant feature and should be considered accordingly.

Several psalms reflect the issue of illness and may include the element of imprecation, but the most significant of these is Ps 69. This psalm has been interpreted in a range of ways, and its long and complex form certainly leaves open a range of possibilities. As noted above, Schmidt regarded this as one of the prayers of the accused, drawing on the last part of v. 4 in which the psalmist claims to have been forced to return goods that were not stolen. However, the psalmist goes on to admit guilt in general terms—hardly what we would expect in a genre that has as its primary concern the protestation of innocence. So, although this is a prayer of someone who has been accused, it is only a minor element. More importantly, v. 20 notes that as a result of the activities of enemies, the psalmist is now in a weakened state, while the language of waters passing over are typical of psalms in which illness seems to be prominent, or at least where the psalmist describes significant suffering.[31] However, it is also clear here that illness and the activities of enemies are linked,[32] which is why there is another extended imprecation in vv. 22–28.

It should be observed that the imprecation derives from a range of experiences that are outlined in vv. 5, 7 and 12, all of which indicate the presence of at least gossip, though gossip of a nature that leads the psalmist to believe that death was imminent (vv. 1–3, 14–18). It is out of the context of this reproach that the psalmist prays against the enemies. Although the imprecation is extended, it should be noted that its requests are linked to the actions of the enemies toward the psalmist. The psalmist has experienced both illness and accusation, and vv. 22–25 ask for the enemies to experience illness, while the request in vv. 26–28 is that their guilt in making false accusations should be made known. All of this is premised on the psalmist's position as outlined in vv. 29, again suggesting that the imprecation is linked to the effect that the enemies have had. It is the certainty that God hears the plea of the righteous that leads to the promise of praise in vv. 30–33, which in turn leads to the hopeful ending of the psalm.

Again, we should note that although the language of the imprecation is harsh, there is no attempt to claim the right of unlimited retribution. What is passionately desired is that God would bring justice, and do so in light of the *lex talionis*, so that those who afflict the righteous should receive a just punishment that fits the crime. That this is surrendered to God is made clear by the psalm's conclusion.

---

31. E.g., Ps 88:7.
32. It should be noted that the integrity of the psalm is often challenged, thus separating these themes, but it has been well defended by Leslie C. Allen, "The Value of Rhetorical Criticism in Psalm 69," *JBL* 105 (1986) 577–98; and J. H. Coetzee, *Die Spanning tussen God se "verborge wees" en Sy "ingrype om te red". 'n Eksegetiese Ondersoek na 'n Aantal Klaagpsalms* (D.D. thesis, University of Pretoria, 1986) 170.

Although other psalms could be considered, there is no doubt that Pss 109 and 69 are the most troubling individual imprecations. Seen in context, however, they function to inculcate attitudes in prayer whereby the right to retribution is surrendered to Yahweh. The wider context of the book, with its eschatological shaping, allows for the possibility that the execution of this justice might be outside of history, but this is not necessary. What matters most is that justice is something only Yahweh can bring, and it is this that these imprecations passionately request.

Communal Psalms

The situation with the communal psalms is slightly different, in that the limitation of retributive violence in the complaint psalms is not limited by the law of exact retribution because it is a law about the punishment of individuals for crimes. Because a form-critical division in the communal laments is slightly less useful in that we are invariably dealing with the actions of national enemies, we will not further subdivide this material. In considering the communal complaints, we will examine Ps 137, principally because it is regarded as the worst of the imprecations,[33] and Ps 79 because its imprecation can be understood as asking for considerably more to be done to those who have attacked Israel than Israel themselves experienced. Nevertheless, we shall see that in both cases the imprecations in these psalms ask for divinely enacted punishment that matches the harm that has been inflicted. That is, although the *lex talionis* is not strictly applicable, it still provides the pattern for these prayers.

Turning first to Ps 137, we can see immediately that it is a psalm of memory, built around the recollections of the experience of Babylon in vv. 1–4, a desire not to forget Jerusalem in vv. 5–6, and finally a request that Yahweh remember and repay Edom and Babylon exactly (Piel of *šlm*) for what they have done in vv. 7–9. The level of torment in vv. 1–3 is clear, as Zion was effectively mocked by the Babylonians, because the "Songs of Zion" would be texts such as Pss 46–48, all of which celebrate Yahweh's choice of Zion. It is in light of this that the psalmist poses the rhetorical question of v. 4, which effectively claims that there was no way for one to show loyalty to Yahweh and sing such songs simply to amuse tormentors. Indeed, in vv. 5–6 the psalmist shows a desire to remember Jerusalem instead, even to the point of expressing a self-curse should Jerusalem no longer be the chief joy of the poet.[34]

It is from this that we come to the imprecation in vv. 7–9. The language here is undoubtedly harsh, but we should again note some of the key fea-

---

33. Craig C. Broyles, *Psalms* (NIBCOT; Peabody, MA: Hendrickson, 1999) 479, says simply "Most psalms are cherished by Christians; this one is not."

34. Reference to the right hand "forgetting" is odd unless it is the skill of playing the harp. However, if there is a slight transposition of the text then it would be a request for the right hand to wither.

tures that we have observed in the prayers of the individual. First, the request is directed to Yahweh, and the one who can be said to be blessed in the final verse is not another human, but Yahweh alone, because Yahweh is the one who can offer exact retribution. That is to say, both the Edomites and the Babylonians should receive back only what they have done. In fact, Isa 13:16 anticipates this as the end of the Babylonians, so there is an extent to which this prayer is shaped by meditation on Scripture. In addition, Isa 14:21 uses similar language to describe the end of the Babylonian dynasty. In all, therefore, the benediction is something that Yahweh alone can fulfill, and all of the passionate rage that is present is surrendered here to him. Again, if we ask when Yahweh might do this, then we are left with no immediate answer, but the Bible insists that it is finally up to Yahweh to bring justice. The importance of the psalm, however, is that it models for the community the same position as that of the individual, which is that retributive justice can be requested, but not in an unlimited way. This justice, once requested, is surrendered to Yahweh in prayer, as nothing further can be done.

Psalm 79 might be considered as an exception to the pattern we have so far noted, as the psalmist asks in v. 12 that God repay those who have defiled Jerusalem[35] sevenfold for the taunts that they have raised against God. As always, these imprecations must be placed within their immediate context in the psalm. In vv. 1–4 the psalmist describes the actions of those who defiled Jerusalem and the widespread damage they have done, leaving many dead and unburied. In v. 4, the key root *ḥrp* is introduced, referring to the taunts of the nations that surrounded Judah, presumably Edom, Moab, and perhaps Ammon. Psalm 79 thus emerges out of a context similar to that of Ps 137. In v. 4, these taunts are directed against Judah, but in v. 10 the neighbors' taunts are now said to be against God himself. But because Judah is understood as God's people, we can see that those who deride them also deride God.[36]

Coming out of the questions in vv. 1–4, the psalm then poses two questions, each of which introduces a new section of the psalm. In v. 5, the psalmist asks "How long" in terms of Yahweh's anger toward his people, while v. 10 asks why the nations should be able to ask where God is. In effect, these questions ask God to balance two related issues. In v. 5–9, the psalmist

---

35. The particular events to which Ps 79 refers are not made explicit and accordingly are the source of considerable debate. But with Frank-Lothar Hossfeld and Eric Zenger (*Psalms 2: A Commentary on Psalms 51–100* [Minneapolis: Fortress, 2005] 304–5), the Babylonian destruction of the temple seems most likely, though fortunately a final decision on this is not needed for our purposes. For an exilic origin in contrast to the other Asaph psalms, see Beat Weber, "Zur Datierung der Asaph-Psalmen der 74 und 79," *Bib* 81 (2000) 521–32. However, the reference to Jerusalem makes clear that the nation affected was Judah, not the Northern Kingdom of Israel.

36. We see this pattern also in 1 Sam 17, where *ḥrp* is also a *Leitwort*. Goliath initially defied (*ḥrp*) the armies of Israel (1 Sam 17:10). But David sees this as defying God's army (17:26, 36) and ultimately as defying Yahweh (17:46).

acknowledges the nation's sin (vv. 8–9), something only Yahweh can resolve, while also asking that he act against the invading nations. As such, there is acceptance that some punishment was appropriate. But in vv. 10–13, the emphasis is more on international perceptions of God's justice, though this emerges also from the plea of v. 9 that Yahweh act because he is the God of Judah's salvation. Forgiveness of Judah as Yahweh's people is thus foundational to the ultimate experience of God's justice, but the psalm also insists that God's justice be seen in the nations. The importance of this is emphasised by the repetition here of several key terms from vv. 1–4, thus indicating that God's justice must be seen to relate to the specific situation and not be deferred to some later point.

More importantly for our purposes, there is a close link between the actions of the invaders and what the psalm requests. Where they have poured out blood (v. 3), the psalm asks Yahweh to pour out his anger on these nations (v. 6) and that the outpoured blood of God's servants be redressed (v. 10).[37] Judah has experienced God's wrath, because of their sin, and now the nations that have so devastated Jerusalem and the temple need to receive the same. It is in this context that we need also to read the request for sevenfold repayment for the nations' reproaching Yahweh. "Sevenfold" here should be read against its background in Lev 26:18, where Yahweh promises to punish Israel sevenfold for their sin. In context, this is not an unlimited punishment, nor is it massively out of proportion to the crime, but rather it is a complete punishment. The psalm draws on this background to ask that the nations be fully punished for their attitude to Yahweh, but it does not ask for more than this, and neither does it seek justification for enacting violence against these nations. Justice is something that ultimately can only be given by God, and this psalm is a passionate request for that but no more. When faced with the boastful claims of the superpowers of the time, the psalmists know that they can pray. Having prayed, though they long to praise God for this justice, they accept that justice is something only God can enact.

Conclusion

Can Christians therefore use these psalms in prayer? The answer is that we can, but in doing so we must realize their place within the book of Psalms and also within the wider body of Scripture. In the end, these psalms ask us to take a position of powerlessness and to approach God only from that position. Violence is something that lurks in the heart of all, but it is not something that we may finally enact simply because we have been injured by

---

37. *něqāmâ* is often rendered as vengeance or similar. But the links between what has been done and what is requested makes it clear that redress is what is requested here. Cf. Goldingay, *Psalms* (BCOTWP; Grand Rapids: Baker Academic, 2007) 2:527. Allen P. Ross, *A Commentary on the Psalms* (KEL; Grand Rapids: Kregel, 2013) 2:678, says it is simply an appeal for "a just judgment."

someone else, nor may we request unlimited retribution.[38] Lamech's song (Gen 4:23–24) is something against which the whole of Scripture reacts. We cannot take a facile "New Testament supplants the Old" view either, because as we have seen the New Testament (and Jesus himself) continues to use imprecation. Rather, we have to ask what these psalms model to us and what resources they offer in prayer. As we do this, we are challenged in terms of our own tendency toward a desire to enact retribution, and we are challenged to see that it is only when we view ourselves as powerless that we can begin to hope for God's justice.[39]

What these psalms model to us is that we can indeed pray for justice in a world where violence continues, and where God's people are often at the receiving end of that violence. But for the psalms it is never the right of any individual or the people of God corporately to enact this violence. Within the Psalms, the king may legitimately act as Yahweh's representative to use violence as is needed, and no more, to ensure that justice is brought about. But within the larger movement of the Bible as a whole, we see that this authority is now given to Jesus. As we have noted, the king in Psalms was already becoming an eschatological figure, so it is consistent that Jesus should occupy this role eschatologically. In any case, violence such as was needed to bring about justice belongs to God alone in the Psalms, and this continues to be the case in the New Testament. We may pray, and pray passionately, for divine justice and know that it may be enacted in history or deferred eschatologically, but there we must leave it. Hence, these psalms describe and experience violence because of the nature of this world and having received it turn to God in prayer. And it is in prayer that our violence is left, asking for justice and nothing more than is just.

---

38. Hence John N. Day (*Crying for Justice: What the Psalms Teach Us about Mercy and Vengeance in an Age of Terrorism* [Grand Rapids: Kregel, 2005] 14) sees the use of these psalms by Christians as an "extreme ethic" in contrast to love and blessing which he regards as our "characteristic ethic."

39. Along similar lines, Jerome F. D. Creach, *Violence in Scripture* (Interp; Louisville, KY: Westminster John Knox, 2013) 194, observes that these psalms "can only be prayed rightly by and on behalf of the powerless."

Chapter 6

Suffering Has Its Voice: Divine Violence, Pain, and Prayer in Lamentations

HEATH A. THOMAS

Introduction

Jesus' cry of dereliction remains something of an enigma. Mark presents Jesus' words in Aramaic, suggesting that Jesus was not merely quoting the Psalms to fulfill Scripture as the Davidic sufferer *par excellence*. Jesus' usage of Aramaic indicates a human sufferer speaking with ordinary language to complain to God about extraordinary pain: "My God, my God, why have you forsaken me?" (Mark 15:34).

His complaint raises questions concerning divine violence and human suffering. Did Jesus really not understand his situation? Could he really not explain his suffering? In the logic of the apostle Mark and other Gospel writers, it certainly *appears* that Jesus could rationally and logically explain why he was dying on the cross because the Gospels reinforce the notion that Jesus came, in fact, to suffer and die in order to, among other things, renew Israel and reconcile all nations to God. Still, this fact in no way diminishes the force of his lament to God. Jesus cried out to God because he was, at that instant, God-forsaken, and this moment comprises a crucial bridge that links the humanity and deity of Jesus as recorded in the Gospels.[1] Jesus' cry from the cross exemplifies how complaint prayer can navigate the suffering that emerges as a result of divine violence.

In the life of the Church today, it is possible to suggest that complaint prayer remains unnecessary, apart from the example of Jesus. Human suffering, even when experienced at the hand of God, is not a problem, because God remains interminably free to do as he wishes; he is God, after all. If he is violent and causes pain, that violence is not without purpose. So the thinking goes, the purpose of divine violence is to build the soul of the believer. God enables (or allows) pain to produce virtue(s): kindness, patience,

---

1. See the discussion of Richard Bauckham, *Jesus and the God of Israel: God Crucified and Others Studies on the New Testament's Christology of Divine Identity* (Grand Rapids: Eerdmans, 2008) 254-68.

longsuffering, or endurance. Some New Testament exemples seem to point in this direction (e.g., Rom 5:2-4; Phil 3:10; Col 1:24; 2 Tim 1:12; 1 Pet 1:6-9; 3:8-22; 4:1-19; Jas 1:2; 5:7-10). The human response, then, should be silence, patience, even gratitude for divine violence. We could call this a theodic response.[2] The book of Lamentations offers this response to divine violence and pain as well (Lam 3:25-39).

But a theodic response is not the *only* way that Scripture negotiates divine violence, which complicates the issue of human response. Jesus did not respond with silence or gratitude on the cross. And Scripture provides evidence for complaining (or even protesting) divine violence through prayer. For instance, sufferers cry out "Why, O God, do you reject us forever?" (Ps 74:2). Or, "My God, my God! Why have you forsaken me?" (Ps 22:2). Or, "Why O LORD, do you stand far off?" (Ps 10:1). Other prayers do the same (Pss 17:1; 44:23). Even the martyrs under the throne in heaven use similar language in their appeal to God: "O Sovereign Lord, holy and true, how long before you will judge and avenge our blood on those who dwell upon the earth?" (Rev 6:10). These are all complaint prayers, which offer a vocabulary for addressing divine violence and human pain.

Kristin Swenson recognizes that complaint prayer engages the "dark side" of God in a particular way. These prayers provide "language for expressing pain, a grammar of pain, which continues to resonate for people struggling with difficulties understanding and describing their particular experiences of suffering."[3] Complaint prayers are neither impious nor petty, because they address complexities, difficulties, and pain without blinking, and they do so with a radical faith in God. They do not explain away divine violence or "cure" pain, but they do offer a way to grapple with violence and pain from the foundation of faith.

This essay explores divine violence and pain, particularly from the book of Lamentations. I shall argue that Lamentations identifies and engages divine violence and resultant pain through both complaint and confessional prayer. Although other ways of praying certainly appear in Lamentations (silent prayer, meditation, and petitionary prayer for example), this essay focuses on complaint and confession exclusively.[4] This decision is due in part to the fact that complaint and confessional prayer both encompass the other prayer-forms to one degree or another, and it is due in part to what

---

2. This term derives, clearly, from the notion of a particular understanding of "theodicy," where God's actions are justified as appropriate, even good, in the face of suffering and pain. For the complexity of theodicy especially on display in the Bible, see Antti Laato and Johannes C. de Moor, eds., *Theodicy in the World of the Bible* (Leiden: Brill, 2003).

3. Kristin M. Swenson, *Living through Pain: Psalms and the Search for Wholeness* (Waco, TX: Baylor University Press, 2005) 74.

4. For the diversity of prayer-types in the book, see: Heath A. Thomas, "Relating Prayer and Pain: Psychological Analysis and Lamentations Research," *TynBul* 61 (2010) 183-208.

can be covered in this study.⁵ The rationale for this thesis is fairly straightforward. Prayer in the face of divine violence offers a distinctive approach to a difficult issue that may be helpful for people of faith, particularly the ancient people of Judah, and by analogy, the modern Church. Although previous research argues for the vitality of lament in the Christian life, it excludes prayer against divine violence.⁶

Three points clarify the approach offered here. First, this essay shall proceed by investigating what the text indicates rather than providing a larger systematic and philosophical framework within which the data of Lamentations might be fixed. The latter approach, while helpful in its own way, remains more theoretically focused than what appears here. I am interested in how ancient Judahites responded to their experience of violence and pain at the hand of God, rather than how one can demonstrate the rationality or acceptability of a violent God. It is an argument that explores the question of divine violence from the cultural center of their faith and particularly their prayers, rather than "placing God in the dock," so to speak, and interrogating the rationality and justice of his actions from another standpoint, such as philosophy or systematic theology.

The textual approach advocated here provides a different valence to the question of divine violence than does philosophical investigations of the same. Philosophical investigations often treat theodicy or God and the problem(s) of evil by asking questions about the coherence of Christian belief and the problem of evil. One could inquire about the logical or evidential problems of evil in order to resolve them in a philosophical or apologetic manner. Evans takes this kind of approach in his recent, helpful, and stimulating work on the problem of evil and its defeat in Christian belief.⁷ But Lamentations does not tackle the problem in that way. One could say, rather, that Lamentations' challenge is how it negotiates the "experiential problem" of divine violence. It experiences divine violence as a problem and wrestles with it through prayer. This is not to say that Lamentations' wrestling with divine violence presents a better mode of engagement, but only a different one. Perhaps Lamentations' approach, and this essay's approach, can be helpful for future philosophical and systematic investigations of the question of divine violence.

Second, this essay takes care in delineating the terminology of "pain" and "violence." Taking the former first, "pain" remains a multifaceted reality that cannot be reduced only to a physical experience. Instead, "pain" can encompass a variety of experiences: physical, emotional, psychological,

---

5. See ibid., for how complaint and confession relate to other prayer forms in the book.

6. Nicholas Wolterstorff, "If God Is Good and Sovereign, Why Lament?" *CTJ* 36 (2001) 42–52.

7. Jeremy A. Evans, *The Problem of Evil: The Challenge to Essential Christian Belief* (Nashville: B&H Academic, 2013).

social, and so on. Its dynamic quality makes its definition elusive. And yet, as Swenson notes of pain, "you know it when you encounter it."[8] Identified in the context of this essay, pain has to do with the complex physical, emotional, psychological, social, and even spiritual experience(s) that hurts the one(s) who undergoes it. This hurt may be a negative occurrence (often it is), even if one associates the pain with some sort of insight, growth, or deeper appreciation of life. Take, for example, the "pain" of exercising or breaking up scar tissue after surgery. These remain simultaneously negative and beneficial experiences. One cannot, however, divorce pain from the constructive aspect of the experiences by virtue of their benefit for the sufferer(s). Those who undergo such pain often do not voluntarily go through it again. Why? Precisely because it is painful! So pain is a negative experience, even if one "gains" something constructive from it.

For our purposes, "violence" is an act or deportment that causes pain (physical, social, emotional, psychological, or even spiritual) to an Other.[9] The definition(s) and conceptualization(s) of violence deserve rigorous reflection in light of current literature on the topic, which is why this essay defines it as it does.[10] Violence may be associated with pain, but it may not necessarily be associated with "harm" or "evil." I avoid these moral categories, because one must develop criteria to establish them.

Divine violence may be painful, but not necessarily evil. To provide a clarifying example, consider how Hebrew literature identifies "discipline." In Proverbs, discipline is a corrective action (indeed, a *physical* corrective action) that cannot be understood without its connection with pain. Note Prov 29:15: "The rod and reproof give wisdom, but a child left to himself brings shame to his mother." The teaching here remains unambiguous. As I have defined terms above, no doubt this action against the child with the rod would be painful and violent. But for the sage, the "rod" of discipline is not a malignant tool of terror. It is not evil, because it is an instrument for help rather than harm (see also Prov 13:24; 22:15; 23:13; 29:15).

The distinction is significant, especially because such violent "discipline" comes at the hand of God. As the sage states: "Do not reject the discipline (*mûsār*) of the LORD, my son; do not abhor his rebuke. For whom the LORD loves, he disciplines, like a father whose son he delights" (Prov 3:11–12). To return to the analogy of breaking up scar tissue, a painful act, even a violent one, may not be equated with a harmful, evil act. In the remainder of the Hebrew Scriptures, God disciplines his people (often with a "rod") as a form of correction. Such action against his people, however, is characterized as a beneficent action of a parent disciplining a child (Deut 8:5; 11:2; 2 Sam 7:14; Mic 6:9; Jer 31:18; Ps 23:4; 93:4; Prov 6:23; cf. Lam 3:1). In this way, divine

---

8. Swenson, *Living through Pain*, 4.
9. Building from Larry Ray, *Violence and Society* (London: Sage, 2011) 7–9.
10. Slavoj Žižek, *Violence: Six Sideways Reflections* (London: Picador, 2008); Ray, *Violence and Society*; Hannah Arendt, *On Violence* (San Diego: Harcourt Brace, 1970).

discipline is violent and painful but nonetheless an act of care. Although violent, in these texts such action does not register as "harmful," or "evil." Lamentations 3:25–39 utilizes this vein of thought and identifies divine action against his people precisely as a form of discipline, admittedly violent.

Finally, the argument offered here does not offer an apologetic for the rationality, propriety, or defensibility of divine violence within the contours of Old Testament theology that fully explains pain and violence. Such work, as others have shown in this volume and in others, is valuable.[11] The Old Testament does offer theodic explanations of divine action (including divine violence) in other biblical works, particularly in the Deuteronomistic Historical book(s), in the book of Jeremiah, and in the Minor Prophets.[12] But advancing a "theodicy" or a theology of divine violence is not the aim of this essay. Rather, it is a particular engagement of the question of divine violence from Lamentations.

Divine Violence and Lamentations

Lamentations is an underutilized resource for the problem of divine violence. Current literature often underplays or ignores it, perhaps due to an assumption that the book is really about the "mercies of the LORD" (Lam 3:21) and so unlikely help when looking for resources on the topic.[13] The central position of Lam 3 and its use of Exod 34:6 (often called the *Gnadenformel* or "grace formula") in Lam 3:21–24 may authorize a one-sided perspective of divine love.[14] But Lamentations powerfully identifies and negotiates divine violence.

This section explores three major blocks of text and their presentations of divine violence: Lam 1:10, 16 and Lam 2:1–9. These passages employ language that scholars typically associate with violence: physical force exerted against the abused. However, in light of the definition articulated above, *any* act or deportment that causes pain to an Other equates to violence,

---

11. See esp. Evans, *The Problem of Evil*; Heath A. Thomas, Jeremy Evans, and Paul Copan, eds., *Holy War in the Bible: Christian Morality and an Old Testament Problem* (Downers Grove, IL: IVP Academic, 2013); Paul Copan, *Is God a Moral Monster? Making Sense of the Old Testament God* (Grand Rapids: Baker, 2010).

12. Note the different "theodicies" at work in the Old Testament explored in Laato and de Moor, eds., *Theodicy*.

13. See its neglect in Eric A. Seibert, *Disturbing Divine Behavior: Troubling Old Testament Images of God* (Minneapolis: Fortress, 2009); idem, *The Violence of Scripture: Overcoming the Old Testament's Troubling Legacy* (Minneapolis: Fortress, 2012); Jerome F. D. Creach, *Violence in Scripture* (Interp; Louisville, KY: Westminster John Knox, 2013); Thomas Römer, *Dark God: Cruelty, Sex, and Violence in the Old Testament* (trans. S. O'Neill; New York: Paulist, 2013).

14. So suggests Ulrich Berges, "The Violence of God in the Book of Lamentations," in *One Text, a Thousand Methods: Studies in Memory of Sjef van Tilborg* (ed. P. C. Counet and U. Berges; BIS 71; Leiden: Brill, 2005) 21–44 (esp. pp. 22–23). For the grace formula, see Hermann Spieckermann, "Barmherzig und gnädig ist der Herr...," *ZAW* 102 (1990) 1–18.

including spiritual, psychological, or social pain. For this reason, passivity, distance, and presence cause pain and thereby can be identified as forms of divine violence in Lamentations.[15] These threads weave together in the poetry of Lamentations to create a horrific fabric of suffering.

Divine Passivity (Lamentations 1:10)

Lamentations presents divine violence through God's passivity in Lam 1:10. The text reads:

> An enemy spread his hand over all my precious things,
> For she watched nations penetrate her sanctuary
> Which You had decreed (to) her: "They shall not enter into your assembly."[16]

The correspondence between body and temple stands out, and the poetic use of personification particularly enables this association.[17] Zion appears as a woman and a nameless, faceless enemy places his "hand" over her "precious things." "All her precious things" likely denotes temple implements, but with the body analogy, "precious things" may also denote jewelry that adorns the female body or the body itself. In any case, enemy action is aggressive, and the next line carries the assault further to speak of sexual violation.

Verse 10b horrifically depicts a monstrous desecration. The verb from the Hebrew root *bw'*, "he entered into," evokes sexual abuse especially when coupled with the term *miqdāš*, "sanctuary."[18] Zion's "sanctuary" is her temple, but in the body // temple correspondence, the sacred space is Zion's genitalia. In this metaphor, the enemy has *raped* Jerusalem: he "penetrated" her sanctuary; he desecrated her. Wanton rape sullies and shames the holy body of Zion.

In light of her abuse, the speaker addresses God directly in v. 10c, which raises the issue of divine passivity. The "you" of the third verset likely is God, who pronounced the former decree to Zion ("They shall not enter into your assembly"). The language of Deut 23:3–4 resonates with v. 10c and may lie in the background. God's former command that prevents the Moabites and Ammonites from entering God's sanctuary now serves as the ground for the complaint in v. 10c. The speaker uses the former decree as a foundation to protest the impropriety of Zion's violation. God said this would not happen then, so it should not happen now. But the rape scene in v. 10 inflames the intensity of the protest. God should have been true to his former command, because his passivity has led to the wanton rape of the city itself. This violation cannot go unnoticed. Zion suffers at the hands of

---

15. Elizabeth Boase, "The Characterisation of God in Lamentations," *ABR* 56 (2008) 32–44.

16. All translations from the original languages are mine.

17. Alan Mintz, *Ḥurban: Responses to Catastrophe in Hebrew Literature* (JTLMA; Syracuse: Syracuse University Press, 1996) 25.

18. A. Berlin, *Lamentations* (OTL; Louisville, KY: Westminster John Knox, 2002) 55.

enemy violence (the nation/enemy who rapes her), but the speaker's comment in v. 10c decries God's passivity. God sits by while the violation occurs. Divine passivity in the face of Zion's rape leaves the speaker wondering about God's painful disregard, which is an act of violence against God's people.

Divine Distance (Lamentations 1:16)

Lamentations 1:16 presents divine violence as distance. Distance is slightly different from passivity, because the text suggests God's spatial separation from the sufferer. Personified Jerusalem's speech depicts God's distance in disturbing detail. The text reads:

> On account of these I weep, my eye constantly descending with water.
> For far from me is a comforter, the one who restores my life.
> My children have become desolate, for the enemy is superior.

Personified Jerusalem weeps "constantly" over the pain she endures. The duplication of "my eye" in the first verset reflects deep hurt, implying the persistent weeping.[19] This technique effectively enables the reader to recognize Zion's suffering, like her tears, as unremitting.[20]

But what *causes* her weeping and suffering? Jerusalem only says that it is "on account of *these* [*things*]." The antecedent to "these things" may be divine activity described in Lam 1:13–15. Still, there is no reason to limit the things for which Jerusalem weeps. To this point, divine activity (vv. 13–15), enemy activity (vv. 9–10), degradation (vv. 1–2), and perhaps anxiety over sin (v. 11) all cause pain for Zion.[21] In light of the variety of sufferings she mentions in her speech, it is more sensible to understand "these things" as broadly as possible. The full account from vv. 1–15 identifies different points of her pain.

Her pain *also* includes the fact that she has no comforter in Lam 1:16b. As described in Lam 1:2b, 7c, 9b, Jerusalem cries over the lack of a "comforter." Who is this comforter? In v. 16, the comforter she laments is God himself. The phrase "the one who restores my life" likely alludes to Ps 23:3, where the psalmist says about the deity, "He restores my life."[22] Read with the intertext of Ps 23:3, then, personified Jerusalem has connected her weeping to divine *distance*. The comforter she longed for is God, but he is far removed from her pain. Because he is not present, her soul cannot be restored. The spatial adjective *far* only reinforces this idea. God *is* or *can be* the one who restores the soul, but for Lamentations, he stands far off, preventing any restoration at all. Although he has been known in the past as a "comforter" and "restorer" (Lam 1:16), or elsewhere as a "redeemer" (Lam 3:58) and "vindicator" (Lam

---

19. Hans J. Boecker, *Klagelieder* (ZB; Zürich: Theologischer Verlag, 1985) 21.
20. Heath A. Thomas, *Poetry and Theology in the Book of Lamentations: The Aesthetics of an Open Text* (HBM 47; Sheffield: Sheffield Phoenix, 2013) 120, for discussion and the defense of the grammar.
21. For v. 11 as a confession of sin, see Heath A. Thomas, "The Meaning of *zōlēlâ* (Lam 1:11) One More Time," *VT* 61 (2011) 489–98.
22. God is also described as the one who "restores life" in Ruth 4:15.

3:59), at the present moment his violence against Zion appears as nothing but distance.

The pain associated with distance reappears in the prayer of Lam 3:49–50:

> My eye flows and it is not still; there is no rest;
> Until he looks down and sees: the LORD from the heavens.

Tears fall as God stands far off. As in Lam 1:16, God reigns in heaven, but suffering remains on earth. The pain that derives from divine distance leaves sufferers knocking on heaven's door, awaiting God's response: "until he looks down and sees." The poetry longs for a response from, and an encounter with, God. But for now, God sits in heaven, "far off" from the cries and pain of his suffering people.

Divine Presence (Lamentations 2:1–9)

Thirty active verbs accumulate within the brief span of Lam 2:1–9, brutally depicting divine violence against his people and land.[23] God destroys Jerusalem and Judah *directly* with "his hand" or *indirectly* with an invading army. God slaughters the "precious things" of Jerusalem's eye in Lam 2:4b. These "precious things" are ambiguous. They may represent temple implements or, more provocatively, they represent the *children* of Jerusalem. Lamentations 2:4c–9 reveals God's rejection of his temple, cult, and city. The city and temple are burned, rejected, and destroyed. Jerusalem's leadership perishes at the hand of Israel's God as well, as Lam 2:1 also indicates. In Lam 2:4c, he pours out his wrath "like fire" into the "tent of the daughter of Zion." Verse 4 recalls the language of the "Tent of Meeting" in pentateuchal texts.[24] God's act of pouring fire in Lam 2:4c presents a reversal of fortunes. In the past God's presence appeared as a cloud to consecrate the tabernacle (Exod 40:35), but now he is fiery wrath that pours on the temple (Lam 2:4c). God's presence appears as horribly violent in this presentation.

---

23. Lam 2:1a: "He beclouded"; Lam 2:1b: "He cast from heaven to earth the beauty of Israel"; Lam 2:1c: "He did not remember his footstool"; Lam 2:2a, 5a–b: "He swallowed"; Lam 2:2a: "He did not pity"; Lam 2:2b: "He tore down"; Lam 2:2c: "He hurled to earth and profaned her kingdom and officials"; Lam 2:3a: "He cut off every horn of Israel"; Lam 2:3b: "He withdrew his right hand"; Lam 2:3c: "He burned in Jacob"; Lam 2:3c: "He consumed everything"; Lam 2:4a: "He strung his bow"; Lam 2:4b: "He slaughtered"; Lam 2:4c: "He poured out wrath like fire"; Lam 2:5b, 6a: "He annihilated"; Lam 2:5c: "He increased mourning and lamentation"; Lam 2:6a: "He treated violently"; Lam 2:6b: "He abolished"; Lam 2:6c, 7a: "He spurned"; Lam 2:7a: "He repudiated"; Lam 2:7b: "He delivers the walls of Jerusalem's citadels into the hand of an enemy"; Lam 2:8a: "He planned to annihilate the walls of dear Zion"; Lam 2:8b: "He stretched out a line and did not turn back his hand from swallowing"; Lam 2:8c: "He put rampart and wall into mourning"; Lam 2:9a: "He destroyed and shattered Zion's bars."

24. Exod 27:21; 28:43; 29:4, 10, 11, 30, 32, 42, 44; 30:16, 18, 20, 26, 36; 31:7; 35:21; 38:8, 30; 39:32, 40; 40:2, 6, 7, 12, 22, 24, 26, 29, 32, 34, 35. This language is carried through to Leviticus as well, in Lev 1:1.

The verses also reveal God's rejection of all prior systems and structures in Jerusalem: familial, cultic, pastoral, political, or metropolitan. He abolishes festival and Sabbath (2:6); destroys pastureland and habitations (2:1); fortified cities (2:1); and rejects his altar, sanctuary (2:7), and temple (2:4). The text announces that God spurns king and priest (2:6). He exiles Jerusalem's king and princes (2:9), and he denies *torah* (2:9). He enacts the failure of prophecy (2:9). As an outcome of God's activity, elders sit on the ground (2:10a) and maidens grieve (2:10c). Finally, we see children and infants dying on God's day of wrath (2:11–12). The devastation of every structure in society here stands as a result of divine violence, victims of God's wrath.

Divine metaphors heap up in poetry to portray God's violent presence. He is a destructive cloud, perhaps even a terrific storm. Cloud imagery appears in Lam 2:1. The only instance of *cloud* as a verb in the Hebrew Scriptures is in Lam 2:1a: "he has beclouded." Re'emi and Lee identify cloud imagery with theophany in Hebrew Scripture.[25] Normally, the cloud signifies God's favor, as in the Sinai theophany of Exod 19:9, where God descends in a cloud after defeating Egypt. This imagery also appears in Exod 34:5–6, where God descends in a cloud and promises his presence. Dobbs-Allsopp proposes that this imagery can be inverted so God fights *against* his people, as Lam 2:1a suggests.[26] So Lam 2:1a unveils God's violent presence: the theophanic "cloud" and storm rages against God's land and people on his day of wrath.

The violent presence of God appears also as a raging, burning "fire" in Lam 2:1–9. Divine fire belongs to divine warrior imagery, prevalent in both the Hebrew Scriptures and in Canaanite literature.[27] Scholars associate the imagery of "fire" with lightning bolts: "The image of the 'devouring fire' seems to be predominantly expressive of the divine warrior's wrath and destruction," drawn from Canaanite theological traditions.[28] So God comes from the clouds and has arrows of lightning (Lam 2:4a) that ravage pastureland, cities, and temple.[29] The text rightly proclaims that the fire of the Lord consumed *everything*.

Finally, God appears in this text as an enemy warrior. To be precise, storm and fire imagery stand secondary to the primary image of the divine warrior. Storm and fire images help give color and shape to the divine warrior

---

25. Robert Martin-Achard and S. Paul Re'emi, *God's People in Crisis: Amos and Lamentations* (ITC; Grand Rapids: Eerdmans, 1984) 92; Nancy C. Lee, *The Singers of Lamentations: Cities Under Siege, from Ur to Jerusalem to Sarajevo* (BIS 60; Leiden: Brill, 2002) 133.

26. F. W. Dobbs-Allsopp, *Weep, O Daughter of Zion: A Study of the City-Lament Genre in the Hebrew Bible* (BibOr 44; Rome: Pontifical Biblical Institute, 1993) 62; Frank Moore Cross, *Canaanite Myth and Hebrew Epic: Essays in the History of the Religion of Israel* (Cambridge: Harvard University Press, 1973) 156–77.

27. Antje Labahn, "Fire from Above: Metaphors and Images of God's Actions in Lamentations 2.1–9," *JSOT* 31 (2006) 239–56.

28. P. D. Miller, "Fire in the Mythology of Canaan and Israel," *CBQ* 27 (1965) 256–61 (esp. p. 259).

29. Cross, *Canaanite Myth and Hebrew Epic*, 161–63.

image. Ancient Near Eastern iconography depicts the divine warrior with a bow in hand, often grasping the bow from the heavens.[30] Hebrew Scriptures portray God as an archer with bow or arrows, possibly understood as thunderbolts and lightning, as in Lam 2:4a.[31] In that text, God strings his bow. It is taught, and the arrow is positioned to fire into the target.[32] The divine warrior strikes his people with destructive force.

When read alongside other texts in the Hebrew Scriptures, Lam 2:1–9 further depicts the divine warrior's violent presence. Boecker recognizes allusions to Exodus in Lam 2:3b, 4a. In Exod 15:6, God's right hand wins glory for himself and his right hand shatters his enemy. Whereas God formerly fought against Israel's enemies with the strength of his right hand, Lam 2:3b, 4a reverses this tradition. Now he fights against his people with a bow in his right hand, and he withdraws from the enemy his right hand.[33] The reversal of Exod 15:6 in Lam 2:3b, 4a suggests a dark divine victory song: as in the Song of the Sea, God remains victorious, but his victory is now over his *own people* rather than *Egypt*. The reality that God did "not pity" (Lam 2:2a) reveals he has enacted divine war against his own people. The language of "not pitying" a nation is evocative of texts associated with divine warfare (e.g., Deut 7:2–16; 1 Sam 15:3).[34] Lamentations 2:2 reads, "The Lord swallowed, *he did not pity*, all the habitations of Jacob. He tore down in his rage the fortified cities of dear Judah. He hurled to earth, he profaned kingdom and her officials." Just as he commanded divine war against enemy nations, he has now commanded divine war against his own people. The comparative "like an enemy" and "like a foe" provocatively proves this in Lam 2:4–5. He is pictured as an enemy warrior, a foe who brandishes a bow against his people. These verses depict God as the violent warrior whose presence brings trauma, devastation, and death.

Conclusion

In light of the discussion above, it becomes apparent that the problem of divine violence is perhaps more acute than previously recognized. God's violence in Lamentations associates with his activity, as is normally af-

---

30. Martin Klingbeil, *Yahweh Fighting from Heaven: God as Warrior and as God of Heaven in the Hebrew Psalter and Ancient Near Eastern Iconography* (OBO 169; Gottingen: Vandenhoeck & Ruprecht, 1999), figure 88.

31. Deut 32:23, 24; Job 6:4; 34:6; Pss 18:14; 21:12; 38:2; 64:7; 77:17; 120:4; 144:6; Isa 41:2, Hab 3:9; Zech 9:13.

32. The tensed bow seems to be the force of "strong (in) his right hand." Boecker rightly translates the Heb., "erhoben seine Rechte (raised in his right hand)" (*Klagelieder*, 38).

33. Ibid., 38–39.

34. See Heath A. Thomas, "A Neglected Witness to 'Holy War' in the Writings," in Heath A. Thomas, Jeremy Evans, and Paul Copan, eds., *Holy War in the Bible: Christian Morality and an Old Testament Problem* (Downers Grove, IL: IVP Academic, 2013) 77–78.

firmed, but also his distance and passivity. This fact expands on what counts as violent action and thereby what creates pain among God's people. But this brings us to the second aim of the essay, to explore how God's people respond to violence and pain. God's distance and passivity, as well as his activity, are seen to be taken up, in general, in and through prayer.

Retribution and Confession as Response

One response arrives in an affirmation of the retribution principle that leads to prayer of confession. The retribution principle is a way of identifying a sin-and-punishment scheme. As one sins, one undergoes punishment as a result.[35] In Lamentations, punishment comes directly from God's hand.[36] Retribution, then, teaches theodicy. Because sin deserves punishment, and the one who experiences pain is a sinner, then God is justified in his violence. A number of texts lead to this conclusion, but I focus on only one.[37] Lamentations 3:25–39 offers a retributive answer to the problem of divine violence, which then demands a particular human response: penitential acts and penitential prayer. Boda notes the penitential quality of prayer in these verses, providing God's people a way to negotiate his wrath and move them forward with hope.[38] In so doing, the text presents an appropriate way to live within (and perhaps beyond) the present state of suffering in a loose argument that proceeds through the verses. So penitential prayer, as a response to divine violence, confirms the retribution principle.[39]

If Lam 3:24 adjures hope in God, then vv. 25–30 admonish *why* it is "good" to hope in him. "The LORD is good to the one who waits, to the soul who seeks him" (Lam 3:25). Verses 25–26 confirm the covenantal relationship between God and his people taught in vv. 22–23 (through the language of Exod

---

35. The inverse of this, of course, is true as well. If one obeys the will of God (lives a righteous life), then one will be rewarded with blessing. See the discussion in Laato and de Moor, eds., introduction to *Theodicy*, xxx–xxxviii.

36. However, the Hebrew Scriptures also provide evidence where the direct action of God is *not* in view, so that we may say that retribution is a result of how God makes the world: God created a world in which sin has its full effects in the life of the sinner. Sin is accompanied by punishment, but the punishment is a result of the sin "coming back upon the head of the sinner" rather than God directly punishing the sinner by direct divine causation. This latter view appears in the wisdom literature of the Old Testament, and in some prophetic texts as well (as in Obad 1:15). See the discussion of Terence E. Fretheim, *Reading Hosea–Micah: A Literary and Theological Commentary* (Reading the Old Testamennt; Macon, GA: Smyth & Helwys, 2013).

37. Elizabeth Boase assesses the difference between retributive and educative theodic tendencies in these verses, but here I suggest that retributive thought plays a significant role throughout Lam 3:25–39. See Boase, "Constructing Meaning in the Face of Suffering: Theodicy in Lamentations," *VT* 58 (2008) 449–68.

38. Mark J. Boda, "The Priceless Gain of Penitence: From Communal Lament to Penitential Prayer in the 'Exilic' Liturgy of Israel," *HBT* 25 (2003) 51–75.

39. Thomas, "Relating Prayer and Pain," 199–204.

34:6). As his covenant people, vv. 25–27 teach the *way* that God's people should react to God's goodness. The community should "seek" God and "wait" on him with silent expectation for his coming salvation.[40] As the faithful wait expectantly on the LORD, they should embrace the yoke of his judgment as well as the pain that accompanies it in v. 27. This embrace of pain appears to be a virtue in vv. 28–30. The text admonishes:

> Let him sit alone and be silent, for he has laid (it) upon him.
> Let him lay his mouth in the dust; perhaps there is hope.
> Let him surrender his cheek to the one who smites him; let him be satisfied with scorn.

Judgment ("the yoke") stands as a *good* for the sufferer, because God has enacted it (God "laid it upon him," v. 28). Embracing judgment as "good" means agreeing with God's verdict: punishment is a result of sin. As sufferers debase themselves in penitence, there may yet be hope beyond humiliation and pain (v. 29).

Laying one's mouth in dust, giving the cheek over to the one who hits, and being filled with shame confirm the retributive principle and provide the way forward for human response. Each of these actions comprises part of a larger matrix of penitential acts. Penitence gives way to the reestablishment of justice between two parties, especially in a covenantal relationship. In this light, penitence paves the way for restoration. Without penitence, restoration and healing in the divine-human sphere will not happen, and so penitential acts remain productive toward restoration.[41] Verse 39 will teach that in penitence, the only prayer that is valid is confession of sin.

However, prior to turning to v. 39, vv. 31–33 reveal God's worth, because he reverses judgment when God's people repent. These verses read:

> For he will not spurn forever.
> For if he torments; even so he comforts, for great is his mercy.
> For he does not afflict from his heart,[42] nor grieve the children of man.

Divine justice appears as a reversal from judgment to salvation. Lamentations 3:31 recalls and inverts divine rejection through the repetition of "spurn" from Lam 2:7:

> The Lord spurned his altar. (Lam 2:7)
> For the Lord does not spurn forever. (Lam 3:31)

---

40. The verb *wĕyāḥîl* (v. 26) is difficult. The verb as pointed in the MT is unfamiliar. I follow the LXX which reads a Hiphil imperfect 3ms (√*yḥl*) and translates *kai hupomenei*.

41. It is appropriate to temper this statement, however, because the certainty of restoration does not appear in Lamentations. Lamentations 3:29 captures the tenuous anticipation of restoration: "*perhaps* there is hope." Emphasis mine.

42. The present study agrees with Lindström, who views "from his heart" as referring to an arbitrary punishment of God (see Num 16:28). Thus, the poet affirms God's punishment, as it is not an arbitrary decision. Fredrik Lindström, *God and the Origin of Evil: A Contextual Analysis of Alleged Monistic Evidence in the Old Testament* (ConBOT 21; Lund: CWK Gleerup, 1983) 222.

The finality of judgment in the former texts proves only a temporary reality in the latter texts. Further, the repetition of the Hebrew root *ygh*, "torment," reinforces the logic of reversal as well. Whereas in Lam 1:5b, 12c, God "tormented" Zion for her sins, in Lam 3:32 and 33 God meets his "torment" with divine "comfort": a direct response to Lam 1:2b, 7c, 9b, 16b, 17a, 21a. For this study, it is interesting that divine *distance* is shown to be a passing reality that will be reversed by the mercy of God.

What initiates the reversal? The immediate context links the reversal with penitent actions (vv. 25–30). And by virtue of this reversal, God's judgment does not constitute a final word. Comfort, removal of scorn, and restoration appear on the horizon for the penitent of heart, who recognize God's violence is disciplinary (in some way) but not damning.

Lamentations 3:33 protects the justice of God by affirming that he does not afflict "from his heart." For Berges, this affirmation reveals that God's "wrath does not belong to his characteristics and that his image is not determined by it."[43] Another way to understand this affirmation comes from Westermann, who thinks it means that God is not capricious in his punishment.[44] Rather, when he afflicts, he comforts; his mercies are great, and he does not exert judgment in a manner that is exploitative or unjustified. God's judgment remains only a step toward his comfort.

Lamentations 3:34–36 exonerates God of any appearance of wrong. The text reads:

> To crush under his feet, all the prisoners of the earth;
> To pervert the justice of a man before the presence of Elyon;
> To suppress a person in his suit; does not the Lord see?

These verses reveal that God actively *sees* and *understands* all sorts of injustice that permeate the world. There is no question of his lack of care or his lack of action. God "sees" perversions and injustice and so cannot and will not enact such injustice himself. Following that line of thought, I understand the last line of v. 36 to be an *affirmation* of God's sovereignty and justice, rather than an affirmation of God's *lack* of justice. God is not a "blind" deity unable to see wrong.[45]

Verses 37–39 advance the theodicy developed in vv. 25–36 and teach that confession of sin remains the appropriate prayer in light of the argument of the previous verses. The text reads:

> Who has said this and it come to pass except the Lord commands it?
> Does not evil and good proceed from the mouth of the Most High?
> Why should a human complain, a man, over his sin?

---

43. Berges, "The Violence of God," 41.
44. Claus Westermann, *Die Klagelieder: Forschungsgeschichte und Auslegung* (Neukirchen-Vluyn: Neukirchener Verlag, 1992) 148–49.
45. See the different exegetical possibilities on v. 36 in Thomas, *Poetry and Theology*, 189–94.

Correspondence of Hebrew constructions between "except the Lord commands it" (Lam 3:37b) and "does not the Lord see" (Lam 3:36b) confirms the interrogative function of both, linking the two verses together structurally.[46] These verses suggest that everything comes as a result of God's command, thereby reinforcing God's sovereignty. Verse 39 teaches that in light of his control, his punishment, and human sin, God's people should respond *not* with complaint over God's violence but with confession of sin. The word √'*nn* in the Hithpolel appears only in Lam 3:39 and in Num 11:1: "The people took to complaining (√'*nn*) bitterly before the LORD." "Complaining" in the wilderness (Num 11:1) remains sinful and rouses divine anger, causing Moses to intercede for the people, ameliorating his wrath.[47] Reading Num 11:1 as a co-text with Lam 3:39 illumines the latter text. Lamentations 3:39 admonishes God's people to avoid complaining over anything other than one's sin! God's violent punishment is justified in the past, and God's people were judged for their complaint. God's punishment also is justified now, and the only petition that should arise should center on the sins of God's people: the heart of confessional prayer.

All told, Lam 3:25–39 offers powerful testimony to the retributive principle at work in the book and teaches confession. It affirms that God enacted justified violence against his people and that they should bear the punishment through penitential acts, silence, and patience. In this way, the violence is painful, but not necessarily morally evil. In light of the pain of divine violence, prayer is possible, but only a particular type: confession of sin. What hope can be found here arrives in the fact that God's judgment is neither capricious nor final. God may be trusted because he is good, because his covenant love (v. 32) enables him to afflict *and* pardon. God may be trusted as well because he is in control and does not punish without cause. For this reason, God's people should understand their predicament as an instance of divine punishment for sin. Penitence and confession, then, will bring relief (v. 32).

Complaint as Response

Despite its force, even in Lamentations, a retributive response to divine violence through confession does not completely compel. In fact, as will be shown below, complaint prayer most often provides direct engagement to the complexity of divine violence in the book. Consider the force of Lam

---

46. Lindström, *God and the Origin of Evil*, 223–24.

47. Contrast this with pre-Sinai wilderness wandering pericopes in Exodus 15–18. These texts present suffering as an opportunity to reveal the LORD's deliverance rather than his anger. Brevard Childs notes this in his *Exodus* (OTL; Philadelphia: Westminster, 1974) 258–74; and it is exploited systematically into a larger understanding of lament traditions in the Hebrew Scriptures by Samuel Balentine, *Prayer in the Hebrew Bible: The Drama of Human-Divine Dialogue* (OBT; Minneapolis: Fortress, 1993) 189–98.

3:42: "We have transgressed and rebelled, (but) you have not forgiven!" This text indicates a particular movement when retributive solutions to divine violence do not work. Note the placement of this verse, this prayer, which immediately follows the theodic affirmation from Lam 3:25–39. Lamentations 3:42 offers a different response to penitence and confession in the face of the retribution principle. The verse does not diminish or deny confession, because the first half of the verse confirms the act of confessional prayer ("We have transgressed and rebelled"). But the second half of the prayer goes further, because confession has not been effective in alleviating pain and persistent violence ("you have not forgiven"). Verse 42 reveals that the comfort and forgiveness anticipated in Lam 3:26 and 32 do not appear. It presents a different kind of prayer: complaint prayer that redresses divine violence.

Complaint prayers may seem illogical. After all, why pray to the one who has just caused pain, especially if the prayers do not confirm retribution or alleviate suffering? To raise one example, consider that one stream of Jewish tradition responds to the Holocaust (*Shoah*) by foreclosing not just on retributive prayer but on *any prayer*. In light of the divine violence perpetuated or allowed by God in the *Shoah*, this stream of Jewish tradition regards prayer itself as incomprehensible, impossible.[48] In contrast, complaint prayer persists throughout the corpus of Lamentations, where sufferers pray *to* God *against* God.

Lamentations 2:20–22, which is one of Lamentations' most strident prayers, illustrates the power of complaint prayer in the book. However, complaint prayer recurs in Lam 3:42–59; 5:1, 19–22. These texts protest a number of things that God has done (or not done), such as not forgiving his people in spite of their confession of sin (Lam 3:42), slaughtering his people without pity (Lam 3:43), ignoring prayer (Lam 3:44), standing aloof from the cries of his people (Lam 3:50, 56), avoiding action against wrong (Lam 3:59), and persisting in punishing (Lam 5:19–22). While none of these explicitly question the propriety of punishment, they all redress divine violence in a way that moves beyond the retributive responses of Lam 3:25–39. The poetry personifies the city of Zion as a forlorn mother in Lam 2:20–22. Personification gives suffering and devastation a human voice and human relationships. As a "mother," Zion is bereft of her "children," her inhabitants. God brings violence and causes this pain, and it is to him that she turns.

Zion cries out with anguished voice to God over his own actions against her, and in particular, her people. Her prayer identifies and then questions divine violence, particularly his abusive activity. The text of 2:20–22 reads:

---

48. Specifically, Elie Wiesel and Primo Levi move toward this approach as argued by John K. Roth, "Deliver Us from Evil? Kuhn's Prayer and the Masters of Death," in *Fire in the Ashes: God, Evil, and the Holocaust* (ed. D. Patterson and J. K. Roth; Seattle: University of Washington Press, 2005) 243–57.

> Look, O LORD, and consider to whom you have dealt with in this way!
> Should mothers eat their own fruit, little children raised to health?
> Should priest and prophet be slaughtered in the sanctuary of the Lord?
> Young and old lie down the ground of open places;
> Maidens and young men fell by the sword.
> You slaughtered in the day of your wrath, you butchered, you did not pity.
> You called as on a festal day terrors on every side.
> There was not—in the day of the wrath of the LORD—fugitive or survivor.
> Those whom I raised and reared, enemies finished them.

Iteration of "day of the LORD" language affirms that God's action is judgment: "in the day of his anger" (Lam 2:1c) // "in the day of your wrath" (Lam 2:21) // "in the day of the wrath of the LORD" (Lam 2:22). But this language refuses merely to confirm God's actions, because v. 20 opens an extended prayer about this judgment. Lamentations 2:20–22 comprises part of a larger, formulaic set of prayers in Lamentations, which are marked by the vocative form of the divine name + either the dual imperative "look and consider" or by √r'h combined with the vocative form of the divine name. Often the particle *kî* follows the address, marking the motivation for the petition. Lamentations 2:20 is part of this larger formulaic prayer group: Lam 1:9c, 11c, 20a; 2:20a; 3:59; 5:1b. These formulaic prayers are petitionary in nature, asking God to witness whatever pain that has been expressed in them, with the hope that he will either alter the situation or remove the pain.[49] But prayer in general extends beyond these formulaic exemplars in the book. This specific prayer, like other prayers in Lamentations, aims at gaining God's attention so that he sees the plight of the people and their unthinkable situation. In v. 20a, God's violence is in view: he must consider what he has done and change it!

And what has God done, according to her prayer? His actions emerge through a "horrific pun" that appears between √*ll*, "you dealt with," v. 20a, and √*ll*, "little children," v. 20c.[50] God's actions (√*ll*) create the situation where mothers eat their own "little children raised to health" (√*ll*). These suffering little children appeared in Lam 1:5c (√*ll*) and in Lam 2:11c (√*ll*). But in her prayer, the childrens' plight is more terrible, because mothers consume their "fruit," a food which the next line identifies as "little children (√*ll*)." How can this be? The opening line of the prayer names God as the violent source of this situation. Although he has brought judgment (this

---

49. For an exploration of formulaic prayer in Lamentations and its impact, see Heath A. Thomas, "The Liturgical Function of the Book of Lamentations," in *Thinking Towards New Horizons: Collected Communications to the XIXth Congress of the International Organization for the Study of the Old Testament, Ljubljana 2007* (ed. M. Augustin and H. M. Niemann; BEATAJ 55; Frankfurt am Main: Peter Lang, 2008) 137–47; idem, "Relating Prayer and Pain," 183–208.

50. F. W. Dobbs-Allsopp, *Lamentations* (IBC; Louisville, KY: Westminster John Knox, 2002) 99.

cannot be gainsaid in light of Lam 2:1–9), nonetheless, the prayer complains that his action brings inconceivable pain which cannot be right. Zion prays that God "look" and "consider" the injustice of divine violence in this situation. Retribution does not suffice, and confession does not fit for prayer.

She also prays that God would "look and consider" the death of his own representatives and Zion's future. Both priest and prophet are slaughtered in the sanctuary of the Lord (v. 20c). There is no doubt that priest and prophet clearly stand as guilty of sin in Lamentations (Lam 2:14; 4:13–14). But in Zion's prayer these mediaries are presented as victims of divine violence. Zion's prayer also affirms that his violence has brought human catastrophe. Zion's future is lost in v. 21, as evidenced in the death of the young men and elders coupled with the death of teenagers in the prime of life. The old cannot teach the young; they are gone. But there are no young either. There is only death at the hand of God, leaving Zion without a people, a future. Concluding with three verbs that designate God's action, Zion summarizes the problem: "you slaughtered," "you butchered," "you did not pity." When read with the force of the interrogative from v. 20a, these actions remain in question from the perspective of Zion. How can this be? The prayer, then, complicates flat retributive responses to divine violence. Zion's prayer effectively redresses the justice of divine violence against sinful prophets and a sinful people. She asks whether this action should occur!

Finally, she complains because God has enabled enemies to destroy her. The second-person verb "you summoned" in v. 22 continues the divine address begun in v. 20 that extends through v. 21. Thus, God has "summoned" what Zion calls "terrors on every side" for a festal celebration. But the centerpiece of the party is nothing other than the children that Zion has "raised and reared." Zion's children do not sing in the celebration, they perish. The final line of the prayer haunts the hearer: "Enemies finished them."

Zion's speech in these verses remains theologically provocative, indeed controversial. Adele Berlin suggests that one should not characterize these words as prayer, because Zion's words remain accusatory and protesting. They are filled with anger and disgust toward God and cannot be counted as viable prayer.[51] Her point, however, overstates the case. Although Zion's words do not turn to praise, it is unclear why they do not count as prayer. Westermann believes that the juxtaposition of divine violence and Zion's complaint in Lam 2 comprises a unique testimony in the Hebrew Scriptures, indeed, a contribution in the life of prayer. He identifies Lam 2:20–22 as a lament prayer whose aim is to draw the sufferer to "pour out" her heart to God.[52] In my estimation, Westermann's view is appropriate to the words of Lam 2:20–22. Although strident and confrontational, the words in vv. 20–22 remain prayer: they pour out the pain-filled heart to God. Still,

---

51. Berlin, *Lamentations*, 76.
52. Westermann, *Die Klagelieder*, 136.

the theological challenge of Zion's complaint cannot go unnoticed. God's violence appears in the poetry before these verses, but in Lam 2:20–22, complaint prayer gains its full voice.

Such vociferous and resistant prayer represents another response to divine violence other than confession. Although it is tempting to read complaint as resisting and overturning the retributive principle at work in Lamentations, it is perhaps better to say that it simply provides another response to negotiate divine violence other than retribution. Without attempting to reconstruct the growth or development of the text, in its final presentation, the prayers of Lamentations work corporately to provide different ways to negotiate divine violence.[53] At some points in the poetry, pentitential prayer seems to be a way to negotiate pain and divine violence. However, at other points, contentious complaint prayers rise to the fore, as in Lam 2:20–22. Complaint prayer enables the sufferer to redress God about divine violence and the experience of pain. It enables the sufferer to pray to God about God. Almost paradoxically, a view to God's sovereignty and power stands intact in this construal of complaint prayer. God is sovereign to hear and respond, and that is why the complaint is uttered *to God*. Simultatenously, God's actions are questioned in complaint prayer . . . but from the foundation of faith, that God will hear and respond to counter his own violence.

Conclusion

This essay demonstrated different responses to the pain created by divine violence in and through prayer. Divine violence has been identified in three ways here: through divine passivity, distance, and activity. These three facets serve to broaden the scope of what divine activity can be deemed as "violent" in light of the definition given in the introduction to this essay. Moreover, all three modes of divine action should be understood as bringing pain, and thereby be deemed as "violent." Finally, this study explored how Lamentations negotiates violence and pain primarily through prayer, especially confession and complaint.

What implications emerge from this study? At the outset, it is appropriate to suggest that the horrific challenge of divine violence in all of its complexity must be named. One cannot overlook or marginalize divine violence. It is not tangential to the life of faith, but it must be engaged head on.[54] When divine violence is engaged in Lamentations, the aggressive actions of Lam 2:1–9 count as divine violence, to be sure. But divine violence appears in a broader scope as well. Divine distance and passivity must also be counted as violence, as we discovered in Lam 1.

---

53. For different ways that the responses to divine action are understood in the growth of the book, see the discussion of Thomas, *Poetry and Theology*, 4–49.

54. Philip Jenkins agrees in his interesting work *Laying Down the Sword: Why We Can't Ignore the Bible's Violent Verses* (San Francisco: HarperOne, 2011).

Second, this essay suggests that one way to grapple with the experience of pain and divine violence is through prayer. There is nothing shy or evasive about prayer, either in confession or complaint. Rather, both prayers address the experiential problem of divine violence full in the face. Prayer remains a vital means to address God about negative experiences without resorting to objectifying God in a way that diminishes his relatedness with his people. Prayer enables questions and complaints to rise to God from the relational foundation that, while asymmetrical in terms of power, nonetheless remains fundamentally a communion between God and his people. One cannot overcome the asymmetrical power relationship while at the same time retaining the Creator-creature distinction. Of course, future study will want to explore the asymmetrical nature of the relationship that creates a system of violence, perhaps along the lines of Žižek's analysis of violence.[55] But that is beyond the scope offered here.

Because God's people may speak to their God in prayer, this prayer enables suffering to have its voice. We must fight the temptation to avoid addressing divine violence altogether. Articulating divine violence and pain through prayer has benefits. Prayer "prevents the pray-er from sublimating rage or from obsessing over it. It also releases anger and deters the pray-er from engaging in violent action" against others.[56] Complaint prayer especially sets a context for questioning God in a healthy way. Prayer provides a relational context for God's people to engage their God over the challenges of divine violence.

For example, let us return once again to Jesus' cry of dereliction from the cross. On the cross, Jesus did not stand outside of his experience to explain divine violence at the cross. Rather, he cried out to God in prayer to connect to the Father and to wrestle with his experience of divine violence. Although divine abandonment brings the atonement, it is still violent, and Jesus prayed to God over his experience of divine violence.

As an analogue, Lamentations knows and can articulate the nature and reasons for divine violence and pain that the petitioners experience. But cognition or explanation of these realities is not the primary point of the poetry. Lamentations, rather, establishes and displays the sense of communion and spirituality between the petitioners and God (as did Christ on the cross in his cry of dereliction). Ultimately, the Father *did* respond to the Son. And Lamentations' petitioners hope that God will provide response to their prayers as well (which, on the response from the larger Old Testament, God does).[57] Lamentations provides a context for a spirituality that takes divine violence back to God in prayer to await his response.

---

55. Žižek, *Violence*.
56. Thomas, "Relating Prayer and Pain," 202.
57. Isa 40–66; Zech 1–2, for example. See Norman K. Gottwald, *Studies in the Book of Lamentations* (SBT 14; London: SCM, 1962) 44–46; Christopher Seitz, *Word without End: The Old Testament as Abiding Theological Witness* (Grand Rapids: Eerdmans, 1998) 130–49.

Lamentations negotiates divine violence, then, in a multifaceted way in and through prayer: whether confession or complaint. In either case, what both prayers expect is divine response: either God's forgiveness or other divine responses that would give relief to Lam 1:10, 1:16, or 2:1–9.

Finally, a word needs to be said about the stance of prayers in Lamentations. Its prayers remain open to divine response, *whatever the response* may be. This openness can be identified as the difference between a request and a demand. A request (even if confrontational and contentious in complaint prayer) does not demand God to respond. Both confession and complaint prayer in Lamentations, I suggest, share a common theology rooted in the justice of God in communion with his people. One discovers this theology in the *rhetoric of prayer* itself. Prayer goes to the God of Israel, who, at least in the minds of the petitioners, believe God is good to act justly when hearing cries of confession, or complaint, even if the cries of distress arise from the violence of God himself. Prayers of confession and penitence are sensible, if the poet(s) believed that through them God would be moved to act out of his just power to forgive. Alternatively, the experience of divine violence can be described, affirmed, and resisted in complaint prayer. But complaint prayer only remains sensible, if the poet(s) believed that through the rhetoric of protest, God would be moved to act in his power and justice. The prayer works, if it affirms that God is powerful and just to act even against his own behavior. So for both confession and complaint, God's justice remains the theological foundation on which both prayers operate.

Because of this foundation, both confession and complaint prayers remain doggedly dependent on God. No attempt is made at independence from God so as to judge him objectively. Some think otherwise. Dobbs-Allsopp, for example, suggests that in rage and disgust (in Lam 2:20–22), Zion slowly walks away from God and avoids his face.[58] However, it does not appear that she wants to move away from God in any real sense. He is still the source of hope and the one who will adjudicate her experience and respond to her prayer justly. This hope reveals that, in both confession and complaint prayer, God and his justice are affirmed even as they are questioned. Because of this hope, God's people negotiate and renegotiate the pain of divine violence through the vehicle of prayer.

Admittedly, the approach to divine violence explored here does not (and cannot) explain divine violence comprehensively. But it remains difficult to state comprehensively how and why pain occurs, especially if it is from God. It is probably better, at least for the experiential problem of divine violence, that our response should be prayer, as the poets of Lamentations realized. The gift of the book of Lamentations teaches the value of prayer

---

58. Dobbs-Allsopp, *Lamentations*, 102. He does not deal well, however, with the second-person verbs that continue in v. 22. Although the vocative of the divine name is absent, this does not mean that Zion walks away from God.

in the face of divine violence. Both confession and complaint give suffering its voice in the face of violence and thereby advance a logic of hope. It is hope found not in a rational or systematic explanation or defense of God, but rather in God himself, "until he looks down and sees, the LORD from the heavens" (Lam 3:50).

Chapter 7

"I Will Send Fire":
Reflections on the Violence of God in Amos

M. Daniel Carroll R.

It has long been a staple in Old Testament ethics that the prophets were champions of the poor and courageous defenders of social and economic justice. In the 19th century, some scholars envisioned the 8th-century prophets as the pinnacle of Israelite religion, of a pure "ethical monotheism" unencumbered by a stifling ritual and establishment priesthood.[1] Since that time, the view that the prophets were ethical beacons has continued to the point that the term *prophetic* now refers to a strong moral stance. In common parlance, to be "prophetic" is understood to mean that an individual, organization, or movement is willing to stand up for the marginalized.

Latin American liberation theology turned to the prophetic literature as a pillar of their biblical case for social critique and transformation. Biblical scholars such as José Porfirio Miranda, Severino Croatto, and Jorge Pixley produced significant works on the prophets.[2] Theologians Gustavo Gutiérrez and Ignacio Ellacuría looked to those biblical books as models of voices that condemn injustice and offer a vision of a future world without injustice.[3] Others such as Carlos Mesters introduced their audiences to their

---

1. For a discussion of this view in relationship to Amos, see my *Amos: The Prophet and His Oracles: Research on the Book of Amos* (Louisville, KY: Westminster John Knox, 2002) 5–7.

2. José Porfirio Miranda, *Marx and the Bible: A Critique of the Philosophy of Oppression* (trans. J. Eagleson; Maryknoll, NY: Orbis, 1974); J. Severino Croatto, *Isaías: La palabra profética y su relectura hermenéutica*, vol. 1: *El profeta de la justicia y de la fidelidad (1–39)* (Buenos Aires: La Aurora, 1989); vol. 2: *La liberación es posible (40–55)* (Buenos Aires: Lumen, 1994); idem, *Imaginar el futuro: Estructura retórica y querigma del Tercer Isaías, Isaías (56–66)* (Buenos Aires: Lumen, 2001); Jorge Pixley, *Jeremiah* (St. Louis: Chalice, 2004); cf. my *Contexts for Amos: Prophetic Poetics in Latin American Perspective* (JSOTSup 132; Sheffield: Sheffield Academic Press, 1992) 109–20, 289–306, 312–19; idem, *Amos—The Prophet and His Oracles*, 53–72.

3. Gustavo Gutiérrez, *On Job: God-Talk and the Suffering of the Innocent* (trans. M. J. O'Connell; Maryknoll, NY: Orbis, 1987) 19–49; Ignacio Ellacuría, "Utopia and Prophecy

revolutionary message at a popular, or lay, level.⁴ In apartheid South Africa, the *Kairos Document* differentiated between "state" and "church" theologies, which refused to stand up for change, and a "prophetic" theology that recognized the centrality of the theme of oppression in the Bible and stood in solidarity with the efforts at social transformation.⁵

This positive appreciation of the prophetic message now is challenged in some circles. A few scholars say that the prophetic commitment to the poor is overstated, or that these texts may be suspect, as they reflect the ideological persuasion of elites who produced this literature.⁶ Another group, more strident and finding an echo in the broader culture wars against the Bible, disapprove of the violence of the prophetic words of judgment with their sweeping announcements of natural disasters and destructive invasions that would bring suffering on the guilty and innocent alike.⁷ I cite three examples of those who question the prophetic books as a whole, but one also can find critiques of individual books such as Isaiah and Amos.⁸

In *Hope amid the Ruins*, Carol Dempsey appreciates the prophetic demand for justice and the hopeful visions of renewal and restoration, but she assesses the punitive judgment passages to be historically conditioned and, consequently, troublesome for modern readers.⁹ The chastisement is too brutal and comprehensive, Dempsey claims, and the images of God as a

---

in Latin America," in *Mysterium liberationis: Fundamental Concepts of Liberation Theology* (ed. I. Ellacuría and J. Sobrino; trans. J. R. Brockman; Maryknoll, NY: Orbis, 1993) 289–328.

4. Carlos Mesters, *El profeta Jeremías: Boca de Dios, boca del pueblo* (trans. J. Gómez; Bogotá: San Pablo, 1994).

5. Kairos Theologians, *The Kairos Document: Challenge to the Church: A Theological Comment on the Political Crisis in South Africa* (2nd ed.; Grand Rapids: Eerdmans, 1986).

6. For the former, see Cyril S. Rodd, *Glimpses of a Strange Land: Studies in Old Testament Ethics* (OTS; Edinburgh: T. & T. Clark, 2001) 170–74, 296. For the latter, Walter J. Houston, *Contending for Justice: Ideologies and Theologies of Social Justice in the Old Testament* (rev. ed.; London: T. & T. Clark, 2008). Houston contends, however, that the postexilic educated patron class that he believes produced Amos maintained its social conscience and a sense of responsibility (58–61, 71–73, 93–98). See also the sources in n. 7.

7. Some feminists characterize the prophetic literature as sexist, even misogynist, presenting a generally violent attitude toward women. See J. Cheryl Exum, "The Ethics of Biblical Violence against Women," in *The Bible in Ethics: The Second Sheffield Colloquium* (ed. J. W. Rogerson, M. Davies, and M. D. Carroll R.; JSOTSup 207; Sheffield: Sheffield Academic Press, 1995) 248–71; Renita Weems, *Battered Love: Marriage, Sex, and Violence* (Minneapolis: Fortress, 1995).

8. E.g., Andrew Davies, *Double Standards in Isaiah: Re-evaluating Prophetic Ethics and Divine Justice* (BIS 46; Leiden: Brill, 2000); Mark Gray, *Rhetoric and Social Justice in Isaiah* (LHB/OTS 432; London: T. & T. Clark, 2006); David J. A. Clines, "Metacommentating Amos," in *Interested Parties: The Ideology of the Writers and Readers of the Hebrew Bible* (JSOTSup 205; Gender, Culture, Theory 1; Sheffield: Sheffield Academic Press, 1995) 76–93.

9. Carol J. Dempsey, *Hope amid the Ruins: The Ethics of Israel's Prophets* (St. Louis: Chalice, 2000).

cruel husband and divine warrior are unacceptable. Even so, the prophetic word has both positive and negative elements for ethical reflection today. That is, this literature

> is not without its shortcomings, flaws, imperfections, and unsettling images, all of which often betray certain cultural, historical, social, and religious influences that reflect the ancient world and the people's attempt to try to make sense of their lived experience in relationship to their experience of their God. Yet the prophets' focus on creation, covenant, Torah, and right relationship helps to make the texts' flaws palatable, which allows for the emergence of a timeless and prophetic ethical vision.[10]

The double entendre of the title of Julia O'Brien's *Challenging Prophetic Metaphor* conveys the thrust of her work: the portrayals of Yahweh challenge our contemporary ethical sensibilities, and so their underlying ideologies must be challenged.[11] To the unacceptable concepts of God as "abusing husband" and "angry warrior" she adds that of the "authoritarian father," who mistreats his "defenseless daughter" Jerusalem and Edom, unfairly depicted in the text as the "selfish brother." Her discussion of divine anger is more sophisticated than Dempsey's (she can value that response to injustice but not how God acts on his wrath), as is her hermeneutical conviction that ideological critique of the text combined with self-evaluation is the best way forward.

In two recent publications, Eric Seibert builds on the work of these and other scholars to question divine violence.[12] He surveys attempts to defend God's actions and to minimize the negative impact that these passages might have on readers. The problem, Seibert believes, is that these efforts and Christians generally take these texts at face value as correct views of Yahweh and human reality. Instead, he contends, they should be recognized for what they truly are: texts reflective of and limited by the worldviews of their contexts. He argues for a Christocentric hermeneutical grid that recognizes that the true God of Christian faith, represented in the person of Jesus, is nonviolent.[13] We should read the Bible with respect, Seibert says, but also with responsible discernment. Its value for us comes not in

---

10. Ibid., 127–28.
11. Julia M. O'Brien, *Challenging Prophetic Metaphor: Theology and Ideology in the Prophets* (Louisville, KY: Westminster John Knox, 2008).
12. Eric A. Seibert, *Disturbing Divine Behavior: Troubling Old Testament Images of God* (Minneapolis: Fortress, 2009); idem, *The Violence of Scripture: Overcoming the Old Testament's Troubling Legacy* (Minneapolis: Fortress, 2012).
13. Seibert stands within the Anabaptist tradition. For negative responses from that perspective, see W. Derek Suderman, "Wrestling with Violent Actions of God: A Response to Eric Seibert's *Disturbing Divine Behavior*"; Ken Esau, "Disturbing Scholarly Behavior: Seibert's Solution to the Problem of the Old Testament God"; Waldemar Janzen, "Teaching the Old Testament: The 'Problem' of the Old Testament Revisited," *Direction* 40 (2011) 151–62, 163–78, 179–97, respectively.

accepting all that it says but in dialoguing critically with it in order to sift out what can be embraced from what must be disallowed. It is important to acknowledge and transcend the moral and theological shortcomings of the Old Testament to be able to read the text nonviolently and not be swayed by its destructive ideologies. Toward that end, Seibert offers strategies that he believes can improve Christian engagement with the Old Testament.[14]

How does one respond to these negative evaluations of the prophetic literature? In what follows, I do not deal directly with the range of theological, hermeneutical, and ecclesiastical arguments made by these scholars. My goal is more focused. Fundamental to the debate over the violence of God is the question whether our theology will countenance a God who judges. Old Testament scholar Dale Patrick recently published *Redeeming Judgment*, which covers the entire canon in order to reclaim the centrality of divine judgment as a biblical theme that has become unfashionable.[15] Seibert, for example, argues that the God presented by and in Jesus does not judge in history by sovereignly causing catastrophes.[16] This essay, however, accepts that Yahweh does judge (e.g., Gen 18:25; Pss 50:6; 96:13)[17] and explores the nature and purpose of divine violence in his historical judgments to ascertain better what the biblical text affirms about his person and commitments.

What is lacking in these publications that decry God's violence, I feel, is a satisfying and realistic theology of divine judgment. It is not satisfying in that they can lack a close reading of the biblical text that is more attuned to literary-theological details and that coheres with what is communicated in the breadth of the canon. It is less than realistic in that it does not grapple better with the fact that humanity lives in a world of cruel tragedies largely of its own making and that this is the ugly and unfair world within which God acts.

The book of Amos[18] will be my source for this brief foray into the issue of divine violence. It is an appropriate text, because judgment is central

---

14. Seibert, *Disturbing Divine Behavior*, 223–40; idem, *The Violence of Scripture*, 95–146.

15. Dale Patrick, *Redeeming Judgment* (Eugene, OR: Pickwick, 2012). For Amos, see 195–207.

16. Seibert, *Disturbing Divine Behavior*, 200–2, 243–61. He also argues that passages that suggest that Jesus believed in divine judgment could very well not be original.

17. For a helpful survey of the Old Testament material on justice, see Richard Schultz, "Justice," *NIDOTTE* 4:837–46. For the vocabulary of and metaphors in the Old Testament for anger, both human and divine, see Matthew R. Schlimm, *From Fratricide to Forgiveness: The Language and Ethics of Anger in Genesis* (Siphrut 7; Winona Lake, IN: Eisenbrauns, 2011) 48–88, 185–201; for the prophetic literature in particular, see David T. Lamb, "Wrath," *DOTPr*, 878–83.

18. I use the canonical form of the book, which I believe is the most appropriate text for Christian theological ethics. See my "Ethics and Old Testament Interpretation," in *Hearing the Old Testament: Listening for God's Address* (ed. C. G. Bartholomew and D. J. H. Beldman; Grand Rapids: Eerdmans, 2012) 204–27; cf. R. W. L. Moberly, *Old Testament Theology: Reading the Hebrew Bible as Christian Scripture* (Grand Rapids: Baker Academic, 2013) 282–88.

to its message. Judgment also is a key theme in the Book of the Twelve, and ideally a study of this theme in Amos would be located within its treatment in that broader corpus.[19] This essay, however, is limited to that one prophetic text, which has its own distinctive contribution to make to this debate.

Amos and the Violence of God

Detailing the Divine Violence in Amos

Eryl Davies articulates the theological challenge of prophetic judgments in his book *The Immoral Bible*:

> The punishment which God inflicts upon his own people sometimes appears to be intolerably cruel, and in some prophetic passages the punitive intent of the divine will seems difficult to justify, for God's anger does not appear to be a just and proportional response to human sin ... when God's fury is unleashed upon his people, he shows little self-restraint, and consequently the innocent are made to suffer as much as the guilty.... At times, the punishment inflicted by God appears to be unreasonable and even irrational.[20]

The book of Amos opens with a statement relating the ministry of the prophet to an earthquake ("two years before the earthquake"; 1:1). Other verses in the book might refer to this natural disaster, too, and they declare in various degrees of directness that this destruction comes by Yahweh's hand (2:13; 3:14–15; 4:11, 13; 6:9–11; 8:8; 9:1, 5, 9).[21] Earthquakes can be devastating, and the loss of life and livelihood is indiscriminate. This must have been a uniquely powerful earthquake, because Zechariah mentions it more than two centuries later (14:5). In the recent past, Israel also had suffered hunger, drought, and crop failures (4:6–9).

To these devastations can be added passages that announce war, the conquering of cities, and exile for Israel and other peoples.[22] These communal

---

19. For brief discussions of the theology of the Twelve, see Stephen G. Dempster, *Dominion and Dynasty: A Theology of the Hebrew Bible* (NSBT 15; Downers Grove, IL: InterVarsity, 2003) 182–88; Heath Thomas, "Hearing the Minor Prophets: The Book of the Twelve and God's Address," in *Hearing the Old Testament: Listening for God's Address* (ed. C. G. Bartholomew and D. J. H. Beldman; Grand Rapids: Eerdmans, 2012) 356–79.

20. Eryl W. Davies, *The Immoral Bible: Approaches to Biblical Ethics* (London: T. & T. Clark, 2010) 7–8.

21. D. K. Ogden, "The Earthquake Motif in the Book of Amos," in *Goldene Äpfel in silbernen Schalen: Collected Communications to the XIIIth Congress of the International Organization for the Study of the Old Testament, Leuven 1989* (ed. K.-D. Schunk and M. Augustin; BEATAJ 20; Frankfurt am Main: Peter Lang, 1992) 69–80; K. J. Dell, "Amos and the Earthquake: Judgment as Natural Disaster," in *Aspects of Amos: Exegesis and Interpretation* (ed. A. C. Hagedorn and A. Mein; LHB/OTS 536; London: T. & T. Clark, 2011) 15–40.

22. For the terrible realities of ancient warfare, see Michael G. Hasel, *Military Practice and Polemic: Israel's Laws of Warfare in Near Eastern Perspective* (Berrien Springs: Andrews University Press, 2005) 51–123; Israel Ephʿal, *The City Besieged* (CHANE 36; Leiden: Brill, 2009); the "Tactics" sections in Boyd Seevers, *Warfare in the Old Testament: The*

traumas also are connected to God. Divine agency is underscored by the first-person verbs in the Oracles against the Nations (1:3–2:16): "I will send fire" (1:4, 7, 10, 12, 14; 2:2, 5),[23] "I will break" (1:5), "I will cut down" (1:5, 8; 2:3), "I will turn my hand" (1:8), and "I will kill" (2:3). These actions are connected to warfare. The descriptions of the consequences of God's actions are dire. The text speaks of the loud sounds of combat (1:14; 2:2), the destruction of fortresses (1:4, 7, 10, 12, 14; 2:2, 5), the death of leaders (1:5, 8; 2:3) and entire populations (1:8; 2:3), and of the deportation of the defeated (1:5, 15).

The involvement of Yahweh in the imminent military defeat of Israel is clear in oracles directed at the Northern Kingdom throughout the book. The decision to weigh down the cart that is Israel leads all kinds of troops to flee at the end of chap. 2 (2:13–16). In chap. 3, the calamity caused by Yahweh and announced by a trumpet blast (3:6) involves an unnamed foe tearing down and plundering Samaria's fortresses, the sanctuary of Bethel, and the elite's mansions (3:11, 13–15). Yahweh is a roaring lion that leaves only bits and pieces of his people (3:12; cf. 1:2; 3:4, 8). In chap. 4, women of means are led away through breaches in the fortress walls (4:3; cf. 6:7), and the reader is told that in the past Yahweh had tried to use death in battle to bring the nation to repentance (4:10). In chap. 5, Israel's armies and militias are decimated, akin to an abused virgin left to die in the field (5:2), and the wailing of mourners resounds through the streets of all its towns (5:16–17). The "day of Yahweh" will bring not victory, as many expected, but rather terrible darkness and deportation to a land beyond Damascus (5:18–20, 26–27); there is only a faint hope that "perhaps" a remnant might be spared (5:15). Chapter 6 says that Yahweh hates Israel's fortresses (6:8), and his judgment will leave only rubble. The reader witnesses a scene of family members looking for those buried under collapsed buildings (6:9–11). The chapter closes with the declaration that God is sending an enemy army that will oppress the nation from border to border (6:14). In chap. 7, after the prophet's intercession spares Israel the devastation pictured in the first two visions in the chapter, the third represents metaphorically the flimsiness of the fortresses of Israel as made of walls of tin[24] that Yahweh will pull down (7:7–8), and through the prophet God decrees the exile and humiliation of the chief priest of Bethel and his family (7:17). Chapter 8 describes the bodies of the dead scattered on the temple floor and the weeping of the singers (8:3). The people mourn, and Yahweh leaves them a dearth of food and drink (8:10–14). In the final chapter, Yahweh brings the temple down on the heads of the worshipers (9:1) and will hunt down those who try to flee. None will escape the judg-

---

Organization, Weapons, and Tactics of Ancient Near Eastern Armies (Grand Rapids: Kregel, 2013) 66–76, 132–40, 172–76, 234–46, 266–69, 290–95.

23. The threat of fire reappears later in the book (5:6; 7:4).

24. Translating the term *'anak* as "tin," not "plumbline." See Shalom M. Paul, *Amos* (Hermeneia; Minneapolis: Fortress, 1991) 233–35. For a recent survey of views, see R. Reed Lessing, *Amos* (CC; St. Louis: Concordia, 2009) 459–62, although he does not opt for this interpretation.

ment (9:2–4) of Yahweh, the all-powerful Creator (9:5–6), who will destroy the nation and scatter its people (9:8–10).

These frightful experiences of a terrible natural disaster and the horrors of war are exacerbated by the fact that the book of Amos notably emphasizes a potentially problematic name of God: *Yahweh 'ĕlōhê ṣĕbā'ôt* (NIV: the LORD God Almighty; NRSV: the LORD, the God of hosts; CEB: the LORD, the God of heavenly forces), an epithet with military connotations of Yahweh as divine warrior.[25] This name and title combination and other configurations with slight modifications appear nine times in judgment oracles and hymnic passages (3:13; 4:13; 5:14–16, 27; 6:8, 14; 9:5).[26] Scholars debate whether *ṣĕbā'ôt* ("hosts") refers to the nation's armies, celestial hosts, or the heavenly divine council, or whether it is an abstract plural signifying power (hence, the translation "Almighty"). In the broader context of the book of Amos, one or more of these is a viable option. The mention of the stars and creation in two hymnic passages could point to the celestial realm (5:8; 9:6), even as 3:7 apparently alludes to the heavenly council. The bringing of attacking armies against other nations and Israel could point to human referents, and the incomparable might of Yahweh is indisputable in the book. In any case, this title of Yahweh is linked straightforwardly with armed conflict.

Reflections on Divine Violence in Amos

Undoubtedly, the book of Amos would have much to answer for in today's theological climate. The violence of Yahweh is ubiquitous in its pages and seemingly woven into his very person. Does that surface impression do justice to the full characterization of God in this prophetic text? I respond to this query in four parts.

The Importance of Background Studies

Interaction with this material in Amos should begin by locating its vocabulary within its *cultural context*. This is a claim also made by critics of the Old Testament God, but, whereas they point to this as a reason to distrust what it says about Yahweh because of outdated modes of reflecting on God, I move in a different direction.

This initial step recognizes that many descriptions of judgment are stereotypical, employing vocabulary that is found throughout the ancient

---

25. Sa-Moon Kang, *Divine War in the Old Testament and in the Ancient Near East* (BZAW 177; Berlin: de Gruyter, 1989); Horst Dietrich Preuss, *Old Testament Theology* (trans. L. G. Perdue; Louisville, KY: Westminster John Knox, 1995) 1:128–38; Stefan Paas, *Creation and Judgment: Creation Texts in Some Eighth Century Prophets* (OTS 47; Leiden: Brill, 2003) 231–44; cf. Tremper Longman III and Daniel G. Reid, *God Is a Warrior* (SOTBT; Grand Rapids: Zondervan, 1995).

26. Stephen Dempster argues that the placement of God's names has structural implications for the book in "'The LORD Is His Name': A Study of the Distribution of the Names and Titles of God in the Book of Amos," *RB* 98 (1991) 170–89.

Near East.²⁷ The wording of passages such as these often is formulaic, as well as hyperbolic and highly emotive. On the one hand, these lines confirm the defeat of the enemy in accepted nationalistic and religious language, whether in anticipation of victory or in retrospect to glorify the protagonist's deity and army. At the same time, the vocabulary of these messages was to generate fear and obedience in a vassal people toward their sovereign king and his god.

That the judgments in the Oracles against the Nations are so repetitive in their vocabulary, the instrument of judgment unspecified, and the time of punishment indeterminate, suggests that these words in Amos 1–2 are stereotypical. These oracles voice in contextual jargon that Yahweh would one day punish these nations. Because they are such broad depictions of invasion and siege, to what degree then do these totalizing descriptions of Amos reflect actual historical events? They could very well be representative of the rhetoric of that day, with its attending ideological and theological purposes, not precise snapshots of what Yahweh had decreed. Historically, we know that Assyria fulfilled these general oracles, but as originally given they could very well be formulaic pronouncements of future judgment for wrongdoing, not precise predictions of what was going to happen decades later.

This background orientation can explain the significance of the vocabulary. It places the issue of divine violence and these depictions of war into their proper cultural perspective. It also should serve to caution the interpreter against imposing a 21st-century reading on these texts, one that is overly literal and determined by what that same lexicon might mean today. Nevertheless, while this more appropriate historical standpoint does help interpret the language better and avoid sweeping pronouncements about Yahweh, we must acknowledge that it does not solve the moral dilemma. This brings me to my second point.

The Nature of Judgment

In addition to the need to place greater attention to the ancient setting, the interpreter also should observe that the prophetic books give explicit reasons for God's judgments.²⁸ The book of Amos teaches that *divine*

---

27. K. Lawson Younger Jr., *Ancient Conquest Accounts: A Study in Ancient Near Eastern and Biblical History Writing* (JSOTSup 98; Sheffield: Sheffield Academic Press, 1990); Aaroud van der Deijl, *Protest or Propaganda: War in the Old Testament Book of Kings and in Contemporaneous Ancient Near Eastern Texts* (SSN 51; Leiden: Brill, 2008); C. L. Crouch, *War and Ethics in the Ancient Near East: Military Violence in Light of Cosmology and History* (BZAW 407; Berlin: de Gruyter, 2009); for Amos, see pp. 97–116; cf. D. Brent Sandy, *Plowshares and Pruning Hooks: Rethinking the Language of Biblical Prophecy and Apocalyptic* (Downers Grove, IL: InterVarsity, 2002) 75–102. At the same time, these lexical and theological/ideological commonalities do not negate the unique elements of what is found in the Old Testament.

28. Form critics have long recognized the structural patterns of judgment oracles, which demonstrate the connection between indictment and punishment. A classic study

violence is as a response to human violence. In other words, human violence is judged with violence. The prophet condemns the peoples in the Oracles against the Nations for their cruelty in war: for threshing Gilead (whether metaphorically or as actually torturing victims, 1:3), for the taking and selling of war captives (1:6, 9), for blood lust in battle (1:11), for the gruesome abuse of women (1:13), and for dishonoring the dead of the defeated (2:1). God's punishment is that those who employ military might for territorial or economic gain will themselves suffer defeat by a more potent foe. The judgment mirrors the crime, and at the same time is designed to stop it. Divinely sanctioned violence is not random; it is designed to punish the perpetrators of human violence.[29] God uses the violence endemic to humankind (cf. Gen 6:11) and turns these nations over to the fruit of their pitiless aspirations and commitments. The opening formula of each oracle (literally, "I will not cause *it* to return"; 1:3, 6, 9, 11, 13; 2:1) could refer to the announcement of punishment (Num 23:20; Isa 45:23; 55:11) or to the judgment itself, which has already gone out and will not be turned back.[30] Importantly, in these oracles God is concerned for and acts on behalf of those who are *not* the people of God. All of humanity is in his purview, when it comes to the violation of justice and its victims.[31]

What, though, of the violent invasion that Israel will suffer as its punishment?[32] Unlike the judgment on the other nations, the text does not denounce Israel for attacking its neighbors. The book does mock the self-deceiving celebration of military victory in 6:13 and depicts Israel as small and weak (7:2, 5). Some of the Oracles against the Nations could refer to Israel's defeats (e.g., 1:3, 9, 11), and 4:10 mentions loss in battle. Instead of military campaigns, however, the book concentrates instead on Israel's internal transgressions, its oppression of the poor.[33] Tamez, Hanks, and others

---

is Claus Westermann, *Basic Forms of Prophetic Speech* (trans. H. C. White; Louisville, KY: Westminster John Knox, 1991).

29. See, e.g., Jerome F. D. Creach, *Violence in Scripture* (Interp; Louisville, KY: Westminster John Knox, 2013) 163–75.

30. The vague pronominal suffix "it" is taken by most English versions to refer to God's wrath (NASB, NRSV, ESV, CEB). The NIV 2011 leaves the translation imprecise. For a survey of options, see Paul, *Amos*, 46–47.

31. John Barton has argued the prophet and Yahweh presuppose ancient universal norms for conduct in war, general moral limits in combat which all could accept. See his *Amos's Oracles against the Nations* (SOTSMS 6; Cambridge: Cambridge University Press, 1980); idem, *The Theology of the Book of Amos* (OTT; Cambridge: Cambridge University Press, 2012) 57–61.

32. Almost two-thirds of references to God's wrath in the prophetic literature are directed at Israel and Judah (Lamb, "Wrath," 880–81). That it concerns primarily God's people demonstrates that it is not a nationalistic reflex, even as this fact raises its problematic nature for the believing community.

33. The Israel oracle (2:6–16) has the same introductory formula as those against the nations, stylistically (and theologically) connecting socioeconomic abuse with the war crimes of 1:3–2:3. Scholars disagree about the significance of the covenant in the message

have demonstrated that the vocabulary of injustice in the Old Testament is connected to the violence manifest in the structural mistreatment of the vulnerable.[34] The book of Amos is no exception in exposing and condemning "this plague of predatory violence."[35] In 2:7, 5:11, and 8:4 the poor are "trampled"; in 4:1 they are "crushed"; and 3:10 cites the hoarding of violence and destruction in Samaria's fortresses. The vulnerable are bought and sold (2:6; 8:6), unfairly taxed (2:8; 5:11), and denied justice in the courts (2:7a; 5:12). These are the actions of a set of elites (merchants, political leaders and officials), who use their power to exploit others in order to enjoy a life of ease and plenty (4:1; 5:11; 6:3–6; 8:5). Although the text does not explain the mechanisms of injustice,[36] the moral outrage is clear. Once again, human violence triggers a judgment of violence, an invasion (and the earthquake). Throughout the Old Testament, Yahweh responds to the cry of the oppressed by punishing those who practice injustice. Both in regards to international and national transgressions, the book of Amos explains why judgment is coming; it is not the product of divine whim. God had been involved in the past history of Israel and the nations (e.g., 2:9–10; 3:1; 4:6–11; 9:7); his participation would continue through judgment and beyond.

The book of Amos, along with the prophetic literature generally, also teaches that divine punishment is vitally connected and corresponds to the transgression. One scholar who has developed extensively this idea of *lex talionis*, or poetic justice, in relation to God's judgments is Terence Fretheim.[37] Although I am not entirely comfortable with all of his formulation,[38] I be-

---

of Amos. For surveys of views, see my *Amos: The Prophet and His Oracles*, 16–18; John Barton, *The Theology of the Book of Amos*, 107–12.

34. Elsa Tamez, *Bible of the Oppressed* (Maryknoll, NY: Orbis, 1982); Thomas D. Hanks, *God So Loved the Third World: The Biblical Vocabulary of Oppression* (trans. J. Dekker; Maryknoll, NY: Orbis, 1983); cf. Pedro Jaramillo Rivas, *La injusticia y la opresión en el lenguaje figurativo de los profetas* (Institución San Jerónimo 26; Navarra: Verbo Divino, 1992). For current systemic and criminal violence against the poor, see Gary A. Hogan and Victor Boutros, *The Locust Effect: Why the End of Poverty Requires the End of Violence* (New York: Oxford University Press, 2014).

35. This phrase is taken from Hogan and Boutros, *The Locust Effect*, xi.

36. For a survey of hypotheses, see my "Social Science Approaches," in *DOTPr* 734–47.

37. Terence E. Fretheim, "Divine Judgment and the Warming of the World: An Old Testament Perspective," in *God, Evil, and Suffering: Essays in Honor of Paul R. Sponheim* (ed. T. E. Fretheim and C. L. Thompson; WWSup 4; St. Louis: Luther Seminary, 2000) 27–29; idem, "Theological Reflections on the Wrath of God in the Old Testament," *HBT* 24 (2002) 19–24; idem, "God and Violence in the Old Testament," *WW* 24 (2004) 18–28; idem, *God and World in the Old Testament: A Relational Theology of Creation* (Nashville: Abingdon, 2005) 158–65. Cf. Dale Patrick, *Sin and Judgment in the Prophets: A Stylistic and Theological Analysis* (SBLMS 27; Chico, CA: Scholars Press, 1982), for Amos, 21–25; idem, *Redeeming Judgment*, 199–201; John Goldingay, *Old Testament Theology*, vol. 2: *Israel's Faith* (Downers Grove, IL: InterVarsity, 2006) 596–615.

38. Fretheim limits the foreknowledge and power of Yahweh more than I do. In his view, God is constrained by creation and its moral order. I also would not marginalize

lieve that he correctly observes that Yahweh works through a moral order grounded in creation and the very nature of things, where consequences fit the transgression and often are generated by it. This truth lays much of the violence that humanity suffers at the feet of other humans. God can no longer be blamed so easily for why or how he judges, for judgment is the just desserts of that to which humans have dedicated their lives, efforts, resources, and intelligence: the weaponry, the art of warfare, and the mechanisms of exploitation. Judgment, in other words, is a harrowing window into the darkness of the human soul, even as it is a necessary component of a complex theodicy that requires that human evil be punished.[39]

Fretheim also recognizes that the divine choice (and risk) to judge *in history* and *through human agents* is a messy business. These divine agents—in the prophetic books often the armies of empires—vent their fury and ambitions in attacking communities and overstep the bounds of decency. As a consequence, in the inescapable interconnectedness of human existence, all suffer in the violence brought on by sin, irrespective of the degree of involvement in the transgressions condemned by the prophet.[40] This biblical fact has been taken as evidence that God's wrath is irrational and uncontrolled, but actually the breadth of suffering is wrought by unrestrained human violence.

In Amos research there have been several attempts to get around God's decision to mobilize these instruments of judgment and their extensive impact. Some interpret the totalizing passages of national disaster in light of others that make distinctions within the people (7:9; 9:8–10). They argue that the only targets of God's judgment will be members of the government, unethical merchants, and other oppressors.[41] While it is true that

---

the juridical dimension of God's judgment in favor of a fundamentally act-consequence model, where God "mediates the consequences that are intrinsic to the wickedness itself" instead of making forensic judgments (*God and World in the Old Testament*, 165; cf. *Creation Untamed: The Bible, God, and Natural Disasters* [TECC; Grand Rapids: Baker Academic, 2010] 48–55, 112–14). Both aspects, I believe, are evident in the prophetic literature (cf. Robert B. Chisholm Jr., "Retribution," *DOTPr* 671–76). In his discussion of *lex talionis*, Crouch states that the fact that in his judgments Yahweh does what he condemns suggests that Yahweh does not find war "fundamentally objectionable," a conclusion that I believe misses the point of the text.

39. See the thoughtful work by Peter Admirand, *Amidst Mass Atrocity and The Rubble of Theology: Searching for a Viable Theodicy* (Eugene, OR: Cascade, 2012).

40. Fretheim, "Theological Reflections on the Wrath of God," 24–25; "The Character of God in Jeremiah," in *Character and Scripture: Moral Formation, Community, and Biblical Interpretation* (ed. W. P. Brown; Grand Rapids: Eerdmans, 2002) 219–23 (pp. 211–30); "'I was only a little angry': Divine Violence in the Prophets," *Interp* 58 (2004) 368–73 (pp. 365–75); *God and World in the Old Testament*, 161–63.

41. Harold Reimer, *Richtet auf des Recht! Studien zur Botschaft des Amos* (SBS 149; Stuttgart: Katholisches Bibelwerk, 1992) 16–17, 22–27, passim; Karl A. Möller, *A Prophet in Debate: The Rhetoric of Persuasion in the Book of Amos* (JSOTSup 372; Sheffield: Sheffield Academic Press, 2003) 139–41.

there are degrees of guilt, war and earthquakes are never so discriminating. For others, the answer to the dilemma of reconciling the descriptions of sweeping destruction with these other statements in the book lies in sorting out the possible redaction history of the production of the book. Robert Coote, for example, argues that the original version of the prophet's message restricted punishment to those who had committed sociopolitical and economic crimes. According to his reconstruction, later additions to the text extended the punishable sins to the religious sphere, with the result that the entire nation was made out to be guilty.[42] A recent attempt along redactional lines is found in the work of Graham Hamborg. He identifies the abuse, the violators, and the victims of each in what he believes are the four layers of the book's creation (he focuses specifically on 2:5–16).[43] Of course, compositional hypotheses of this sort cannot be proven. In any case, these studies are not helpful for the task at hand. They do not get at the ethical challenge of the canonical text, which is the target of today's debates.

Can we entertain the possibility that all Israel at some level is sinful, even as its leaders commit transgressions that the prophets explicitly denounce? Sin (whether religious, ideological, racial or ethnic, socioeconomic, and political) is more complex than scholars realize. There can be multiple kinds of participation by the wider population. I mention three examples, out of many that could be cited: the support of Nazi ideology given by the German people (including institutions one would think would have stood as bulwarks against such atrocities: Protestant denominations, the Catholic Church, and the universities) and the broad involvement in the marginalization of the Jews; the racist attitudes against blacks and the multiple social and legal mechanisms of exclusion in the United States and the Republic of South Africa; and the hateful, vengeful acts of state terrorism and the tribal and Islamic sect loyalties in several countries (and across borders) in the Middle East today. In each case, confirmation of hateful exclusion has been sought in religious convictions, and most everyone is complicit in some form or fashion in these sociocultural transgressions, whether officially, personally, actively, or passively. It is possible to stage the Nuremburg trials, set up truth commissions, change zoning and voting laws, and remove dictators, but the deeply rooted problems of the marginalization and elimination of the "other" persist across demographic and social divides. These dispositions are embedded in the ethos, mores, and laws of society and are endorsed by religion.[44] They cannot be circumscribed to the leadership,

---

42. Robert B. Coote, *Amos among the Prophets: Composition and Theology* (Philadelphia: Fortress, 1981) 16–19, 22–24, 46–53, 62–65.

43. Graham R. Hamborg, *Still Selling the Righteous: A Redaction-Critical Investigation of Reasons for Judgment in Amos 2:5–16* (LHB/OTS 555; London: T. & T. Clark, 2012).

44. Note the insightful reflections of Miroslov Volf on the exclusion of the "other" in *Exclusion and Embrace: A Theological Exploration of Identity, Otherness, and Reconciliation* (Nashville: Abingdon, 1996).

even though those persons deserve the greatest condemnation. Few are truly innocent, but clearly there are those who are most responsible for these sinful states of affairs and for the suffering that their decisions and actions precipitate.

These dense cultural, ethnic, sociopolitical, legal, economic, and religious realities, I believe, can help explain to a degree why in the Old Testament entire nations are judged, even as specific persons and groups are censured for their greater blame. In the prophetic books, these guilty individuals are the subjects of woe passages ("woe to those who") and usually are found among the elites; occasionally, they are singled out by name. What is more, the judgments that the prophets announce, whether these come in the form of armed conflict or natural disasters, cannot be tidy. Entire nations are doomed, but especially their leadership. Unfortunately, these disasters affect those who are not worthy of the punishment for these particular transgressions. They are the victims of the societies' sin, and now will suffer as well in the judgment.

These various knotty elements of divine judgment are found in the book of Amos. Members of the groups in control, the chief sinners of the Northern Kingdom, are described in terms of their evil character traits and actions (e.g., 2:6-8; 3:10; 4:1; 5:11-13; 6:3-7; 8:4-6); the only two that are identified are the king (Jeroboam in 1:1; 7:9-10) and the high priest of Bethel (Amaziah in 7:10-14).[45] At the same time, apparently all (irrespective of social strata) celebrate the distorted ideology of national might and victory (4:4-13; 5:4-6, 18-20; 6:13). Of course, this theology also legitimated the lifestyle of the powerful (2:8; 3:15; 6:3-7; 7:10, 13; 8:4-6).[46] The whole nation would pass through the comprehensive judgment described earlier in this essay (e.g., 3:1-2; 6:14), even as the prophet defended the vulnerable and singled out a few for special censure.

The misery triggered by human sin is hard to bear. This complicated, but realistic, perspective on how judgment in history happens brings me to my third point.

The Pathos of God

It is clear in the Old Testament that Yahweh does not take joy in judgment. What to do with this biblical conviction vis-à-vis the images of the divine judge? It is important to appreciate that Yahweh's mercy and wrath are joined together in the Old Testament prophets. Both are foundational to his person (e.g., Jer 18:1-10; Joel 2:12-14; Jonah 4:2; Nah 1:2-8; cf. Exod 34:6-7). It will not do, then, to bifurcate these two dimensions, as many critics of the God of the Old Testament do. Instead of holding both together, they view them as competing, independent reflections on God.

---

45. The interplay between national judgments and the singling out of kings also is found in the oracles against other peoples in the Oracles against the Nations (1:5, 8, 15; 2:3).

46. We will return below to the matter of religion and ideology.

Walter Brueggemann, for instance, whose many insights into the creative power of prophetic language to affect the religious and sociopolitical imagination I very much applaud,[47] has categorized judgment texts as part of Israel's "counter-testimony"—that is, disturbing portrayals of God, which he juxtaposes with little commingling to the "core testimony" of Israel. This "core testimony" is the "characteristic" way of talking about the biblical God, who is faithful and gracious to his people. He claims that these two discreet tracks are different sides of Israel's experience with God and ultimately point to an "unresolved ambiguity" and "profound disjunction" in God's own interior being. To mix them would undermine the theological tension that is fundamental to the faith of the Old Testament.[48]

Brueggemann is at his best when exploring how the rhetorical force of the prophetic announcements of loss unmasks the pretentious and damaging lies of the dominant worldview and offers alternative possibilities for the future; he also appreciates the connection between sin and the moral fabric of the world. But Brueggemann struggles with clearly articulating (even though his prose is impressive and a delight to read) the association of words of judgment with God's direct intervention in history—that is, with making a strong correlation between the rhetoric and its theological insights of the text and the actual world within which God's people and the nations move and live.

In several studies on Jeremiah, Kathleen O'Connor appeals to Trauma and Disaster studies to suggest that what we read in that book is a survival strategy of a defeated people trying to make theological sense of a world destroyed.[49] By declaring that the Babylonian invasion was God's response to their sins, the people are able to verbalize their suffering and begin to take responsibility for the fall of Jerusalem and its rebuilding. The book's troublesome oracles, in other words, are anguished reflections of a hurting people and may not reveal what Yahweh is truly like. O'Connor does well to appeal to research that can unpack the language of the prophets in ways that those of us who live in peace cannot grasp easily. Her work underscores the startling realism of the text, but, again, must we redefine God so that he

---

47. Note his classic study, *The Prophetic Imagination* (2nd ed.; Minneapolis: Fortress, 2001). This notion of the prophetic imagination has been central to his publications for decades.

48. Idem, *Theology of the Old Testament: Testimony, Dispute, Advocacy* (Minneapolis: Fortress, 1997) 227–28, 267–313, 373–403, 502–27; more recently, *The Practice of Prophetic Imagination: Preaching an Emancipating Word* (Minneapolis: Fortress, 2012) 45–70.

49. K. M. O'Connor, "The Book of Jeremiah: Reconstructing Community after Disaster," in *Character Ethics and the Old Testament: Moral Dimensions of Scripture* (ed. M. D. Carroll R. and J. E. Lapsley; Louisville, KY: Westminster John Knox, 2007) 81–92; idem, "Reclaiming Jeremiah's Violence," in *The Aesthetics of Violence in the Prophets* (ed. J. M. O'Brien and C. Franke; LHB/OTS 517; New York: T. & T. Clark, 2010) 37–49; idem, *Jeremiah: Pain and Promise* (Minneapolis: Fortress, 2012); cf. L. Stulman and Hyun Chul Paul Kim, *You Are My People: An Introduction to Prophetic Literature* (Nashville: Abingdon, 2010).

is not connected to judgment, in whole or in part? Where do we draw the line between human theologizing and genuine revelation into the person of God? In another publication, she posits that the tears of God for the suffering of Judah contradict his character as judge.[50]

I would suggest that the paradoxes within the person of God in the prophets are better understood not by pitting his mercy so starkly against his wrath,[51] but by locating the mystery of the conjunction of Yahweh's compassion and anger of Yahweh in his *pathos*. Abraham Heschel has explicated the topic of God's pathos in exemplary fashion.[52] He says: "It is because God is the source of justice that His pathos is ethical; and it is because God is absolutely personal ... that this ethos is full of pathos."[53] Yahweh is invested in justice (in the actions and attitudes of individuals and nations) and deeply cares both for the victims of injustice and for the people who languish under judgment. Although God does chastise, he does so with deep sorrow. Blatant disregard for human life and oppression do provoke God's anger, but the cost of righteous punishment also deeply pains him (e.g., Isa 16:9–11; Jer 9:1, 10, 17–24; 48:29–33).[54] Punishment pains God, because of his personal relationships with his people, humanity, and creation.

This perspective finds an echo in the book of Amos. I claim that Yahweh does not delight in hearing the screams in battle (1:14), the weeping of mourners (5:16–17; 8:10; cf. 1:2; 6:9–10), and the groans of the poor.[55] In 5:1–3, Yahweh lifts up a lament (*qînâ*) for Israel through his prophet because

---

50. Idem, "The Tears of God and Divine Character in Jeremiah 2–9," in *God in the Fray: A Tribute to Walter Brueggemann* (ed. T. Linafelt and T. K. Beal; Minneapolis: Fortress, 1998) 172–85.

51. This is one of Fretheim's critiques of Brueggemann and O'Connor. See his "Some Reflections on Brueggemann's God," in *God in the Fray: A Tribute to Walter Brueggemann* (ed. T. Linafelt and T. K. Beal; Minneapolis: Fortress, 1998) 24–37; idem, "The Character of God in Jeremiah," 214–17. L. Juliana M. Classens argues for appreciating other metaphors for God to counter the recent one-sided emphasis on divine violence, in *Mourner, Mother, Midwife: Reimagining God's Delivering Presence in the Old Testament* (Louisville, KY: Westminster John Knox, 2013).

52. Abraham Heschel, *The Prophets* (New York: Harper & Row, 1962; repr., New York: Perennial Classics, 2001) 285–382. Matthew R. Schlimm analyzes and distinguishes the dissimilar views on divine pathos of Heschel, Fretheim, and Brueggemann in "Different Perspectives on Divine Pathos: An Examination of Hermeneutics in Biblical Theology," *CBQ* 69 (2007) 673–94.

53. Heschel, *The Prophets*, 290. For more discussion of justice, see pp. 249–81; on Amos, see pp. 32–46.

54. In addition to Heschel, for the sorrow of God, see Fretheim, *The Suffering of God: An Old Testament Perspective* (OBT; Minneapolis: Fortress, 1984) 107–66; "Theological Reflections on the Wrath of God," 6–8; "The Character of God in Jeremiah," 212–13; "'I was only a little angry,'" 373–75; idem, *Creation Untamed*, 93–121. The divine embrace of human pain, of course, finds its fullest expression in the cross of Jesus Christ. See esp. Jürgen Moltmann, *The Crucified God: The Cross of Christ as the Foundation and Criticism of Christian Theology* (trans. R. A. Wilson and J. Bowden; Minneapolis: Fortress, 1993).

55. Also note expressions of Yahweh's anger in 5:21; 6:8; 8:7.

of its terrible losses, which will be the result of the coming military conflict associated with his judgment. Though prophets sometimes raise a taunt over those who deserve punishment (e.g., Isa 14:4–23; Ezek 26:17; 28:11–19; Hab 2:6–20), that is not the case here. Yahweh grieves the agony of punishment. The woe of 5:1–3 echoes the wailing of his people in 5:16–17, the corresponding pericope in the chiastic structure of 5:1–17.

What is more, God's judgments in the book of Amos are neither arbitrary nor hurried. Yahweh repeatedly had sent local disasters to prompt a change in his people so as to forestall judgment, but the nation did not return to him (4:6, 8, 9, 10, 11). In response to the prophet's pleas in the first two visions, Yahweh "changed his mind" (*nāḥam*) about the disasters that he was going to send (7:3, 6; cf. Jer 18:8, 10; Jonah 3:10; 4:2). Restraint, patience, and a willingness to change his plans of punishment precede the eventual divine decree of unavoidable wrath on Israel. Even the Oracles against the Nations (chaps. 1–2) demonstrate divine tolerance. Whatever the exact significance of the repeated phrase "For three transgressions, no four," these words convey a pattern of sin, in which one transgression *at last* forces God to send judgment.[56] Once again, there is forbearance, even toward peoples who do not know Yahweh.

The punishments of an earthquake and an invasion are harsh and overwhelming, but they are not sent precipitously or without cause. These are actions driven by God's ethical demands yet tempered by his longsuffering mercy. These words by Fretheim are apropos:

> These references to divine wrath are coherent only if placed along a time line, so that one can speak of delay, a time of provocation, a time of execution, and an end. God's anger is *historical* anger.... The texts never suggest that God was provoked from all eternity by any sin that would ever be committed... and that each such "historical" provocation is an actualization of that prior provocation. *Wrath is a contextualized reality.*[57]

God's pathos—his emotional engagement with his and other peoples, with the cause of justice, and with his punishment—should inform our response to and involvement in issues of justice. Ideally, our righteous anger at injustice is grounded in God's. We are made in his image, so indignation at the abuse of justice is to be expected. As in the case with God, our disapproval of wrong should find concrete expression through deterrents, judgments as it were: systems of penalties locally, nationally, and internationally to safeguard justice as best we can as humans and to punish its violation.

Ideological Reversal

A fourth way the book of Amos engages the issue of the violence of God is the reversal of Israel's religious ideology. This is done in at least two ways.

---

56. There are several options in Amos research about the meaning of the graded numerical saying "for three sins ... even for four." See conveniently Paul, *Amos*, 27–30.

57. Fretheim, "Theological Reflections on the Wrath of God," 14.

To begin with, the book closes with a passage (9:11–15) that describes a future setting under a Davidic monarchy (of which we will say more later), the return to the land, a time of food and drink aplenty and of Israel's peaceful coexistence with its enemies and other nations, and permanent rootedness in their towns and farms. Everyone's activity at that time will be directed toward constructive ends and toward sustaining and enjoying life; no more will human hands devote themselves to killing, oppressing, and destroying. All of these images are an intentional reversal of their transgressions and of their present and imminent suffering.[58]

The soon-coming judgment announced by Amos is not Yahweh's final word. Whatever Israel and other peoples would go through due to the will of the sovereign God, it is aimed ultimately at renewal. Judgment is not the work of an impulsive, vindictive, heartless, or detached deity; it is a step toward blessedness and salvation, both particular (his people) and universal (all nations). I do not say this to minimize in any way the awfulness of judgment or to instrumentalize it flippantly as a necessary means to a greater end. But we need to recognize that the purposeful movement toward salvation through judgment is the consistent message of the prophetic literature.

From this perspective, the judgment-redemption link is grounded in God's relationships with the earth, his people, and humanity, and these relationships are inseparable from his commitment to justice. It is not surprising, then, that predictions of international justice to be established by the Coming One find a prominent place in the prophetic visions of the future (e.g., Isa 11:1–5; 42:1–4; Jer 23:1–6; 33:14–16), even if it is not mentioned plainly in Amos 9:11–15. Judgment is the gateway to true, efficacious, global justice; it is salvific in purpose. With this justice comes global peace, which is pictured in some picturesque images in other prophetic books (e.g., Isa 11:6–11; 65:17–25); the scene of societal and agricultural bliss in Amos 9:11–15 communicates the end of all violence.

What we lack in recent debates is a more robust appreciation of Yahweh's demands and their link to his obligations to creation and humanity.[59] God will not let his "strange work" (NIV) of judgment (Isa 28:21) be

---

58. Commentators often have dismissed 9:11–15 as a later addition, because of the consistent message of judgment in the rest of the book. This is not the place to defend its authenticity (see, e.g., Paul, *Amos*, 288–95; Francis I. Andersen and David Noel Freedman, *Amos* [AB 24A; New York: Doubleday, 1989] 885–93, 912–26; Terence E. Fretheim, *Reading Hosea–Micah: A Literary and Theological Commentary* [Reading the Old Testament; Macon: Smyth & Helwys, 2013] 157–58), except to observe the striking vagueness of these words in contrast with the detailed descriptions of the future in other prophetic books. These lines are a general hope for change, not a precise prediction or *vaticinium ex eventu*. They are part of the prophetic protest against the present. In any case, as mentioned earlier, readers must deal with the present shape of the book in their theological and ethical reflections (see p. 116 n. 18).

59. Fretheim argues similarly in "Theological Reflections on the Wrath of God," 25–26; "The Character of God in Jeremiah," 217–19; "God and Violence in the Old Testament," 24–25; *God and World in the Old Testament*, 189–98.

his concluding work.⁶⁰ Significantly, in Amos and other prophetic books, those who will enjoy that new day are the remnant, a concept that assumes judgment has passed (Amos 5:15; 9:14).⁶¹ If judgment is a crucial component of a viable theodicy that deals with evil, so too is the hope of future restoration when wrongs that merited judgment will be made right and renewal enjoyed. In the prophetic literature, these divine actions occur on this earth and in history.⁶² This vision of the future incorporates forgiveness and the cleansing from transgression and the possibility of worshiping God anew.⁶³ These elements are not developed in Amos, but they are treated in other prophetic books.

In sum, the prophetic theme of the Day of the LORD continually brings together judgment and restoration. The "day" or "days" in the book of Amos all refer to the coming wrath (e.g., 3:14; 5:18, 20; 6:3; 8:3), except for the instance at 9:11, which begins with "in that day." In other words, punishment and renewal are both parts of the future plans of God.

Second, the book of Amos presents a sustained critique of the religious construct that sanctifies the sociopolitical and economic status quo. The prophet condemns the ideology of Israel and its fruits, which trigger divine judgment. I have described this religious censure extensively in other publications,⁶⁴ but allow me to summarize the argument briefly. Amaziah, the high priest at Bethel, tellingly declares to Amos, "This is the king's sanctuary and the temple of the kingdom" (7:13). The prophet, however, will not certify these religious ideas and institutions. Instead, the message is that Yahweh will destroy the sanctuaries at Bethel and Gilgal (and probably Sa-

---

60. Note Heschel's comments in *The Prophets*, 223–29.

61. Gerhard F. Hasel, *The Remnant: The History and Theology of the Remnant Idea from Genesis to Isaiah* (3rd ed.; Andrews University Monograph Studies in Religion 5; Berrien Springs, MI: Andrews University Press, 1980). For Amos, see 173–215; cf. Sang Hoon Park, "šĕ'ēr," *NIDOTTE* 4:11–17.

62. In the New Testament, of course, there are the additional eschatological hopes of personal redemption and heaven, as well as the prediction in the closing chapters of Revelation of the new heaven and earth.

63. For eschatology as key for theodicy, see Admirand, *Amidst Mass Atrocity and The Rubble of Theology*. The category of eschatology also is needed for the redemption of the memories of atrocities. See Miroslov Volf, *The End of Memory: Remembering Rightly in a Violent World* (Grand Rapids: Eerdmans, 2006); Admirand, *Amidst Mass Atrocity*, 25–32, 141–42, 264–67, 285–94, passim. Issues of memory have been fundamental to the work of truth and reconciliation commissions in contexts of terrible violence. Note, e.g., Michael A. Hayes and David Tombs, *Truth and Memory: The Church and Human Rights in El Salvador and Guatemala* (Leominster: Gracewing, 2001).

64. E.g., M. Daniel Carroll R., "'For So You Love to Do': Probing Popular Religion in the Book of Amos," in *Rethinking Contexts, Rereading Texts: Contributions from the Social Sciences to Biblical Interpretation* (ed. M. D. Carroll R.; JSOTSup 299; Sheffield: Sheffield Academic Press, 2000) 168–89; idem, "Can the Prophets Shed Light on Our Worship Wars? How Amos Evaluates Religious Ritual," *SCJ* 8 (2005) 215–27; cf. Daniel I. Block, "Worship," *DOTPr*, 867–78.

maria), where the populace thought they met him in their ceremonies (3:14; 4:4–5; 5:4–6; 7:9; 8Amos:3; 9:1). In God's sight, their worship was sin (4:4–5; 5:21–25), and so a devastating encounter with Yahweh awaited them (4:12–13; 5:17).

The national political and religious ideology (common in the ancient world) was that the deity, Yahweh, was committed to his people and that the political and moral order was sustained and protected by his representative, the king. It ignored past disasters and misrepresented the present and future. It sustained the belief that Israel enjoyed God's favor under Jeroboam II. The Oracles against the Nations and 4:6–11 expose the lie: war and want were the realities of their actual experience, and things would get much worse. The confident, celebratory royal ideology believed that the Day of Yahweh would be light, that it heralded triumph and blessing. Apparently, all clung to and celebrated these twisted perceptions (5:18–20; cf. 4:4–5; 5:14; 6:1–3; 9:10), perhaps even those within Israel who were exploited by that socioreligious world, whose expectation was for patriotic national glory or for the end of their suffering.[65] Linville's comment reflects this observation:

> Belief in a triumphant day of vindication over one's enemies is as easily ascribed to victims of injustice as it is to myopic, complacent and comfortable elite who think present good fortune is only indicative of greater glory to come. . . . But is the victim's faith that the day would bring vindication and justice really less naïve than the confidence of their oppressors?[66]

It is announced that the Day of Yahweh would mean defeat and exile, and Israel's fortresses and armies would not be able to stop the onslaught. But, as already stated, there was hope beyond that debacle. That future hope would include raising up the fallen tabernacle of David, a political order based in the south. The dynasty of Jeroboam II of Israel could not save the nation and would have no part of that coming restoration (9:11). The ideological lie would be proven false and toothless. From the beginning of the book, the Northern Kingdom's government and religion are declared illegitimate. Yahweh roars from the temple in Zion, from Jerusalem the capital of Judah (1:2), not from Bethel or Samaria.

It is easier to worship a benevolent deity, not a demanding and uncomfortable one, who makes demands and judges human sin. These are difficult words, and I want to make it clear that I am not caricaturing modern critics of the God of the Old Testament by impugning their motives or equating

---

65. The complex relationship between religion and injustice explored by Marxism and Latin American liberation theology is pertinent here. All can defend religion, even as it as functions as an opiate and an instrument of oppression and false consciousness. For more on these issues as they pertain to Amos, see my *Contexts for Amos*, 109–22, 289–306; cf. Enrique Dussel, *Las metáforas teológicas de Marx* (Estella: Editorial Verbo Divino, 1993).

66. James R. Linville, *Amos and the Cosmic Imagination* (SOTSMS; Aldershot: Ashgate, 2008) 116.

them with the religious leaders and the religious framework of eighth-century Israel. Some of those who question Yahweh are people I know and whose sincerity I do not doubt. It simply is to establish the point that we must be wary of redefining Yahweh by eliminating what we do not like in the secure settings of much of our reflections. I am not sure if efforts to propose a nice God who does not judge forcefully would make much sense on the streets of Aleppo in the midst of the ongoing horrors in Syria today or in the mountains of Guatemala during the 36 years of our civil war, or whether the cries for justice—and for judgment!—during the Civil Rights Movement or in the days of apartheid in South Africa would accept a sanitized, benevolent version of Yahweh, who will not punish *in history*. Desperate cries for justice would not allow it.

Conclusion

The God of the Old Testament is a violent God. What does that conviction mean when comprehended within the breadth of the biblical revelation? This essay offers tentative thoughts about this theological conundrum, particularly as it pertains to the prophetic literature. I have used Amos as my source. My points are four. First, we should read this literature with the proper cultural lens to evaluate what truly is being communicated in the judgment passages. Second, divine judgment often corresponds to what humans have done. We suffer our own transgressions, all of us, even as some are more responsible. Third, reflecting on divine judgment leads us to the pathos of God. He is emotionally engaged in judgment and does not chastise capriciously. He must punish; justice demands it, though it is not tidy. Nevertheless, he is pained to execute his wrath, and in his mercy is willing to stay judgment and change his plans. Fourth, the eschatological hope at the end of the book tells us that judgment is not the end of the work of God; God's goal is redemption and restoration. That hope does not negate the reality of judgment. The reality of the coupling of wrath and hope reveals that a religion, which focuses solely on his goodness and human flourishing, may be comforting but does not know the fullness—indeed the mystery—of the character of Yahweh.

God is both love and a consuming fire. The inseparable fact within the biblical record is underscored by Walter Moberly:

> For there is, irrespective of human preference, a mysterious reality with which humans have to do, which they do not have the power to change (however much they may indeed have freedom of interpretation and exploration within certain limits), and which they ignore at peril of self-deception and blindness; when, however, this reality is rightly understood and responded to, it is good and gracious beyond imagining.[67]

---

67. R. W. L. Moberly, "Is Monotheism Bad for You? Some Reflections on God, the Bible, and Life in the Light of Regina Schwartz's *The Curse of Cain*," in *The God of Israel* (ed. R. P. Gordon; UCOP 64; Cambridge: Cambridge University Press, 2007) 101.

Chapter 8

Toward an End to Violence: Hearing Jeremiah

Elmer A. Martens

Those who hold that the prophets, including Jeremiah, portray a God who has an appetite for violence have numerous texts they can marshal to support their claim. The current cultural mood is fixated on the subject of violence, partly because of the frequent reports of incidents of violence globally, and partly, one might conjecture, because of a philosophical framework set by philosophers a generation ago. Questions of power and violence occupied deconstructionist philosophers.[1] In religious circles, the works of René Girard, especially his book *Violence and the Sacred,* gained wide attention.[2] Recently biblical scholars and theologians have taken up the subject of God as violent.[3]

This essay, focusing on Jeremiah, seeks to address the imbalance that is created when attention is given primarily to texts that present a God who is violent. Significant texts, not to mention the structure of Jeremiah's book as a whole, will not allow the portrait of a violent-only kind of God to stand. Admittedly, a prophet such as Jeremiah is often preoccupied with the topic of God's wrath and the imminent destruction by the Babylonians.

Author's note: I wish to express appreciation for helpful feedback to scholar colleagues Lynn Jost, Dwight Acomb, Pierre Gilbert, Gordon Matties, and Bob Boyd; to friends Nick Sembrano and Dean Williams; and to the 2014 Seminary class Biblical Theology I at Fresno Pacific Biblical Seminary.

1. Jacques Derrida, *Of Grammatology* (trans. G. C. Spivak; Baltimore: Johns Hopkins University Press, 1976). Derrida holds that "writing cannot be thought outside of the horizon of intersubjective violence" (p. 127). From his chapter "The Violence of the Letter: From Lévi-Strauss to Rousseau," one might well deduce that an interpretation of a text is itself an act of violence. I owe the reference to Nick Sembrano.

2. René Girard, *Violence and the Sacred* (trans. P. Gregory; Baltimore: Johns Hopkins University Press, 1997).

3. E.g., Regina M. Schwartz, *The Curse of Cain: The Violent Legacy of Monotheism* (Chicago: University of Chicago Press, 1997); Philip Jenkins, *Laying Down the Sword: Why We Can't Ignore the Bible's Violent Verses* (New York: HarperOne, 2011); Eric A. Seibert, *The Violence of Scripture: Overcoming the Old Testament's Troubling Legacy* (Minneapolis: Fortress, 2012); Jerome F. D. Creach, *Violence in Scripture* (Interp; Louisville, KY: Westminster John Knox, 2013).

However, a closer look opens up another perspective, for his book contains remarkable assertions which offer a contrary (even if complementary) portrait of God. The purpose of this essay is to present a portrait of God from the book of Jeremiah that at a minimum tempers the portrait of a violent God, and more maximally highlights a trajectory into the New Testament that envisions an end to violence.

Divine Anger: Factoring in the Context of Covenant

Readers of Jeremiah are understandably taken aback by the brash statements of God's anger, a frequent theme. The term *'ap* ("anger") appears in Jeremiah more than in other books. This anger is frequently attributed to Yahweh (e.g., 15:14, "I will make you serve your enemies in a land that you do not know, for in my anger a fire is kindled that shall burn forever"; cf. 33:5).[4] Another root, *ḥrh* ("kindling fire") combines with *'ap* to give the translation "fierceness (burning) of his anger." The desolation of harvest and even the desolation of Israel's land is "because of the fierce anger of the Lord" (12:13; cf. 25:37; 30:24). A third term, *ḥēmâ,* also linked with heat, conveys the concept of an inner intense emotional disturbance. "Therefore, thus says the Lord God: My anger and my wrath (*ḥēmâ*) shall be poured out on this place . . . it will burn and not be quenched" (7:20). By one count, 42 different verses or passages in Jeremiah mention or elaborate on God's anger.[5]

These strong statements about God's disposition could be construed as a huge moral defect in God. However, they ought not be so construed for several reasons, the chief of which is that God is in a covenant relationship with Israel.[6] This sort of bondedness between a people and its God consists of promises and obligations. In this partnership, the chief obligation of Israel is loyalty to its covenant partner, which expresses itself in obedience. This obligation Israel has ignored. Repeatedly, Jeremiah cites instances of disloyalty, all of which culminate in the charge, "They have turned back to the iniquities of their ancestors of old, who refused to heed my words; they have gone after other gods to serve them; the house of Israel and the house of Judah have broken the covenant that I made with their ancestors" (11:10,

---

4. Scripture quotations are from the NRSV unless otherwise noted.
5. E. A. Martens, *Jeremiah* (BCBC; Scottsdale: Herald, 1986) 313–14.
6. The bulk of Bernard W. Anderson's book, *Contours of Old Testament Theology* (Minneapolis: Fortress, 1999) 79–236, is devoted to "Yahweh's Covenant with the People" in which he discusses the Abrahamic, the Mosaic, and the Davidic covenants. Hetty Lalleman comments, "The message of the prophets was primarily based on the covenant between God and Israel" (*Jeremiah and Lamentations* [TOTC 21; Downers Grove, IL: InterVarsity, 2013] 21). In one of the finest concise treatments on "covenant," J. Gordon McConville observes, "Covenant as a theological idea is distinctively biblical. . . . [It] becomes a way of speaking of all of life in subordination to a loving god. As such it can serve as a model for all Christian thinking, including ethical thinking" ("*bĕrît,*" *NIDOTTE* 1:753). Cf. Steven L. McKenzie, *Covenant* (UBT; St. Louis: Chalice, 2000).

emphasis added). Even later, in announcing a new covenant, the reminder about their past is stark, "a covenant that they broke" (31:32).

Covenant is not a mechanical arrangement, as in a contract, where failures to meet obligations are quickly identified and appropriate consequences follow in mechanical fashion. Covenant is a bonding of persons and when, as in the case of Israel and her God, the one party, Israel, betrays her partner, the effects are not only judiciary but personal. Yahweh, Israel's God, is emotionally affected. He is deeply pained by the people's infidelity (2:29–31; 3:19–20; 8:4–7, 18–22; 9:10, 17–19).

Also critical to the discussion of covenant is the reality that the God of the covenant is a God of justice, a concept that is often understood as God acting to punish evil and reward good. But this sort of conclusion must be nuanced. God sees to it that the evil latent in an act results in an appropriate consequence. That is, God ensures that any action issues in "fruit" that is already latent in the act (12:2). Evil actions already have the bad consequences intrinsic to them. It is as though God stands guard ensuring that the cosmic order is maintained. Hence, there is an impersonal dimension to wrath, an expression in response to the violation of a moral order. It is as though wrath goes forth as from within the wicked actions (4:4; 23:19–20).[7] Part of this mediation is for God to employ agents who proceed violently, though God risks violence by association.[8]

But the forensic aspect of God's justice also comes into play. Part of the covenant arrangement between God and Israel involves sanctions. Blessing follows adherence to the covenant (e.g., Deut 28:1–14). Curses follow rupture of the covenant (e.g., Deut 28:15–68). Given ample documentation by the prophet that Israel has been disloyal to the covenant, it becomes a matter of *integrity* whether God will follow through with the covenant curses as he would with covenant blessings.

The forensic side of justice is demonstrated in Jeremiah in several ways, not least of these is the judgment speech form, a feature of which is that it is reason-based. In the two-part judgment speech, the *indictment* constitutes the reason for the *announcement* of dire consequences. One such statement, among many, begins with the indictment, "Have you not brought this upon yourself by forsaking the Lord your God?" which is followed by

---

7. A helpful delineation of the relation between sin and judgment apart from forensic terms is given by Terence Fretheim, *Jeremiah* (SHBC; Macon: Smyth & Helwys, 2002) 34–41.

8. Fretheim helpfully presents a chart (ibid., 36) that details the actions of nations such as Babylon ("he will strike them down"; 21:7) as God's actions ("I will strike down"; 21:6). "These striking parallels suggest that *the portrayal of God's violent action in Jeremiah is conformed to the means that God uses*" (ibid., 39, emphasis his); cf. Fretheim's elaboration on God's acting through means in idem, "The Character of God in Jeremiah," in *Character and Scripture: Moral Formation, Community, and Biblical Interpretation* (ed. W. P. Brown; Grand Rapids: Eerdmans, 2002) 210–23.

the announcement "Your wickedness will punish you" (2:17, 19).[9] It is not as though a deity was on a rampage of violent destruction without reason; the reasons are clearly stated. No, the judgment oracles by their very form refute the view that God is arbitrary in bringing about severe actions.

An understanding of the justice and holiness of God answers the charge made by some that God is capricious. David Plotz, a self-described agnostic Jew, read through the entire Bible with its stories of plagues and murder and its "ruthless vengeance for minor sins (or no sin at all)," and commented, "I can only conclude that the God of the Hebrew Bible, if He existed, was awful, cruel, and capricious."[10] Granted, a statement about God's wrath poured out on humans and animals (7:20) is severe, but is one to conclude that God is capricious? The provocation for this harsh word is the family practice in Judah and Jerusalem of idolatry (7:17–19), a blatant violation of the first commandment and diametrically at odds with God's holiness. Is God capricious when God asserts, "for I have dealt you the blow of an enemy ... because your guilt is great, because your sins are so numerous" (30:14)? The answer must surely be "No!" God offers a clear-cut rationale for his actions of severity. Moreover, it is a rationale that flows out of his nature as the covenant God.

That God is a God of justice means that by his very nature God must be intolerant of evil. He is not a toothless deity. Matters of human injustice call for action by a God of justice.[11] After listing evils, such as going after other gods or indulging in sexual immorality and gross promiscuity, God engages in self-examination with the question, "Shall I not punish them for these things? ... Shall I not bring retribution on a nation such as this?" (5:7–9). God takes account of the deadly nature of sin. Not to act would represent apathy, the opposite of love and goodness. God's acts in history are not capricious; on the contrary, they are in keeping with God's nature and aligned

---

9. Commenting on Jer 2:14–19, Leslie C. Allen comments, "Besides wrong religion, vv. 14–19 also identify a supplementary reason for that punishment, wrong politics, which is consistent with the charge of Judah's inordinate disloyalty to Yahweh" (*Jeremiah* [OTL; Louisville, KY: Westminster John Knox, 2008] 44). Compare similar patterns of indictment/announcement (the numbers in parentheses represent the transition) in 8:12; 11:9–13 (11); 13:20–27 (24); 28:15–16 (16).

10. David Plotz, *Good Book: The Bizarre, Hilarious, Disturbing, Marvelous, and Inspiring Things I Learned When I Read Every Single Word of the Bible* (New York: Harper, 2009) 302; quoted in Seibert, *The Violence of Scripture*, 24. Cf. K. L. Noll, in reference to the stories in 1 Samuel 1–15, states, "The story teller requires a capricious deity to make the plot work" in "Is There a Text in this Tradition? Readers' Response and the Taming of Samuel's God," *JSOT* 83 (1999) 36; quoted in Eric A. Seibert, *Disturbing Divine Behavior: Troubling Old Testament Images of God* (Minneapolis: Fortress, 2009) 147.

11. Commenting on "The Framework of God's Sovereign Justice," Christopher J. H. Wright observes, "There is a huge moral difference between violence that is arbitrary or selfish and violence that is inflicted under strict control within the moral framework of punishment" (*The God I Don't Understand: Reflections on Tough Questions of Faith* [Grand Rapids: Zondervan, 2008] 93).

with values of justice, righteousness, holiness, and especially love. Miroslav Volf, referring to the destruction of life and property in his Croatian homeland, notes also that 800,000 people were hacked to death in one hundred days in Rwanda. He says:

> Though I used to complain about the indecency of the idea of God's wrath, I came to think that I would have to rebel against a God who wasn't wrathful at the sight of the world's evil. God isn't wrathful in spite of being love. God is wrathful because God is love.[12]

Furthermore, God's harsh actions are limited; they do not continue nonstop. Israel asks, "Will he (God) be angry forever?" (3:5). Jeremiah announces in the name of God, "I will not look on you in anger, for I am merciful" (3:12). Fretheim comments on Jer 12:7–13 about the "relational God": "The Godward side of wrath is always grief; and a striking thing about the God of Jeremiah is that both the grief and the anger are revealed to the prophet, who puts both on public display."[13] For some, such a multivoiced presentation invites extended dialogue.[14]

Nor should it be overlooked that whatever destructive actions are envisioned, within the covenant arrangement Israel is shown a way to avert disaster. For example, "If you truly amend your ways and your doings, if you truly act justly one with another . . . then I will dwell with you in this place, in the land that I gave of old to your ancestors forever and ever" (7:5–7).[15] Besides, God gives adequate time for change (11:7–8). What is more, the compassionate side of God is evident when, in the face of a broken covenant, God offers a new covenant. J. Gordon McConville, discussing the theology of the book of Jeremiah, notes, "The underlying theology of covenant receives considerable development in Jeremiah," the most important of which is the new covenant.[16] God offers a way forward even when the covenant is broken.

If one sees clearly the dominance that covenant plays in God's story with Israel, then Yahweh's harsh actions of bringing disaster, even destruction,

---

12. Miroslav Volf, *Free of Charge: Giving and Forgiving in a Culture Stripped of Grace* (Grand Rapids: Zondervan, 2006) 138–39. Quoted by Paul Copan, *Is God a Moral Monster? Making Sense of the Old Testament God* (Grand Rapids: Baker, 2011) 192.

13. Fretheim, *Jeremiah*, 34. For "relational" language, see pp. 31, 33, 39.

14. E.g., Gordon Matties, "The Word Made Bitter: At the Table with Joshua, Buber, and Bakhtin," in *The Old Testament in the Life of God's People: Essays in Honor of Elmer A. Martens* (ed. J. Isaak; Winona Lake, IN: Eisenbrauns, 2009) 307–32.

15. W. L. Holladay's solution to the text variations is well taken: that v. 3 should be read as a Qal verb, "So that I may dwell with you in this place," and v. 7 as a Piel, "I shall let you dwell in this place" (*Jeremiah 1* [ed. P. D. Hanson; Hermeneia; Philadelphia: Fortress, 1986] 236–37). B. W. Anderson, writing on Jeremiah, states, "One of the key verbs in the prophet's vocabulary is the verb *shub*, a verb of turning. In a negative sense the verbal noun means turning away, apostasy; in a positive sense, the verb means a turning to, a return—that is, repentance" (*Contours*, 189).

16. J. Gordon McConville, "Jeremiah: Theology of," *NIDOTTE* 4:764.

take on a different hue. In fact, if one probes more deeply into the covenant structure of the Old Testament and beyond, one will emerge, strange as it might seem, with a portrait of God that merits the caption "The God of Goodness."

Portrayal of a Benevolent God: A Challenge to the View that God Is Malevolent

The foregoing section has called attention to God's wrath. That description of God, we have claimed, is at once differently nuanced when placed in the context of covenant-making and covenant-keeping. Pursuing the prophetic descriptions of Yahweh more generally, the portrait that emerges is one of Yahweh's benevolence. At first sight, such assertions about God's goodness are in conflict with the rendering of God as malevolent. While that anomaly merits discussion, an initial move is to set out the data about God's goodness. A few representative texts limited to Jeremiah quickly document this claim that God is beneficent and good:

- Yahweh has delivered a slave people from Egypt (2:6; 7:22; 11:4; 16:14; 23:31).
- Yahweh has given his people Israel the gift of land. "I brought you into a plentiful land to eat its fruits and its good things" (2:7; cf. 11:5; 32:22).
- Yahweh, self-described as "a fountain of living water" (2:13), has provided for his people.
- Yahweh has mercifully deputized prophets to bring back an errant people (25:3–4).
- Yahweh will establish a new covenant with Israel, adherence to which will bring blessing (31:31–34). God will return Israel to its land (33:1–13). Even more, he promises them a new heart (24:7).
- Yahweh rejoices in goodness. "I will rejoice in doing good to them, and I will plant them in them in this land in faithfulness, with all my heart and all my soul" (32:41). Such a divine disposition is celebrated in song as Israel brings it offerings: "Give thanks to the Lord of hosts, for the Lord is good." (33:11).[17]

On reviewing texts such as these and others, Lamb concludes, "Goodness is such an integral part of Yahweh's character that he cannot help himself; he has to do good."[18]

---

17. Assertions about God's goodness are numerous elsewhere. In the Torah, Deut 7:7–10; 8:2–4; 26:1–11; and in the Psalms where God's goodness is not limited to Israel but extended to peoples generally, Pss 145:9; 25:7–8; 34:8; 52:9; 73:1; 86:5; 100:5; 106:1; 118:1; 119:68; 136:1. See J. Wenham, *The Goodness of God* (Downers Grove, IL: InterVarsity, 1974) 58–88; reprinted as *The Enigma of Evil: Can We Believe in the Goodness of God?* (Grand Rapids: Zondervan, 1985).

18. David Lamb, *God Behaving Badly: Is the God of the Old Testament Angry, Sexist and Racist?* (Downers Grove, IL: InterVarsity, 2011) 121. See also the four chapters devoted to the concept "God Is Good" in *God Is Great, God Is Good: Why Belief in God Is Reasonable and Responsible* (ed. W. L. Craig and C. Meister; Downers Grove, IL: InterVarsity, 2009)

Stressing the goodness of God, however, gives rise to the question, "What about the evil in the world?" If God is both good and all-powerful, there should be no evil in the world such as kidnapping, sex trade, murder, war, and destruction. The objection is forceful, but some answers have been proffered.[19] A few comments, leaning on Jeremiah, supplement and amplify these answers.

Evil in the world is brought about by humans to whom God has given freedom. Jeremiah's visit to the potter's house reinforces the claim that humans have the ability to act in freedom. Yahweh also has the freedom to act. Given human actions, God has the freedom to alter his course of action.[20] Jeremiah's parable of the good and bad figs points to the fact that good can come out of evil. It is the exiles who represent the good figs, but who through God's severe action will be sent into exile. There, however, God will "give them a heart to know that I am the Lord" (24:7). A form of this argument draws on the illustration of a surgeon plunging the knife into a human body. An onlooker might choke at this evil; a fellow physician understands that the "evil" of this act can result in the patient being cancer-free.

As to the claim that God is good and works toward what is good, it is critical that we let God define what is "good." Yahweh's definition of "good" does not necessarily align with what humans might consider to be good. The charge that God is the agent of evil when, for example, the prophet announces, "I will bring to an end in Moab, says the Lord, those who ..." (48:35), or "Moab shall be destroyed as a people" (48:42), must take into account the divine standards of righteousness and the nations' egregious sins (e.g., the "pride of Moab" [48:29]; Moab's "insolence" [48:30]). Two chapters describe the decimation that is to come on Babylon, against whom "the LORD has opened his armory and brought out the weapons of his wrath" (50:25). Among the reasons for such drastic destructive actions is "the wrong that they have done to Zion" (51:24), not to mention imperial arrogance (50:31–32).

Do texts that depict God's violent actions negate the claim that God is good?[21] No, because the larger intention must be noted, namely, that God curbs evil. A benign outcome is intended. Fretheim comments, "God's violence, whether in judgment or salvation, is never an end in itself, but is

---

107–66. See also chap. 3, "Divine Goodness," in C. S. Lewis, *The Problem of Pain* (New York: Macmillan, 1944) 25–42.

19. See Chad Meister, "God, Evil and Morality," in *God Is Great, God Is Good: Why Belief in God Is Reasonable and Responsible* (ed. W. L. Craig and C. Meister; Downers Grove, IL: InterVarsity, 2009) 107–18.

20. I. S. Markham expounds on the open universe in which people and God are active agents. See "Suffering, Providence, and Horrid Religious People," in *Against Atheism: Why Dawkins, Hitchens, and Harris Are Fundamentally Wrong* (Oxford: Blackwell, 2010) 116–27.

21. Texts about God bringing disaster: Jer 6:19, 32:31; 49:5. Cf. "This whole land shall become a ruin and a waste, and these nations shall serve the king of Babylon seventy years" (Jer 25:11).

always exercised in the service of God's more comprehensive salvific purposes for creation."[22] J. F. D. Creach, commenting on the flood, observes, "Hence it becomes apparent that much of the Bible's description of violence and destruction is related directly to God's desire to maintain the proper order in creation."[23] The Bible explains, too, that God's love will outlast his anger. "For men are not cast off by the Lord forever. Though he brings grief, he will show compassion, so great is his unfailing love (*ḥesed*)," (Lam 3:31–32 NIV; cf. Exod 34:6). Despite the caveats that people may mount, the foundational plank is, as Scripture asserts, that God is good.

Such an assertion is not dismissive of evidence that seems contrary, but it is to insist that given such a complex figure as God Almighty, paradox is to be expected. One must make space for mystery and paradox.[24] Paul A. Barker, leaning on R. W. L. Moberly's treatment of Exodus 32–34, observes, "When dealing with the things of God, one can hardly but expect paradox, nuance, subtlety and multi-facetedness."[25] If the assertion about God's goodness is a partial answer to negative images of God, an even stronger assertion is grounded in God's love.

Portrayal of a God Who Loves:
A Challenge to a Violent and Solely Retributive God

The so-called Book of Comfort (chaps. 30–33) holds a central place in Jeremiah's literary work, as is evidenced by the chiastic arrangement of the book. Within Jeremiah's Book of Comfort appears the significant declaration: "I have loved you with an everlasting love (*'ahăbâ*); I have drawn you with loving-kindness (*ḥesed*)" (31:3, NIV). In a surface reading, this sort of assertion seems to clash with the many references to Yahweh's harsh actions. The Hebrew root is *'hb*, a term that signifies love and devotion. The occurrences of the word in the Old Testament are relatively sparse. The verb as applied to God is used 32 times, but in only 23 instances, mostly in the circles of the Deuteronomists, Hosea, and Jeremiah, are Israel or individuals the object of God's love.[26] The term *ḥesed* ("steadfast love") is more

---

22. Terence E. Fretheim, "God and Violence in the Old Testament," *WW* 24 (2004) 25; quoted in Seibert, *Disturbing Divine Behavior,* 79–80.

23. Creach, *Violence in Scripture,* 11. Cf. Stephen B. Chapman, "Martial Memory, Peaceable Vision," in *Holy War in the Bible: Christian Morality and an Old Testament Problem* (ed. H. A. Thomas, J. Evans, and P. Copan; Downers Grove, IL: InterVarsity, 2013) 61: "Moreover, the consistent goal of God's activity in the world is not violence but peace (Ps 46:10[9]; 11:1–7; Zech 9:9–10)."

24. For an elaboration of many of the above points along with his rebuttals, see Seibert, *Disturbing Divine Behavior,* 69–88.

25. Paul A. Barker, *The Triumph of Grace in Deuteronomy: Faithless Israel, Faithful Yahweh in Deuteronomy* (PBM; Eugene, OR: Wipf & Stock, 2006) 3.

26. P. J. J. S. Els, "*'hb*," *NIDOTTE* 1:277–99. Cf. Deut 7:7–8, cf. 7:12–13; 33:3; Hos 3:1; 9:5; 11:1,4; Jer 31:3; Jer 2:2; 31:3.

frequent (246 times, often in Psalms) than is *'ahăbâ* ("love").²⁷ According to Gordon Clark's summary, *ḥesed* is not very close to *'ahăbâ* ("love"): "while it [*ḥesed*] includes 'love,' its connotations are much broader than those of love."²⁸ In this text, however, Yahweh's assertion that his disposition to Israel/Judah is one of love is very weighty, especially when the following exegetical observations are taken into account.

Love is high energy on behalf of another. Israel is in exile, but the divine announcement is, "See, I am going to bring them from the land of the north, and gather them from the farthest parts of the earth" (31:8). No one will be left behind, not the pregnant mother, not the blind, nor the lame. Describing God as "Father" (31:9) presents the image of a strong figure doing a total rescue. Love expends energy on behalf of the weak and unfortunate.

Love is extravagant in seeking another's well-being (31:10–14). The announcement continues with a picture of people "radiant over the goodness of the Lord," evidence of which is an abundance of grain, wine, and oil, along with sheep and cattle. Women shall "rejoice in the dance," and life will be at its finest, "like a watered garden" (31:12–14). With a cornucopia of good things pouring on them, Israel experiences the divine affection, which expresses itself not in a skimpy handout but in lavish provisions for the loved one. The prophet is not blind to that side of God which finds it necessary to "scatter Israel" because of her evil (31:10), but the scattering and the punishment is definitely not God's last word or act. His love moves him to great generosity. Els summarizes Norman Snaith's research on the subject: "God's 'election-love expressed by *'hb* . . . is (a) an unconditional love, (b) a sovereign love, and (c) 'a love in spite of,' an 'over-plus' love."²⁹

Love is eager for intimacy. A passage that highlights the emotive element of God's love is the oracle in Jer 31:15–22. The opening scene is of a mother, Rachel, weeping and lamenting her absent children. Yahweh responds with a comforting word, assuring her that her absent children will return (from exile) and that "there is hope for your future" (31:17). The poem continues with a description of Ephraim, an alternate name in Jeremiah for Israel, who is deeply repentant. God's response is poignant: "Is not Ephraim my dear son, the child in whom I delight? Though I often speak against him, I still remember him. Therefore my heart yearns for him; I have great compassion for him" (31:20; NIV).

---

27. D. A. Baer and R. P. Gordon, "*ḥesed*," *NIDOTTE* 2:210–18. The article lists monographs that offer nuances of meaning. J. A. Thompson claims that *ḥesed* is found "mostly in a covenant or treaty context" (*The Book of Jeremiah* [NICOT; Grand Rapids: Eerdmans, 1980] 566–67).

28. Gordon R. Clark, *The Word* Hesed *in the Hebrew Bible* (JSOTSup 157; Sheffield: JSOT Press, 1993) 267–68.

29. Els, *NIDOTTE* 1:280. Cf. Walter Brueggemann's comment on Jer 31:3: "It is God's heart made visible here which gives Israel a new chance in the future" (*A Commentary on Jeremiah: Exile and Homecoming* [Grand Rapids: Eerdmans, 1998] 283).

The expression "great compassion" translates a word related to *reḥem* ("womb"). Holladay comments, "The emotion of Yahweh over Ephraim is overwhelming: every time he speaks or even thinks of Ephraim, he is overpowered by affection, so that he cannot help showing compassion (*rḥm*) on him."[30] Phyllis Trible has helpfully called attention to the feminine dimension of God's compassion.[31] The scene is eventually one of Israel locked in an embrace with her God (31:22).[32] Love, whatever else it is, is also an emotion. Fretheim, tracing relevant texts, depicts a God of passion who suffers because of the people, with the people, and for the people.[33] At the very least, the image of God as harsh, even violent, must be balanced by an image of God as caring, nurturing, and compassionate.[34] Anger, however dominant in Jeremiah, is not God's defining feature. God's compassion is stronger than his anger. Jeremiah himself (assuming he had a hand in composing Lamentations) came to terms with God's severe actions: "Although he [the LORD] causes grief, he will have compassion (Heb. root *rḥm*) according to the abundance of his steadfast love (*ḥesed*); for he does not willingly afflict or grieve anyone" (Lam 3:32–33). In God, compassion and mercy trump anger. It has been well said: God is angry by necessity, not by nature. By nature, God is love. "Throughout the Bible we see a God who is a concerned lover."[35]

A scholar with a feminist bent, L. Juliana M. Claassens, has helped supply balance to stereotypical portrayals of God. Working from key texts in Jeremiah, she presents God as "Mourner." Specifically, she highlights the poem which, according to her, melds the figure of prophet and God:

> For the hurt of my poor people I am hurt,
> I mourn and dismay has taken hold of me....
> O that my head were a spring of water,
> And my eyes a fountain of tears,
> so that I might weep day and night
> for the slain of my poor people! (Jer 8:21–9:1 [MT 8:21–23])

---

30. W. L. Holladay, *Jeremiah 2: A Commentary on the Book of the Prophet Jeremiah, Chapters 26–52* (ed. P. D. Hanson; Hermeneia; Minneapolis: Fortress, 1989) 192. Holladay offers a full discussion on whether the first line (v. 20b) should be rendered "speak about him" or "speak against him." He thinks that the ambiguity could be part of Jeremiah's intention.

31. Phyllis Trible, *God and the Rhetoric of Sexuality* (OBT; Philadelphia: Fortress, 1978) 48.

32. The statement "A woman surrounds a man" has been variously interpreted: a reference to the virgin birth, women becoming like macho soldiers, and a literary reference inasmuch as two previous oracles about women bracket the reference to Ephraim, a man.

33. Terence E. Fretheim, *The Suffering of God: An Old Testament Perspective* (OBT; Minneapolis: Fortress, 1984) 107–48.

34. The sequel, compassion following wrath, is put into something of a principle by Isaiah: "Though in anger I struck you, in favor I will show you compassion [*rḥm*]" (Isa 60:10b, NIV). Isaiah leaves no doubt that in this polarity of wrath and compassion (if such it is) God's compassion is the last word (cf. Isa 54:8, 10).

35. Copan, *Is God a Moral Monster?* 35.

On the face of it, the speaker is the prophet Jeremiah. But Claassens notes that the poem ends in 9:3 [MT 9:2] with the formula, "says the LORD," which signals that the foregoing is divine speech. She concurs with Kathleen O'Connor that "the prophet's tears merge with the tears of God, who ultimately functions as the principle speaker in the poem."[36] The intent of her analysis is to challenge the dominant portrait of a God who, in warrior fashion, is violent and vindictive, by offering other less-well-known metaphors. "To think of the God who weeps in terms of a wailing or mourning woman [as in Rachel weeping for her children, 31:15–17] offers a unique perspective on the nature of God and provides female imagery for the Divine that balances male imagery."[37]

Finally, in considering the depiction of God, we remark on the structure of the book of Jeremiah. This structure clearly accents God's love over against portrayals of his violence. As shown in this outline, the Book of Comfort appears at the center of the book's chiastic arrangement:

A   God's personal message to Jeremiah (1:4–19)
   B   Sermons warning of disaster (chaps. 2–10)
      C   Stories about wrestling with both people and God (chaps. 11–20)
         D   Disputations with kings and prophets (chaps. 21–29)
            E   The Book of Consolation (chaps. 30–33)
         D′ Rushing headlong to destruction (chaps. 34–39)
      C′ After catastrophe (chaps. 40–45)
   B′ Oracles about the nations (chaps. 46–51)
A′ Historical documentation (chap. 52)[38]

In section B, "sermons warning of disaster" (chaps. 2–10), there are grim depictions of God's destructive action against Jerusalem (e.g., 6:1–12; 8:14–17; 11:9–14), frequently associated with God's anger (4:8; 6:11; 7:20). In the corresponding section B′, "oracles about the nations" (chaps. 46–51), there are more scenes of God unleashing his anger (49:37; 50:13). The arrogance of nations leads them to act violently, but as Creach notes, "God acts against these nations to correct their violence, not to perpetuate more violence."[39]

At the center of this chiastic arrangement is the Book of Comfort (chaps. 30–31[33] with its assertion that God is a loving God. Imagine now a scroll rolled on two rollers, one starting with the beginning of the book;

---

36. L. Juliana M. Claassens, *Mourner, Mother, Midwife: Reimagining God's Delivering Presence in the Old Testament* (Louisville, KY: Westminster John Knox, 2012) 23.
37. Ibid., 34.
38. E. A. Martens, "Jeremiah," in *Isaiah–Lamentations* (by Larry L. Walker and Elmer A. Martens; CBC 8; Wheaton, IL: Tyndale House, 2005) 307–9.
39. Creach, *Violence in Scripture*, 165.

the other starting with the end of the book. Upon "opening" the scroll the reader would be near the midpoint of the book and so face the Book of Comfort. The theological import of the book's structural arrangement with its bookends repeatedly touching on God's wrath, yet with God's love as the chiastic centerpiece, should not be missed. Though the book is bracketed with these harsh actions against Israel and the nations resulting from God's anger against evil-doing, the center of the chiasm, its core message, is one of love: "I have loved you with an everlasting love" (31:3). Both love and anger within God are realities. Of the two, love is the stronger and more defining. To make that point even more forcefully, Jeremiah employs a compelling metaphor.

A Portrait of God as Marital Lover Who Perseveres beyond Disloyalty: A Decisive Challenge to a Negative View of God

Lest one minimize the importance of God's love, it is fitting to emphasize the depth of God's love using the image of marital love, an analogy that C. S. Lewis calls "full of danger."[40] Yahweh rehearses the devotion of Israel in her youth, "your love as a bride" (2:2). Next, Jeremiah's discourse expands on the metaphor of marriage. He details deviance, dalliance, and disloyalty, all of which would justify divorce. The use of this metaphor of marriage harks back to Hosea, chronologically the first to invoke the marriage metaphor to describe the partners, God and Israel (Hos 1–3). Gomer, Hosea's wife, like Israel, is an adulteress. Her adulterous ways are sufficiently devious and deviant that Hosea would have been justified in putting her away through divorce. Instead, Hosea pays a price and takes her back (Hos 3:1–2). Likewise, God's love is extraordinary in that God reaches out even to those who spurn his love.

Jeremiah builds on this metaphor. God, the lover, catalogs his partner's evil, easily sufficient grounds for divorce, ending with the charge, "As a faithless wife leaves her husband, so you have been faithless to me, O house of Israel" (2:4–3:20). However, Yahweh shows them the way back by prescribing a litany of repentance. The promise, based on Yahweh's mercy, is that if they return (šwb), he will heal their faithlessness" (3:11). Tenderness — the opposite of violence — marks Yahweh as lover.

That characteristic of God's persevering love is further underlined in the scene in which Jeremiah himself is at odds with God. In one of his seven laments, Jeremiah accuses God of deception: "Truly, you are to me like a deceptive brook, like waters that fail" (15:18; cf. 20:7). One would think that such outright accusations would bring an end to whatever fraternal relationship still existed. But no, God's reply is not harsh but conciliatory. "If

---

40. Lewis, *The Problem of Pain*, 33.

you turn back, I will take you back, and you shall stand before me" (15:19). God's love endures; in tenderness, God reaches out to the weak.

Jeremiah's portrait of God is of a God who is solicitous for the well-being of Israel and of humans generally. His love is extraordinary. Such a portrait is at variance, and totally so, with the audacious and irreverent statement by Richard Dawkins, the atheist who asserts:

> The God of the Old Testament is arguably the most unpleasant character in all fiction: jealous and proud of it; a petty, unjust, unforgiving control freak; a vindictive blood thirsty ethnic cleanser; a misogynistic, homophobic, racist, infanticidal, genocidal, filicidal, pestilential megalomaniacal, sadomasochistic, capriciously malevolent bully.[41]

At the very least, Dawkins has grossly overstated, and worse, distorted the biblical view of God. More congruent with the Bible's presentation is the comment by Copan, "God gets jealous or angry precisely because he cares."[42]

Conciliatory Messages in Jeremiah: Challenging Violence as a Divine Modus Operandi

Jeremiah's startling message to Judah's King Zedekiah to avert war and violence by submitting to the encroaching enemy, the Babylonians, moves the discussion of violence at once into the political realm. The prophet's equally surprising letter to his fellow countrymen, now in exile, advising them to pray for their enemies, moves the discussion of violence decisively into the realm of religion and spirituality. His conciliatory message is to be heard both in Jerusalem and in Babylon.

In Jerusalem at the turn of the seventh century B.C.E., King Zedekiah is pondering a strategy in the face of the fast-moving Egypt-bound army under the command of Nebuchadnezzar, king of Babylon. The obvious plan is to repel the invading army with military force; the plan is to meet strength with strength. Zedekiah and his advisors are flirting with an Egyptian alliance. The prophet Jeremiah enters the political arena and advises the king to forego any such plan and to submit to the invader. To trust in military alliances is idolatrous (2:16–18).[43] Jeremiah urges King Zedekiah to buckle under to the demands of the oncoming Babylonians and make his peace

---

41. Richard Dawkins, *The God Delusion* (New York: Houghton Mifflin, 2006); quoted in Robert Stewart, "'Holy War,' Divine Action and the New Atheism: Philosophical Considerations," in *Holy War in the Bible: Christian Morality and an Old Testament Problem* (ed. H. A. Thomas, J. Evans, and P. Copan; Downers Grove, IL: InterVarsity, 2013) 265.

42. Copan, *Is God a Moral Monster?* 39.

43. Glen Harold Stassen points to this text as support for one of his steps toward peacemaking practices ("The Prophets' Call for Peacemaking Practices" in *Holy War in the Bible: Christian Morality and an Old Testament Problem* [ed. H. A. Thomas, J. Evans, and P. Copan; Downers Grove, IL: InterVarsity, 2013] 255–59).

with the enemy (27:12; 38:17). That exhortation, given privately to the king (25:4), is also given publicly in the context of a foreign embassy consultation of neighboring nations meeting in Jerusalem, likely in 594 B.C.E. (27:2–11).[44]

In distant Babylon, so it seems, there is also restlessness, and plans are being made to stage an insurrection. If the message to the governing authorities in Jerusalem was toward peaceful coexistence with the enemy, the same message with its conciliatory approach is sent to the Judean captives already in Babylon. In his letter to the exiles in Babylon, the prophet urges, "Seek the welfare of the city where I have sent you into exile, and pray to the Lord on its behalf, for in its welfare you will find your welfare" (29:7). This admonition is radical and counterintuitive; it represented an unequivocal "No!" to any notion of insurgency. Even more unsettling was the further advice to pray for the Babylonian city, advice that called for prayer on behalf of Israel's captors, their enemies.

To pray for the well-being of the city in which the Israelites are captive would not only be against the grain of human instinct, but it challenges the notion that violence is acceptable. One cannot pray for the welfare of the enemy at one point and then turn about and destroy him. An act of intercession demonstrates a concern for the welfare of the other.[45] Such an act is the polar opposite of violence and calls into question the notion that the God of the Old Testament is a war-happy God.

A Scenario of "No Violence": Imagining a New Reality

Given that Jeremiah has conciliatory messages, which gainsay hostility and enmity and point to relationships which are friendly and cordial, and given that the depiction of God in Jeremiah includes portraits of a loving God, one is prepared for a vision of a society marked by an absence of violence.

Hints that this sort of society is possible are found in Jeremiah. The Book of Comfort, both in its poetic form (chaps, 30–31) and subsequent prose version (chaps. 32–33), frequently includes a promise of restoration. The promise, "I will restore their fortunes" functions as its bookends (31:3; 33:26), and is repeated throughout (30:18; 31:23; 32:44, 33:7, 11). The phrase "restore the fortunes" (*šwb šĕbût*), better rendered as "bring about a restoration," is given content in those four chapters.[46] The restoration has to

---

44. For the discussion of the date, see Holladay, *Jeremiah 2*, 115.

45. An illustration is Elisha's counsel to feed the invading Aramean army (2 Kgs 6:11–23). Cf. also M. Daniel Carroll R., "Impulses toward Peace in a Country at War: The Book of Isaiah between Realism and Hope," in *War in the Bible and Terrorism in the Twenty-First Century* (ed. R. S. Hess and E. A. Martens; BBRSup 2; Winona Lake, IN: Eisenbrauns, 2008) 59–78.

46. For an extended discussion of the phrase and its meaning, see my *Motivations for the Promise of Israel's Restoration to the Land in Jeremiah and Ezekiel* (Ph.D. diss., Claremont Graduate School, 1972) 164–96.

do with a spiritual restoration of a once-wayward people (31:15–22) and a physical return of a people from their exile (31:8–9, 16).

The various descriptions of the restoration include the prospects of a worshiping community (31:6–7, 23), an agriculturally prosperous society (31:12), and a safe community (31:24). The picture is one of peaceful coexistence: "And Judah and all its towns shall live there together, and the farmers and those who wander with their flocks" (31:24). The tension and sometimes enmity between the settled folk, the farmers, and the migrating shepherds was an endemic problem of that day. But in the future a new society is envisioned, where there will be harmony and good will. Implied in this portrait is that conflict and certainly violence will be no more.

Similarly, in the prose section of the book the scene of the future is one of peace and security. "I am going to bring it [Jerusalem] recovery and healing. . . . I will heal them and reveal to them abundance of prosperity and security" (33:6). Once again, God's work of restoration results in a society where peace rules; threats of violence are absent. Isaiah, an earlier prophet, graphically portrays a similar scene, at once local and universally generic, in the well-known from-sword-to-plowshare oracle (Isa 2:1–4). Many readers understand fulfillment of this vision to come at a distant, utopian eschatological time. It is better, however, to regard the opening phrase, "In days to come" (*'aḥărît hayyāmîm*), not as a statement about a remote future, but in the sense, as "whenever." The force of the oracle is that "whenever" people stream to the "mountain of the Lord" to be instructed in Yahweh's ways, the outcome will be to beat swords into plowshares. Wars will be no more.[47] Concerning another peaceful scene, one of wolves and lambs lying down together (Isa 11:1–9), Mark McEntire comments, "More than any other text, Isaiah 11 holds out the hope that the violent ways of humanity and the world might come to an end."[48]

The portrait of God is of one who desires a nonviolent world, one where *shalom* is a reality.[49] Might one even say more, namely, that God is a God

---

47. Supporting arguments for this interpretation are found in H. W. Wolff, "Swords into Plowshares: Misuse of a Word of Prophecy?" in *The Meaning of Peace: Biblical Studies* (ed. P. B. Yoder and W. M. Swartley; Louisville, KY: Westminster John Knox, 1992) 110–26. See also my "Toward Shalom: Absorbing the Violence," in *War in the Bible and Terrorism in the Twenty-First Century* (ed. R. S. Hess and E. A. Martens; BBRSup 2; Winona Lake, IN: Eisenbrauns, 2008) 37–38; and Alan Kreider, Eleanor Kreider, and Paulus Widjaja, *A Culture of Peace: God's Vision for the Church* (Intercourse, PA: Good Books, 2005).

48. Mark McEntire, *The Blood of Abel: The Violent Plot in the Hebrew Bible* (Macon, GA: Mercer University Press, 1999) 161.

49. The theme of *shalom* (peace) has been explored by Anabaptist writers, among others. See Perry B. Yoder, *Shalom: The Bible's Word for Salvation, Justice, and Peace* (IMS 7; Nappanee, IN: Evangel, 1987); Willard M. Swartley, *Covenant of Peace: The Missing Piece in New Testament Theology and Ethics* (SPS 9; Grand Rapids: Eerdmans, 2006); Laura L. Brenneman and Brad D. Schantz, eds., *Struggles for Shalom: Peace and Violence across the Testaments* (SPS 12; Eugene, OR: Pickwick, 2014).

of peace? The New Testament goes that far (Heb 13:20). Six times the New Testament speaks of the God of peace.[50] The book of Revelation will not allow us to ignore God as a God of war, but the emphasis on God as a God of peace must not be muted. The Christian gospel remains the "gospel of peace" (Eph 6:15).

A strong caveat needs to be entered at this point. Some recent publications attempt to address the violence of God depicted in the Old Testament by taking their point of departure from the New Testament, claiming that it is in Jesus that God is fully disclosed. Jesus is not ever violent; hence, God is not violent. Any Old Testament mention of God as violent, it is claimed, is a misrepresentation of God. Eric Seibert asserts, "All portrayals of God, especially those that seem problematic, should be brought into conversation with the God Jesus reveals. Those that do not correspond to the character of the God revealed in Jesus should be regarded as distortions of God's nature, distortions that need to be corrected, not defended."[51] While Seibert recognizes, even catalogs, some of the passages presenting an attractive God and pleads for a balanced perspective,[52] it is the instances of disturbing behavior that are in focus in his book, the answer to which is a Christocentric hermeneutic.

While a rebuttal would require a full analysis of his Christocentric hermeneutic, a major objection to such arguments is the dubious authority which is accorded to the Old Testament. Jesus, to whom appeal is made, never disparaged the Hebrew Scriptures, nor did he correct those writings, though he extended their meaning (Matt 5:21–48). These were the Scriptures the apostle had in view when he penned, "All Scripture is inspired by God and is useful for teaching, for reproof, for correction, and for training in righteousness" (2 Tim 3:16). The effort to sanitize the Old Testament problematic passages about God seems altogether too much like an attempt to reshape God in our image. It is humans then who decide what

---

50. Rom 15:33; Phil 4:9; 2 Cor 13:11; 1 Thess 5:23; Heb 13:20; Rom 16:20. In Paul, one reads of "the Lord of Peace" (2 Thess 3:16). So also the third member of the Trinity, the Holy Spirit, is associated with peace (Gal 3:22, 25; Rom 8:6; Eph 4:3). God's kingdom is characterized by the peace of the Spirit (Rom 14:17).

51. Seibert, *Disturbing Divine Behavior,* 227. His detailed arguments are given in chap. 10, "Evaluating Disturbing Divine Behavior by the God Jesus Reveals: Toward a Christocentric Hermeneutic," 169–207. Cf. J. Denny Weaver, *The Nonviolent God* (Grand Rapids: Eerdmans, 2013) 2: "Since the narrative of Jesus in the New Testament pictures Jesus' rejection of violence and his refusal to use the sword, the traditional confession that God is revealed in this story calls for understanding God in nonviolent images. That God should be understood with nonviolent images constitutes the major thesis of this book." Weaver argues strenuously against an atonement theory that presents God as violent. He addresses the violence in the book of Revelation. A careful reading of these texts may be found in Thomas R. Yoder Neufeld, *Killing Enmity: Violence and the New Testament* (Grand Rapids: Baker Academic, 2011).

52. Seibert, *Disturbing Divine Behavior*, 230–31.

is the "correct" portrayal of God. Even though the appeal to the incarnate Christ as representative of God offers some guidelines in depicting God, the end result of the pick-and-choose approach is a subjective portrait of God. It is more faithful to the biblical text to live with the conundrum of a God who defies neat characterization than to wiggle around some inconvenient truths.

Conclusion

Jeremiah's presentation of God is echoed in the New Testament. The dark side of God in which God moves eschatologically to rid the earth and the cosmos of violence is detailed in Revelation, though Paul is also forthright on the subject. Paul says that the Lord Jesus will be "revealed from heaven with his mighty angels in flaming fire, inflicting vengeance on those who do not know God and on those who do not obey the gospel of our Lord Jesus" (2 Thess 1:7–8). But the context in which a discussion about God must proceed is the covenant, as the book of Hebrews, quoting Jeremiah, makes clear (Heb 8–9; cf. Gal 4:21–31). Numerous in the New Testament are the assertions about God's love (e.g., John 3:16; 1 John 4:7–8). Unquestionably, the New Testament carries forward and amplifies Jeremiah's portrait of a God whose nature is one of goodness, love, and kindness.[53] In a most emphatic manner Christ (God) is presented, partly through the image of marriage, not as a vindictive God but as the God who is fully solicitous for his partner's well-being (Eph 5:22–32). Attempts to portray God as vindictive, harsh, and violent must account for this more positive portrayal of Yahweh. The tension regarding the character of God remains, but the accent tips sharply in the direction of God's love, for what greater demonstration could there be of God's love than that he gave himself in Jesus as an expression of his ultimate care for humanity (Rom 5:8; 1 John 3:16)?

Finally, as a practical matter, Jesus, in exhorting his followers to love enemies, reiterates conciliatory action toward the enemy, as did Jeremiah (Matt 5:44–45a; cf. Jer 29:7). This love-of-enemy message by Jesus, already enjoined earlier by Jeremiah, speaks powerfully against violence as a *modus operandi* in any era. New Testament scholar Richard Hays summarizes, "Thus from Matthew to Revelation we find a consistent witness against violence and a calling to the community to follow the example of Jesus in *accepting* suffering rather than *inflicting* it."[54]

---

53. E.g., Matt 7:1; 19:7; Luke 18:19; cf. 1 Pet 2:3; 1 Tim 4:4; Rom 7:16; 8:28; 1 Cor 12:7.

54. Richard B. Hays, *The Moral Vision of the New Testament: Community, Cross, New Creation: A Contemporary Introduction to New Testament Ethics* (San Francisco: Harper, 1996) 332 (emphasis his). The quotation appears in the chapter in which the author marshals arguments from the New Testament refuting the claim that violence is legitimate if it is in defense of justice. "Killing enemies is no longer a justifiable option" (ibid., 336). Chad Meister explains, "Instead of meeting violence with violence, rage with rage, Christians

The book of Jeremiah with its message about a God of covenant who is good, who loves and is persistent in his love, presents a portrait of God that modulates the harsher sounds of a retributive God who deals with nations and his own people in ways that sometimes involve violence. The softer sounds of a gentle God whose mercy is to be accented are heard with clarity in the Book of Comfort, and are greatly amplified in the New Testament portrait of Jesus, the one who came to disclose God (John 1:18). Thus, Jeremiah can readily be located on a trajectory that ends in the New Testament, specifically in Jesus. This God, whose fierce aspect must be acknowledged, yet remains the One who is heard to say, "I have great compassion for him" (Jer 31:20; NIV) and who declares, "I have loved you with an everlasting love" (31:3).

---

are asked to 'turn the other cheek' (See Mt. 5:39; Lk 6:29) and 'not to let the sun go down on their anger' (Eph 4:26). This is about the elimination of the roots of violence—no, more than that: it is about its transfiguration" (Meister, "God, Evil and Morality," 125). Cf. my "Toward Shalom: Absorbing the Violence," 33–57.

Bibliography

Adam, Klaus-Peter. *Der Königliche Held: Die Entsprechung von kämpfendem Gott und kämpfendem Köning in Psalm 18*. WMANT 91. Neukirchen-Vluyn: Neukirchener Verlag, 2001.
Admirand, Peter. *Amidst Mass Atrocity and The Rubble of Theology: Searching for a Viable Theodicy*. Eugene, OR: Cascade, 2012.
Albright, W. F. *Archaeology and the Religion of Israel*. 3rd ed. Baltimore: Johns Hopkins Univeristy Press, 1953.
Allen, Leslie C. *Jeremiah*. OTL. Louisville, KY: Westminster John Knox, 2008.
———. "The Value of Rhetorical Criticism in Psalm 69." *JBL* 105 (1986): 577–98.
Andersen, Francis I., and David Noel Freedman. *Amos*. AB 24A. New York: Doubleday, 1989.
Anderson, Bernard W. *Contours of Old Testament Theology*. Minneapolis: Fortress, 1999.
Anderson, Gary. "What About the Canaanites?" Pp. 27–72 in *Divine Evil: The Moral Character of the God of Abraham*. Edited by M. Bergmann, M. J. Murray, and M. C. Rea. Oxford: Oxford University Press, 2013.
Appleby, R. Scott. *The Ambivalence of the Sacred: Religion, Violence, and Reconciliation*. Carnegie Commission on Preventing Deadly Conflict. Lanham: Rowman & Littlefield, 2000.
Arendt, Hannah. *On Violence*. San Diego: Harcourt Brace, 1970.
Arndt, Emily. *Demanding Attention: The Hebrew Bible as a Source for Christian Ethics*. Grand Rapids: Eerdmans, 2011.
Avalos, Hector. *Fighting Words: The Origins of Religious Violence*. Amherst: Prometheus, 2005.
———. "The Letter Killeth: A Plea for Decanonizing Violent Texts." *JRCP* 1 (2007). N.p. Cited 14 September 2014. Online: www.religionconflictpeace.org/volume-1-issue-1-fall-2007/letter-killeth.
Bacote, Vincent, Laura C. Miguélez, and Dennis L. Okholm, eds. *Evangelicals and Scripture: Tradition, Authority, and Hermeneutics*. Downers Grove, IL: InterVarsity, 2004.
Bainton, Roland. *Christian Attitudes toward War and Peace*. Nashville: Abingdon, 1960.
Balentine, Samuel. *Prayer in the Hebrew Bible: The Drama of Divine-Human Dialogue*. OBT. Minneapolis: Fortress, 1993.
Barker, Kit. "Imprecation as Divine Discourse: Speech Act Theory, Dual Authorship, and Theological Interpretation." Th.D. thesis, Australian College of Theology, 2013.
Barker, Paul A. *The Triumph of Grace in Deuteronomy: Faithless Israel, Faithful Yahweh in Deuteronomy*. PBM. Eugene, OR: Wipf & Stock, 2006.
Barrett, Rob. *Disloyalty and Destruction: Religion and Politics in Deuteronomy and the Modern World*. LHB/OTS 511. London: T. & T. Clark, 2009.
Bartholomew, Craig G. "Listening for God's Address: A *Mere* Trinitarian Hermeneutic for the Old Testament." Pp. 3–19 in *Hearing the Old Testament: Listening for God's Address*. Edited by C. G. Bartholomew and D. J. H. Beldman. Grand Rapids: Eerdmans, 2012.
Bartholomew, Craig G., and David J. H. Beldman, eds. *Hearing the Old Testament: Listening for God's Address*. Grand Rapids: Eerdmans, 2012.
Barton, John. *Amos's Oracles against the Nations*. SOTSMS 6. Cambridge: Cambridge University Press, 1980.
———. "Marcion Revisited." Pp. 341–54 in *The Canon Debate: On the Origins and Formation of the Bible*. Edited by L. M. McDonald and J. A. Sanders. Peabody, MA: Hendrickson, 2002.

———. *The Theology of the Book of Amos*. OTT. Cambridge: Cambridge University Press, 2012.
Bauckham, Richard. *Jesus and the God of Israel: God Crucified and Others Studies on the New Testament's Christology of Divine Identity*. Grand Rapids: Eerdmans, 2008.
Beal, Timothy K. "The System and the Speaking Subject in the Hebrew Bible: Reading for Divine Abjection." *BibInt* 2 (1994): 171–89.
Bekkum, Koert van. *From Conquest to Coexistence: Ideology and Antiquarian Intent in the Historiography of Israel's Settlement in Canaan*. CHANE 45. Leiden: Brill, 2011.
Belcher, R. P. Jr. "Suffering." Pp. 775–81 in *Dictionary of the Old Testament: Wisdom, Poetry & Writings*. Edited by T. Longman III and P. Enns. Downers Grove, IL: IVP Academic, 2008.
Bellis, Alice Ogden. *Helpmates, Harlots, and Heroes: Women's Stories in the Hebrew Bible*. 2d ed. Louisville, KY: Westminster John Knox, 2007.
Benedict, Pope XVI. *Verbum Domini*. Boston: Pauline Books & Media, 2010.
Berger, Doris L. *The Twisted Cross: The German Christian Movement in the Third Reich*. Chapel Hill: The University of North Carolina Press, 1996.
Berges, Ulrich. "The Violence of God in the Book of Lamentations." Pp. 21–44 in *One Text, a Thousand Methods: Studies in Memory of Sjef van Tilborg*. Edited by P. C. Counet and U. Berges. BIS 71. Leiden: Brill, 2005.
Bergmann, Michael, Michael J. Murphy, and Michael C. Rea, eds. *Divine Evil? The Moral Character of the God of Abraham*. Oxford: Oxford University Press, 2011.
Berlin, Adele. *Lamentations*. OTL. Louisville, KY: Westminster John Knox, 2002.
———. *Poetics and the Interpretation of Biblical Narrative*. Sheffield: Sheffield Academic Press, 1983.
Beyerlin, Walter. *Die Rettung der Bedrängten in den Feindpsalmen der Einzelnen auf institutionelle Zusammenhänge untersucht*. FRLANT 99. Göttingen: Vandenhoeck & Ruprecht, 1970.
Birkeland, Harris. *The Evildoers in the Book of Psalms*. Oslo: Jaco Dybwad, 1955.
———. *Die Feinde des Individuums in der israelitischen Psalmenliteratur*. Oslo: Grøhndahl, 1933.
Block, Daniel I. "All Creatures Great and Small: Recovering a Deuteronomic Theology of Animals." Pp. 174–99 in *The Gospel according to Moses: Theological and Ethical Reflections on the Book of Deuteronomy*. Eugene, OR: Cascade, 2012. Reprint of "All Creatures Great and Small: Recovering a Deuteronomic Theology of Animals." Pp. 283–305 in *The Old Testament in the Life of God's People: Essays in Honor of Elmer A. Martens*. Edited by J. Isaak. Winona Lake, IN: Eisenbrauns, 2009.
———. "Deuteronomic Law." In *The Oxford Encyclopedia of Biblical Law*. Edited by B. Strawn and J. Stackert. Oxford: Oxford University Press, forthcoming.
———. *Deuteronomy*. NIVAC. Grand Rapids: Zondervan, 2012.
———. *The Gods of the Nations: A Study in Ancient Near Eastern National Theology*. 2d ed. Eugene, OR: Wipf & Stock, 2013.
———. "How Many Is God? An Investigation into the Meaning of Deuteronomy 6:4–5." *JETS* 47 (2004): 193–212.
———. "Marriage and Family in Ancient Israel." Pp. 33–102 in *Marriage and Family in the Biblical World*. Edited by K. Campbell. Downers Grove, IL: InterVarsity, 2003.
———. "'No Other Gods': Bearing the Name of Yhwh in a Polytheistic World." Pp. 237–71 in *The Gospel according to Moses: Theological and Ethical Reflections on the Book of Deuteronomy*. Eugene, OR: Cascade, 2012.
———. "The Power of Song: Reflections on Ancient Israel's National Anthem (Deuteronomy 32)." Pp. 162–88 in *How I Love Your Torah, O LORD! Studies in the Book of Deuteronomy*. Eugene, OR: Cascade, 2011.
———. "What Do These Stones Mean? The Riddle of Deuteronomy 27." *JETS* 56 (2013): 17–41.

———. "Worship." Pp. 867–78 in *Dictionary of the Old Testament: Prophets*. Edited by M. J. Boda and J. G. McConville. Downers Grove, IL: IVP Academic, 2012.
Boase, Elizabeth. "The Characterisation of God in Lamentations." *ABR* 56 (2008): 32–44.
———. "Constructing Meaning in the Face of Suffering: Theodicy in Lamentations." *VT* 58 (2008): 449–68.
Boda, Mark J. "The Priceless Gain of Penitence: From Communal Lament to Penitential Prayer in the 'Exilic' Liturgy of Israel." *HBT* 25 (2003): 51–75.
Boecker, Hans J. *Klagelieder*. ZB. Zürich: Theologischer, 1985.
Bottéro, Jean. *Religion in Ancient Mesopotamia*. Translated by T. L. Fagan. Chicago: University of Chicago Press, 2001.
Botterweck, G. Johannes, Helmer Ringgren, and Heinz-Josef Fabry, eds. *Theological Dictionary of the Old Testament*. Translated by J. T. Willis, G. W. Bromiley, and D. E. Green. 15 vols. Grand Rapids: Eerdmans, 1974–2006.
Brenneman, Laura L., and Brad D. Schantz, eds. *Struggles for Shalom: Peace and Violence across the Testaments*. SPS 12. Eugene, OR: Pickwick, 2014.
Brett, Mark G. *Decolonizing God: The Bible in the Tides of Empire*. The Bible in the Modern World 16. Sheffield: Sheffield Phoenix, 2008.
Briggs, Richard S. *The Virtuous Reader: Old Testament Narrative and Interpretive Virtue*. STI. Grand Rapids: Baker Academic, 2010.
Bright, John. *The Authority of the Old Testament*. Nashville: Abingdon, 1967.
Broyles, Craig C. *Psalms*. NIBCOT. Hendrickson: Peabody, 1999.
Brueggemann, Walter. *A Commentary on Jeremiah: Exile and Homecoming*. Grand Rapids: Eerdmans, 1998.
———. *Peace*. UBT. St. Louis: Chalice, 2001.
———. *The Practice of Prophetic Imagination: Preaching an Emancipating Word*. Minneapolis: Fortress, 2012.
———. *The Prophetic Imagination*. 2d ed. Minneapolis: Fortress, 2001.
———. *Theology of the Old Testament: Testimony, Dispute, Advocacy*. Minneapolis: Fortress, 1997.
Budin, Stephanie L. *The Myth of Sacred Prostitution in Antiquity*. Cambridge: Cambridge University Press, 2008.
Burgess, John P. *Why Scripture Matters: Reading the Bible in a Time of Church Conflict*. Louisville, KY: Westminster John Knox, 1998.
Burns, John B. "*Qadesh* and *qedesha*: Did They Live Off Immoral Earnings?" *Proceedings* 15 (1995): 157–68.
Byrd, James P. *Sacred Scripture, Sacred War: The Bible and the American Revolution*. Oxford: Oxford University Press, 2013.
Calvin, John. *Commentaries on the Book of Joshua*. Translated by H. Beveridge. Grand Rapids: Eerdmans, 1949.
Carroll R., M. Daniel. *Amos—The Prophet & His Oracles: Research on the Book of Amos*. Louisville, KY: Westminster John Knox, 2002.
———. "Can the Prophets Shed Light on Our Worship Wars? How Amos Evaluates Religious Ritual." *SCJ* 8 (2005): 215–27.
———. *Contexts for Amos: Prophetic Poetics in Latin American Perspective*. JSOTSup 132. Sheffield: Sheffield Academic Press, 1992.
———. "Ethics and Old Testament Interpretation." Pp. 204–27 in *Hearing the Old Testament: Listening for God's Address*. Edited by C. G. Bartholomew and D. J. H. Beldman. Grand Rapids: Eerdmans, 2012.
———. "'For so you love to do': Probing Popular Religion in the Book of Amos." Pp. 168–89 in *Rethinking Contexts, Rereading Texts: Contributions from the Social Sciences to Biblical Interpretation*. Edited by M. D. Carroll R. JSOTSup 299. Sheffield: Sheffield Academic Press, 2000.
———. "Impulses toward Peace in a Country at War: The Book of Isaiah between Realism and Hope." Pp. 59–78 in *War in the Bible and Terrorism in the Twenty-First Century*.

Edited by R. S. Hess and E. A. Martens. BBRSup 2. Winona Lake, IN: Eisenbrauns, 2008.

———. "Social Science Approaches." Pp. 734–47 in *Dictionary of the Old Testament: Prophets*. Edited by M. J. Boda and J. G. McConville. Downers Grove, IL: InterVarsity, 2012.

Cavanaugh, William T. *The Myth of Religious Violence: Secular Ideology and the Roots of Modern Conflict*. Oxford: Oxford University Press, 2009.

Chapman, Stephen B. "Martial Memory, Peaceable Vision: Divine War in the Old Testament." Pp. 47–67 in *Holy War in the Bible: Christian Morality and an Old Testament Problem*. Edited by H. A. Thomas, J. Evans, and P. Copan. Downers Grove, IL: IVP Academic, 2013.

Childs, Brevard. *Exodus*. OTL. Philadelphia: Westminster, 1974.

Chilton, Bruce. *Abraham's Curse: The Roots of Violence in Judaism, Christianity, and Islam*. New York: Doubleday, 2008.

Chisholm, Robert B. Jr. "Retribution." Pp. 671–76 in *Dictionary of the Old Testament: Prophets*. Edited by M. J. Boda and J. G. McConville. Downers Grove, IL: IVP Academic, 2012.

Clark, Gordon R. *The Word Hesed in the Hebrew Bible*. JSOTSup 157. Sheffield: JSOT Press, 1993.

Claassens, L. Juliana M. *Mourner, Mother, Midwife: Reimagining God's Delivering Presence in the Old Testament*. Louisville, KY: Westminster John Knox, 2013.

Claissé-Walford, Nancy L. de "The Theology of the Imprecatory Psalms." Pp. 77–92 in *Soundings in the Theology of the Psalms: Perspectives and Methods in Contemporary Scholarship*. Edited by R. A. Jacobson. Minneapolis: Fortress, 2011.

Clines, David J. A. "Metacommentating Amos." Pp. 76–93 in *Interested Parties: The Ideology of Writers and Readers of the Hebrew Bible*. JSOTSup 205. Gender, Culture, Theory 1. Sheffield: Sheffield Academic Press, 1995.

Coetzee, J. H. *Die Spanning tussen God se "verborge wees" en Sy "ingrype om te red". 'n Eksegetiese Ondersoek na 'n Aantal Klaagpsalms*. D.D. thesis, University of Pretoria, 1986.

Collins, John J. "The Zeal of Phinehas: The Bible and the Legitimation of Violence." *JBL* 122 (2003): 3–21.

Coote, Robert B. *Amos among the Prophets: Composition and Theology*. Philadelphia: Fortress, 1981.

Copan, Paul. *Is God a Moral Monster? Making Sense of the Old Testament God*. Grand Rapids: Baker, 2010.

Copan, Paul, and Matthew Flannagan. "The Ethics of 'Holy War' for Christian Morality and Theology." Pp. 215–39 in *Holy War in the Bible: Christian Morality and an Old Testament Problem*. Edited by H. A. Thomas, J. Evans, and P. Copan. Downers Grove, IL: IVP Academic, 2013.

Cosgrove, Charles H. "Scripture in Ethics: A History." Pp. 13–25 in *Dictionary of Scripture and Ethics*. Edited by J. B. Green. Grand Rapids: Baker Academic, 2011.

Cowles, C. S., Eugene H. Merrill, Daniel L. Gard, and Tremper Longman III. *Show Them No Mercy: Four Views on God and Canaanite Genocide*. Counterpoints. Grand Rapids: Zondervan, 2003.

Craig, William Lane, and Chad Meister, eds. *God Is Great, God Is Good: Why Belief in God Is Reasonable and Responsible*. Downers Grove, IL: InterVarsity, 2009.

Creach, Jerome F. D. *Violence in Scripture*. Interp. Louisville, KY: Westminster John Knox, 2013.

Crenshaw, James L. *Defending God: Biblical Responses to the Problem of Evil*. Oxford: Oxford University Press, 2005.

———. *A Whirlpool of Torment: Israelite Traditions of God as an Oppressive Presence*. OBT. Philadelphia: Fortress, 1984.

Croatto, J. Severino. *El profeta de la justicia y de la fidelidad (1–39)*. Vol. 1 of *Isaías: La palabra profética y su relectura hermenéutica*. Buenos Aires: La Aurora, 1989.

———. *Isaías: La palabra profética y su relectura hermenéutica*, vol. 2: *La liberación es possible (40–55)*. Buenos Aires: Lumen, 1994.

———. *Imaginar el futuro: Estructura retórica y querigma del Tercer Isaías (Isaías 56–66)*. Buenos Aires: Lumen, 2001.

Cross, Frank Moore. *Canaanite Myth and Hebrew Epic: Essays in the History of the Religion of Israel*. Cambridge: Harvard University Press, 1973.

Crouch, C. L. *War and Ethics in the Ancient Near East: Military Violence in Light of Cosmology and History*. BZAW 407. Berlin: de Gruyter, 2009.

Crowell, Bradley L. "Postcolonial Studies and the Hebrew Bible." *CBR* 7 (2009): 217–44.

Dallaire, Hélène M. "Joshua." Pp. 815–1042 in *The Expositor's Bible Commentary: Numbers–Ruth*. Edited by T. Longman III and D. E. Garland. Vol. 2 of *The Expositor's Bible Commentary*. Edited by T. Longman III and D. E. Garland. Rev. ed. Grand Rapids: Zondervan, 2012.

Dallaire, Hélène, and Denise Morris. "Joshua and Israel's Exodus from the Desert Wilderness." Pp. 18–34 in *Reverberations of the Exodus in Scripture*. Edited by R. M. Fox. Eugene, OR: Pickwick, 2014.

Davies, Andrew. *Double Standards in Isaiah: Re-Evaluating Prophetic Ethics and Divine Justice*. BIS 46. Leiden: Brill, 2000.

Davies, Eryl W. *The Immoral Bible: Approaches to Biblical Ethics*. London: T. & T. Clark, 2010.

Davies, John A. "Theodicy." Pp. 808–17 in *Dictionary of the Old Testament: Wisdom, Poetry & Writings*. Edited by T. Longman III and P. Enns. Downers Grove, IL: IVP Academic, 2008.

Dawkins, Richard. *The God Delusion*. New York: Houghton Mifflin, 2006.

Day, John N. *Crying for Justice: What the Psalms Teach Us about Mercy and Vengeance in an Age of Terrorism*. Grand Rapids: Kregel, 2005.

———. "The Imprecatory Psalms and Christian Ethics." *BSac* 159 (2002): 166–86.

———. "The Imprecatory Psalms and Christian Ethics." Th.D. diss., Dallas Theological Seminary, 2001.

Deijl, Aaroud van der. *Protest or Propaganda: War in the Old Testament Book of Kings and in Contemporaneous Ancient Near Eastern Texts*. SSN 51. Leiden: Brill, 2008.

Del Monte, G. F. "The Hittite *Ḥērem*." Pp. 21–45 in *Memoriae Igor M. Diakonof, Annual of Ancient Near Eastern, Old Testament, and Semitic Studies*. Edited by L. Kogan. BB 2; OC 8. Winona Lake, IN: Eisenbrauns, 2006.

Delekat, Leinhard. *Asylie und Schutzorakel am Zionheiligtum: Eine Untersuchung zu den privaten Feindpsalmen*. Leiden: Brill, 1967.

Dell, Katherine J. "Amos and the Earthquake: Judgment as Natural Disaster." Pp. 1–14 in *Aspects of Amos: Exegesis and Interpretation*. Edited by A. C. Hagedorn and A. Mein. LHB/OTS 536. London: T. & T. Clark, 2011.

Dempsey, Carol J. *Hope amid the Ruins: The Ethics of Israel's Prophets*. St. Louis: Chalice, 2000.

Dempster, Stephen G. *Dominion and Dynasty: A Biblical Theology of the Hebrew Bible*. NSBT 15. Downers Grove, IL: InterVarsity, 2003.

———. "'The LORD Is His Name': A Study of the Distribution of the Names and Titles of God in the Book of Amos." *RB* 98 (1991): 170–89.

Derrida, Jacques. *Of Grammatology*. Translated by G. C. Spivak. Baltimore: Johns Hopkins University Press, 1976.

Dobbs-Allsopp, F. W. *Weep, O Daughter of Zion: A Study of the City-Lament Genre in the Hebrew Bible*. BibOr 44. Rome: Pontifical Biblical Institute, 1993.

———. *Lamentations*. IBC. Louisville, KY: John Knox, 2002.

Douglas, Mark. "Violence." Pp. 809–10 in *Dictionary of Scripture and Ethics*. Edited by J. B. Green. Grand Rapids: Baker Academic, 2011.

Dussel, Enrique. *Las metáforas teológicas de Marx*. Estella: Editorial Verbo Divino, 1993.

Eagleton, Terry. *Reason, Faith, and Revolution: Reflections on the God Debate*. TLS. New Haven: Yale University Press, 2010.

Earl, Douglas S. "Holy War and ḥērem: A Biblical Theology of ḥērem." Pp. 152–78 in *Holy War in the Bible: Christian Morality and the Old Testament Problem*. Edited by H. A. Thomas, J. Evans, and P. Copan. Downers Grove, IL: IVP Academic, 2013.

———. "Joshua and the Crusades." Pp. 19–43 in *Holy War in the Bible: Christian Morality and an Old Testament Problem*. Edited by H. A. Thomas, J. Evans, and P. Copan. Downers Grove, IL: IVP Academic, 2013.

———. *The Joshua Delusion? Rethinking Genocide in the Bible*. Eugene, OR: Cascade, 2010.

———. *Reading Joshua as Christian Scripture*. JTISup 2. Winona Lake, IN: Eisenbrauns, 2010.

Ebel, Jonathan H. *Faith in the Fight: Religion and the American Soldier in the Great War*. Princeton: Princeton University Press, 2010.

Ellacuría, Ignacio. "Utopia and Prophecy in Latin America." Pp. 289–328 in *Mysterium liberationis: Fundamental Concepts of Liberation Theology*. Edited by I. Ellacuría and J. Sobrino. Translated by J. R. Brockman. Maryknoll: Orbis, 1993.

Enns, Peter. *The Bible Tells Me So: Why Defending Scripture Has Made Us Unable to Read It*. New York: HarperOne, 2014.

Eph'al, Israel. *The City Besieged*. CHANE 36. Leiden: Brill, 2009.

Ericksen, Robert P. *Theologians under Hitler: Gerhard Kittel, Paul Althaus and Emanuel Hirsch*. New Haven: Yale University Press, 1985.

Esau, Ken. "Disturbing Scholarly Behavior: Seibert's Solution to the Problem of the Old Testament God." *Direction* 40 (2011): 163–78.

Evans, Jeremy A. *The Problem of Evil: The Challenge to Essential Christian Belief*. Nashville: B&H Academic, 2013.

Exum, J. Cheryl. "The Ethics of Biblical Violence against Women." Pp. 248–71 in *The Bible in Ethics: The Second Sheffield Colloquium*. Edited by J. W. Rogerson, M. D. Carroll R., and M. Davies. JSOTSup 207. Sheffield: Sheffield Academic Press, 1995.

Fales, Evan. "Comments on 'Canon and Conquest.'" Pp. 309–13 in *Divine Evil: The Moral Character of the God of Abraham*. Edited by M. Bergmann, M. J. Murray, and M. C. Rea. Oxford: Oxford University Press, 2013.

Firth, David G. *Surrendering Retribution in the Psalms: Responses to Violence in Individual Complaints*. PBM. Milton Keynes: Paternoster, 2005.

———. "The Teaching of the Psalms." Pp. 159–74 in *Interpreting the Psalms: Issues and Approaches*. Edited by P. S. Johnston and D. G. Firth. Leicester: Apollos, 2005.

Flesher, Paul M., and Bruce Chilton. *The Targums: A Critical Introduction*. Waco: Baylor University Press, 2011.

Franke, John R., ed. *Joshua, Judges, Ruth, 1–2 Samuel*. ACCS 4. Downers Grove, IL: InterVarsity, 2005.

Fretheim, Terence E. "The Character of God in Jeremiah." Pp. 210–23 in *Character and Scripture: Moral Formation, Community, and Biblical Interpretation*. Edited by W. P. Brown. Grand Rapids: Eerdmans, 2002.

———. *Creation Untamed: The Bible, God, and Natural Disasters*. TECC. Grand Rapids: Baker Academic, 2010.

———. "Divine Judgment and the Warming of the World: An Old Testament Perspective." Pp. 21–32 in *God, Evil, and Suffering: Essays in Honor of Paul R. Sponheim*. Edited by T. E. Fretheim and C. L. Thompson. WWSup 4. St. Louis: Luther Seminary, 2000.

———. "God and Violence in the Old Testament." *WW* 24 (2004): 18–28.

———. *God and World in the Old Testament: A Relational Theology of Creation*. Nashville: Abingdon, 2005.

———. "'I was only a little angry': Divine Violence in the Prophets." *Interp* 58 (2004): 365–75.

———. *Jeremiah*. SHBC. Macon: Smyth & Helwys, 2002.

———. *Reading Hosea–Micah: A Literary and Theological Commentary*. Macon: Smyth & Helwys, 2013.

———. "Some Reflections on Brueggemann's God." Pp. 24–37 in *God in the Fray: A Tribute to Walter Brueggemann*. Edited by T. Linafelt and T. K. Beal. Minneapolis: Fortress, 1998.

———. *The Suffering of God: An Old Testament Perspective*. OBT. Minneapolis: Fortress, 1984.

———. "Theological Reflections on the Wrath of God in the Old Testament." *HBT* 24 (2002): 1–26.

Fretheim, Terence E., and Karlfried Froehlich. *The Bible as Word of God in a Postmodern Age*. Minneapolis: Fortress, 1998.

Fretz, Mark. "*Herem* in the Old Testament." Pp. 7–44 in *Essays on War and Peace: Bible and Early Church*. Edited by W. M. Swartley. OP 9. Elkhart: Institute of Mennonite Studies, 1986.

Friedman, Richard Elliott. *The Bible with Sources Revealed: A New View into the Five Books of Moses*. San Francisco: HarperOne, 2003.

Gangloff, Frédéric. "Joshua 6: Holy War or Extermination by Divine Command (*Herem*)?" *TRev* 25 (2004): 3–23.

Gaposchkin, M. C. "Louis IX, Crusade and the Promise of Joshua in the Holy Land." *Journal of Medieval History* 34 (2008): 245–74.

Girard, René. *Violence and the Sacred*. Translated by P. Gregory. Baltimore: The Johns Hopkins University Press, 1997.

Goldingay, John. *Israel's Faith*. Vol. 2 of *Old Testament Theology*. Downers Grove, IL: InterVarsity, 2006.

———. *Models for Scripture*. Grand Rapids: Eerdmans, 1994.

———. *Psalms 1–41*. Vol. 1 of *Psalms*. BCOTWP. Grand Rapids: Baker Academic, 2006.

———. *Psalms 42–89*. Vol. 2 of *Psalms*. BCOTWP. Grand Rapids: Baker Academic, 2007.

Gossai, Hemchand. *The Hebrew Prophets after the Shoah: A Mandate for Change*. Eugene, OR: Pickwick, 2014.

Gottwald, Norman K. *Studies in the Book of Lamentations*. SBT 14. London: SCM Press, 1962.

———. *The Tribes of Yahweh*. Maryknoll: Orbis, 1979.

Gray, Mark. *Rhetoric and Social Justice in Isaiah*. LHB/OTS 432. London: T. & T. Clark, 2006.

Green, D. H. *The Millstätter Exodus: A Crusading Epic*. Cambridge: Cambridge University Press, 1966.

Green, Joel B. *Practicing Theological Interpretation: Engaging Biblical Texts for Faith and Formation*. TECC. Grand Rapids: Baker Academic, 2012.

Greenberg, Moshe. "On the Political Use of the Bible in Modern Israel: An Engaged Critique." Pp. 461–71 in *Pomegranates and Golden Bells: Studies in Biblical, Jewish, and Near Eastern Ritual, Law, and Literature in Honor of Jacob Milgrom*. Edited by D. P. Wright, D. N. Freedman, and A. Hurvitz. Winona Lake, IN: Eisenbrauns, 1995.

Gunkel, Herman. *The Psalms: A Form Critical Introduction*. Philadelphia: Fortress, 1967.

Gunn, David M., and Danna Nolan Fewell. *Narrative in the Hebrew Bible*. OBS. Oxford: Oxford University Press, 1993.

Gutiérrez, Gustavo. *On Job: God-Talk and the Suffering of the Innocent*. Translated by M. J. O'Connell. Maryknoll: Orbis, 1987.

Hackett, JoAnn. "Can a Sexist Model Liberate Us? Ancient Near Eastern 'Fertility' Goddesses." *JFSR* 5 (1989): 65–76.

Hamborg, Graham R. *Still Selling the Righteous: A Redaction-Critical Investigation of Reasons for Judgment in Amos 2:5–16*. LHB/OTS 555. London: T. & T. Clark, 2012.

Hanks, Thomas D. *God So Loved the Third World: The Biblical Vocabulary of Oppression*. Translated by J. Dekker. Maryknoll: Orbis, 1983.

Hasel, Gerhard F. *The Remnant: The History and Theology of the Remnant Idea from Genesis to Isaiah*. 3d ed. Andrews University Monograph Studies in Religion 5. Berrien Springs: Andrews University Press, 1980.
Hasel, Michael G. *Military Practice and Polemic: Israel's Laws of Warfare in Near Eastern Perspective*. Berrien Springs: Andrews University Press, 2005.
Harnack, Adolf von. *Marcion: The Gospel of the Alien God*. Translated by J. E. Steely and L. D. Bierma. 1924. Repr., Durham: Labyrinth, 1990.
Hawk, L. Daniel. *Joshua*. Berit Olam. Collegeville: Liturgical Press, 2000.
Hawkins, Ralph K. *How Israel Became a People*. Nashville: Abingdon, 2013.
Hays, Christopher B. *Death in the Iron Age II and in First Isaiah*. FAT 79. Tübingen: Mohr Siebeck, 2011.
Hays, Richard B. *The Moral Vision of the New Testament: Community, Cross, New Creation: A Contemporary Introduction to New Testament Ethics*. San Francisco: Harper, 1996.
Hayes, Michael A., and David Tombs. *Truth and Memory: The Church and Human Rights in El Salvador and Guatemala*. Leominster: Gracewing, 2001.
Hedges, Chris. *War Is a Force that Gives Us Meaning*. New York: Anchor, 2002.
Heimbach, Daniel R. "Crusade in the Old Testament and Today." Pp. 179–200 in *Holy War in the Bible: Christian Morality and an Old Testament Problem*. Edited by H. A. Thomas, J. Evans, and P. Copan. Downers Grove, IL: IVP Academic, 2013.
Heschel, Abraham J. *The Prophets*. New York: Harper & Row, 1962. Repr., New York: Perennial Classics, 2001.
Heschel, Susannah. *The Aryan Jesus: Christian Theologians and the Bible in Nazi Germany*. Princeton: Princeton University Press, 2008.
Hess, Richard S. "'Because of the Wickedness of These Nations' (Deut 9:4–5): The Canaanites—Ethical or Not?" Pp. 17–37 in *For Our Good Always: Studies on the Message and Influence of Deuteronomy in Honor of Daniel I. Block*. Edited by J. S. DeRouchie, J. Gile, and K. J. Turner. Winona Lake, IN: Eisenbrauns, 2013.
_____. *Israelite Religions: An Archaeological and Biblical Survey*. Grand Rapids: Baker Academic, 2007.
_____. "War in the Hebrew Bible: An Overview." Pp. 19–32 in *War in the Bible and Terrorism in the Twenty-First Century*. Edited by R. S. Hess and E. A. Martens. BBRSup 2. Winona Lake, IN: Eisenbrauns, 2008.
Hess, Richard S., and Elmer A. Martens, eds. *War in the Bible and Terrorism in the Twenty-First Century*. BBRSup 2. Winona Lake, IN: Eisenbrauns, 2008.
Hillers, Delbert R. "Analyzing the Abominable: Our Understanding of Canaanite Religion." *JQR* 75 (1985): 253–69.
Hobbs, T. Raymond. *A Time of War: A Study of Warfare in the Old Testament*. Wilmington: Michael Glazer, 1989.
Hoffmeier, James K. "Some Egyptian Motifs Related to Warfare and Enemies and their Old Testament Counterparts." Pp. 53–70 in *Egyptological Miscellanies: A Tribute to Professor Ronald J. Williams*. Edited by J. K. Hoffmeier and E. S. Meltzer. AW 6. Chicago: Ares, 1983.
Hogan, Gary A., and Victor Boutros. *The Locust Effect: Why the End of Poverty Requires the End of Violence*. New York: Oxford University Press, 2014.
Holladay, William L. *Jeremiah 1: A Commentary on the Book of the Prophet Jeremiah, Chapters 1–25*. Edited by P. D. Hanson. Hermeneia. Philadelphia: Fortress, 1986.
_____. *Jeremiah 2: A Commentary on the Book of the Prophet Jeremiah, Chapters 26–52*. Edited by P. D. Hanson. Hermeneia. Minneapolis: Fortress, 1989.
Hossfeld, Frank-Lothar, and Erich Zenger. *Psalms 2: A Commentary on Psalms 51–100*. Edited by K. Baltzer. Translated by L. M. Maloney. Hermeneia. Minneapolis: Fortress, 2005.
_____. *Psalms 3: A Commentary on Psalms 101–150*. Edited by K. Baltzer. Translated by L. M. Maloney. Hermeneia. Minneapolis: Fortress, 2011.

Houston, Walter J. *Contending for Justice: Ideologies and Theologies of Social Justice in the Old Testament*. Rev. ed. London: T. & T. Clark, 2008.
Ilany, Ofri. "From Divine Commandment to Political Act: The Eighteenth-Century Polemic on the Extermination of the Canaanites." *Journal of the History of Ideas* 73 (2012): 437–61.
Isaak, Jon, ed. *The Old Testament in the Life of God's People: Essays in Honor of Elmer A. Martens*. Winona Lake, IN: Eisenbrauns, 2009.
Jacobs, Alan. *A Theology of Reading: The Hermeneutics of Love*. Boulder: Westview, 2001.
Janzen, Waldemar. "Teaching the Old Testament: The 'Problem' of the Old Testament Revisited." *Direction* 40 (2011): 179–97.
Jenkins, Philip. *The Great and Holy War: How World War I Became a Religious Crusade*. New York: HarperOne, 2014.
———. *Laying Down the Sword: Why We Can't Ignore the Bible's Violent Verses*. New York: HarperOne, 2011.
Josephus. *Jewish Antiquities*. Translated by H. St. J. Thackeray et al. 6 vols. Cambridge: Harvard University Press, 1930–69.
———. *The Jewish War*. Translated by H. St. J. Thackeray. 2 vols. Cambridge: Harvard University Press, 1956–57.
Juergensmeyer, Mark, and Margo Kitts, eds. *Princeton Readings in Religion and Violence*. Princeton: Princeton University Press, 2011.
Junger, Sebastian. *War*. New York: Twelve, 2010.
Kairos Theologians. *The Kairos Document: Challenge to the Church: A Theological Comment on the Political Crisis in South Africa*. 2d ed. Grand Rapids: Eerdmans, 1986.
Kaminsky, Joel S. "Joshua 7: A Reassessment of the Israelite Conceptions of Corporate Punishment." Pp. 315–46 in *The Pitcher is Broken: Memorial Essays for Gösta W. Ahlström*. Edited by S. W. Holloway and L. K. Handy. JSOTSup 190. Sheffield: Sheffield Academic Press, 1995.
Kang, Sa-Moon. *Divine War in the Old Testament and in the Ancient Near East*. BZAW 177. Berlin: de Gruyter, 1989.
Kant, Immanuel. *Religion and Rational Theology: The Conflict of the Faculties 7:63* Edited and translated by A. W. Wood and G. di Giovanni. Cambridge: Cambridge University Press, 1996.
Kauffman, Yehezkel. *The Religion of Israel*. Translated by M. Greenberg. New York: Shocken, 1972.
Kelle, Brad E., and Frank Ritchel Ames, eds. *Writing and Reading War: Rhetoric, Gender, and Ethics in Biblical and Modern Contexts*. SBLSymS 42. Atlanta: Society of Biblical Literature, 2008.
Kellner, Menachem. "And Yet, the Texts Remain: The Problem of the Command to Destroy the Canaanites." Pp. 153–79 in *The Gift of Land and the Fate of the Canaanites in Jewish Thought*. Edited by K. Berthelot, J. E. David, and M. Hirshman. Oxford: Oxford University Press, 2014.
Kierkegaard, Søren. *Fear and Trembling*. Garden City: Doubleday Anchor, 1954.
Klingbeil, Martin G. *Yahweh Fighting from Heaven: God as Warrior and as God of Heaven in the Hebrew Psalter and Ancient Near Eastern Iconography*. OBO 169. Göttingen: Vandenhoeck & Ruprecht, 1999.
Kreider, Alan, Eleanor Kreider, and Paulus Widjaja. *A Culture of Peace: God's Vision for the Church*. Intercourse: Good Books, 2005.
Kuan, Kah-Jin Jeffrey. "Biblical Interpretation and the Rhetoric of Violence and War." *AJT* 23 (2009): 189–203.
Laato, Antti, and Johannes C. de Moor. "Introduction." Pp. xxx–xxxviii in *Theodicy in the World of the Bible*. Edited by A. Laato and J. C. de Moor. Leiden: Brill, 2003.
Laato, Antti, and Johannes C. de Moor, eds. *Theodicy in the World of the Bible*. Leiden: Brill, 2003.

Labahn, Antje. "Fire from Above: Metaphors and Images of God's Actions in Lamentations 2.1–9." *JSOT* 31 (2006): 239–56.

Lalleman, Hetty. *Jeremiah and Lamentations*. TOTC 21. Downers Grove, IL: InterVarsity, 2013.

Lamb, David T. "Wrath." Pp. 878–83 in *Dictionary of the Old Testament: Prophets*. Edited by M. J. Boda and J. G. McConville. Downers: Grove: IVP Academic, 2012.

⸺. *God Behaving Badly: Is the God of the Old Testament Angry, Sexist and Racist?* Downers Grove, IL: InterVarsity, 2011.

Laney, J. Carl. "A Fresh Look at the Imprecatory Psalms." *BSac* 138 (1981): 35–45.

Lasine, Stuart. "Fiction, Falsehood, and Reality in Hebrew Scripture." *HS* 25 (1984): 24–40.

Lee, Nancy C. *The Singers of Lamentations: Cities Under Siege, From Ur to Jerusalem to Sarajevo*. BIS 60. Leiden: Brill, 2002.

Leiter, David A. *Neglected Voices: Peace in the Old Testament*. Scottdale: Herald, 2007.

LeMon, Joel M. "Saying Amen to Violent Psalms: Patterns of Prayer, Belief, and Action in the Psalter." Pp. 93–110 in *Soundings in the Theology of the Psalms: Perspectives and Methods in Contemporary Scholarship*. Edited by R. A. Jacobson. Minneapolis: Fortress, 2011.

Lessing, R. Reed. *Amos*. CC. St. Louis: Concordia, 2009.

Levenson, Jon. *Inheriting Abraham: The Legacy of the Patriarch in Judaism, Christianity, and Islam*. Princeton: Princeton University Press, 2012.

Lewis, C. S. *The Problem of Pain*. New York: Macmillan, 1944.

Lindström, Fredrik. *God and the Origin of Evil: A Contextual Analysis of Alleged Monistic Evidence in the Old Testament*. CBOTS 21. Lund: CWK Gleerup, 1983.

Linville, James R. *Amos and the Cosmic Imagination*. SOTSMS. Aldershot: Ashgate, 2008.

Lipinski, Edward. "Cult Prostitution in Ancient Israel." *BAR* 40 (January/February 2014): 48–56, 70.

Longman, Tremper III, and Daniel G. Reid. *God Is a Warrior*. SOTBT. Grand Rapids: Zondervan, 1995.

Luc, Alex. "Interpreting the Curses in the Psalms." *JETS* 42 (1999): 395–410.

Lyons, W. L. *A History of Modern Scholarship on the Biblical Word Herem: The Contributions of Walter C. Kaiser, Jr., Peter C. Craigie, and Tremper Longman, III*. Lewiston: Mellen, 2010.

MacDonald, Nathan. *Deuteronomy and the Meaning of Monotheism*. FAT 2/1. Tübingen: Mohr Siebeck, 2003.

Markham, Ian. *Against Atheism: Why Dawkins, Hitchens, and Harris are Fundamentally Wrong*. West Sussex: Wiley-Blackwell, 2010.

Martens, Elmer A. *Jeremiah*. BCBC. Scottdale: Herald, 1986.

⸺. "Jeremiah." Pp. 293–553 in *Isaiah–Lamentations*, by Larry L. Walker and Elmer A. Martens. CBC 8. Wheaton: Tyndale House, 2005.

⸺. "Motivations for the Promise of Israel's Restoration to the Land in Jeremiah and Ezekiel." Ph.D. diss., The Claremont Graduate School, 1972.

⸺. "Toward Shalom: Absorbing the Violence." Pp. 33–58 in *War in the Bible and Terrorism in the Twenty-First Century*. Edited by R. S. Hess and E. A. Martens. BBRSup 2. Winona Lake, IN: Eisenbrauns, 2008.

Martin-Achard, Robert, and S. Paul Re'emi. *God's People in Crisis: Amos and Lamentations*. ITC. Grand Rapids: Eerdmans, 1984.

Matties, Gordon. "The Word Made Bitter: At the Table with Joshua, Buber, and Bakhtin." Pp. 307–32 in *The Old Testament in the Life of God's People: Essays in Honor of Elmer A. Martens*. Edited by J. Isaak. Winona Lake, IN: Eisenbrauns, 2009.

McCann, J. Clinton Jr. "The Book of Psalms." Pp. 639–1280 in *1 & 2 Maccabees, Introduction to Hebrew Poetry, Job, and Psalms*. Edited by L. E. Keck. Vol. 4 of The *New Interpreter's*

Bible: Commentary in Twelve Volumes. Edited by L. E. Keck. Nashville: Abingdon, 1996.

―――. *A Theological Introduction to the Book of Psalms: The Psalms as Torah.* Nashville: Abingdon, 1993.

McConville, J. G. *Deuteronomy.* AOTC 5. Downers Grove, IL: InterVarsity, 2002.

McDonald, Patricia M. *God and Violence: Biblical Resources for Living in a Small World.* Scottdale: Herald, 2004.

McEntire, Mark. *The Blood of Abel: The Violent Plot in the Hebrew Bible.* Macon: Mercer University Press, 1999.

―――. *Portraits of a Mature God: Choices in Old Testament Theology.* Minneapolis: Fortress, 2013.

McKenzie, Steven L. *Covenant.* UBT. St. Louis: Chalice, 2000.

McNamara, Martin. *Targum Neofiti 1: Genesis.* The Aramaic Bible 1A. Collegeville: Liturgical, 1992.

Meister, Chad. "God, Evil and Morality." Pp. 107–18 in *God Is Great, God Is Good: Why Belief in God Is Reasonable and Responsible.* Edited by W. L. Craig and C. Meister. Downers Grove, IL: InterVarsity, 2009.

Merrick, J., and Stephen M. Garrett, eds. *Five Views on Biblical Inerrancy.* Counterpoints. Grand Rapids: Zondervan, 2013.

Merrill, Eugene H. "The Case for Moderate Discontinuity." Pp. 61–94 in *Show Them No Mercy: Four Views on God and Canaanite Genocide,* by C. S. Cowles et al. Counterpoints. Grand Rapids: Eerdmans, 2003.

Mesters, Carlos. *El profeta Jeremías: Boca de Dios, boca del pueblo.* Translated by J. Gómez. Bogotá: San Pablo, 1994.

Miller, Patrick D. Jr. *The Divine Warrior in Early Israel.* HSM 5. Cambridge: Harvard University Press, 1973.

―――. "Fire in the Mythology of Canaan and Israel." *CBQ* 27 (1965): 256–61.

Mintz, Alan. *Hurban: Responses to Catastrophe in Hebrew Literature.* JTLMA. Syracuse: Syracuse University Press, 1996.

Miranda, José Porfirio. *Marx and the Bible: A Critique of the Philosophy of Oppression.* Translated by J. Eagleson. Maryknoll: Orbis, 1974.

Moberly, R. W. L. "Is Monotheism Bad for You? Some Reflections on God, the Bible, and Life in the Light of Regina Schwartz's *The Curse of Cain.*" Pp. 94–112 in *The God of Israel.* Edited by R. P. Gordon. UCOP 64. Cambridge: Cambridge University Press, 2007.

―――. *Old Testament Theology: Reading the Hebrew Bible as Christian Scripture.* Grand Rapids: Baker Academic, 2013.

―――. "Toward an Interpretation of the Shema." Pp. 124–44 in *Theological Exegesis: Essays in Honor of Brevard S. Childs.* Edited by C. Seitz and K. Greene-McCreight. Grand Rapids: Eerdmans, 1999.

Moll, Sebastian. *The Arch-Heretic Marcion.* WUNT 250. Tübingen: Mohr Siebeck, 2010.

Möller, Karl A. *A Prophet in Debate: The Rhetoric of Persuasion in the Book of Amos.* JSOTSup 372. Sheffield: Sheffield Academic Press, 2003.

Moltmann, Jürgen. *The Crucified God: The Cross of Christ as the Foundation and Criticism of Christian Theology.* Translated by R. A. Wilson and J. Bowden. Minneapolis: Fortress, 1993.

Monroe, Lauren A. D. "Israelite, Moabite and Sabaean War-ḥērem Traditions and the Forging of National Identity: Reconsidering the Sabaean Text RES 3945 in Light of Biblical and Moabite Evidence." *VT* 57 (2007): 318–41.

Mowinckel, Sigmund. *The Psalms in Israel's Worship.* Oxford: Basil Blackwell, 1962.

Nelson, Richard D. *The Historical Books.* IBT. Nashville: Abingdon, 1998.

―――. *Joshua: A Commentary.* OTL. Louisville, KY: Westminster John Knox, 1997.

―――. "Josiah in the Book of Joshua." *JBL* 100 (1981): 531–40.

Neufeld, Thomas R. Yoder. *Killing Enmity: Violence and the New Testament*. Grand Rapids: Baker Academic, 2011.
Niditch, Susan. *War in the Hebrew Bible: A Study in the Ethics of Violence*. New York: Oxford University Press, 1993.
Noll, K. L. "Is There a Text in this Tradition? Readers' Response and the Taming of Samuel's God." *JSOT* 24 (1999): 31–51.
Noll, Mark A. *America's God: From Jonathan Edwards to Abraham Lincoln*. Oxford: Oxford University Press, 2002.
———. *The Civil War as a Theological Crisis*. Chapel Hill: The University of North Carolina Press, 2006.
O'Brien, Julia M. *Challenging Prophetic Metaphor: Theology and Ideology in the Prophets*. Louisville, KY: Westminster John Knox, 2008.
O'Connor, Kathleen M. "The Book of Jeremiah: Reconstructing Community after Disaster." Pp. 81–92 in *Character Ethics and the Old Testament: Moral Dimensions of Scripture*. Edited by M. D. Carroll R. and J. E. Lapsley. Louisville, KY: Westminster John Knox, 2007.
———. *Jeremiah: Pain and Promise*. Minneapolis: Fortress, 2012.
———. "Reclaiming Jeremiah's Violence." Pp. 37–49 in *The Aesthetics of Violence in the Prophets*. Edited by J. M. O'Brien and C. Franke. LHB/OTS 517. New York: T. & T. Clark, 2010.
———. "The Tears of God and Divine Character in Jeremiah 2–9." Pp. 172–85 in *God in the Fray: A Tribute to Walter Brueggemann*. Edited by T. Linafelt and T. K. Beal. Minneapolis: Fortress, 1998.
Ogden, D. K. "The Earthquake Motif in the Book of Amos." Pp. 69–80 in *Goldene Äpfel in silbernen Schalen: Collected Communications to the XIIIth Congress of the International Organization for the Study of the Old Testament, Leuven 1989*. Edited by K.-D. Schunck and M. Augustin. BEATAJ 20. Frankfurt am Main: Peter Lang, 1992.
Origen. *Homilies on Joshua*. Edited by C. White. Translated by B. J. Bruce. FC 105. Washington: The Catholic University of America Press, 2002.
Paas, Stefan. *Creation and Judgment: Creation Texts in Some Eighth Century Prophets*. OTS 47. Leiden: Brill, 2003.
Pardee, Dennis. "Canaanite Dialects." Pp. 103–7 in *The Ancient Languages of Syria-Palestine and Arabia*. Edited by R. D. Woodard. Cambridge: Cambridge University Press, 2008.
Patrick, Dale. *Redeeming Judgment*. Eugene, OR: Pickwick, 2012.
———. *Sin and Judgment in the Prophets: A Stylistic and Theological Analysis*. SBLMS 27. Chico: Scholars Press, 1982.
Paul, Shalom M. *Amos: A Commentary on the Book of Amos*. Hermeneia. Minneapolis: Fortress, 1991.
Peels, Eric. *Shadow Sides: God in the Old Testament*. Carlisle: Paternoster, 2003.
Peters, Benjamin John. *Through All the Plain*. Eugene, OR: Cascade, 2014.
Philo. Translated by F. H. Colson et al. 10 vols. Loeb Classical Library. Cambridge: Harvard University Press, 1949–71.
Pixley, Jorge. *Jeremiah*. Chalice Commentaries for Today. St. Louis: Chalice, 2004.
Plotz, David. *Good Book: The Bizarre, Hilarious, Disturbing, Marvelous, and Inspiring Things I Learned When I Read Every Single Word of the Bible*. New York: Harper, 2009.
Preuss, Horst Dietrich. *Old Testament Theology*. Vol. 1. Translated by L. G. Perdue. OTL. Louisville, KY: Westminster John Knox, 1995.
Prior, John Mansford. "'Power' and 'the Other' in *Joshua*: The Brutal Birthing of a Group Identity." *Mission Studies* 23 (2006): 27–43.
Prior, Michael. *The Bible and Colonialism: A Moral Critique*. The Biblical Seminar 48. Sheffield: Sheffield Academic Press, 1997.
Provan, Ian. *Seriously Dangerous Religion: What the Old Testament Really Says and Why It Matters*. Waco: Baylor University Press, 2014.

Ramage, Matthew J. *Dark Passages of the Bible: Engaging Scripture with Benedict XVI and Thomas Aquinas*. Washington: Catholic University of America Press, 2013.
Ray, Larry. *Violence and Society*. London: Sage, 2011.
Reimer, Harold. *Richtet auf des Recht! Studien zur Botschaft des Amos*. SBS 149. Stuttgart: Katholisches Bibelwerk, 1992.
Rivas, Pedro Jaramillo. *La injusticia y la opresión en el lenguaje figurativo de los profetas*. Institución San Jerónimo 26. Navarra: Verbo Divino, 1992.
Rodd, Cyril S. *Glimpses of a Strange Land: Studies in Old Testament Ethics*. OTS. Edinburgh: T. & T. Clark, 2001.
Rogerson, J. W. *According to the Scriptures? The Challenge of Using the Bible in Social, Moral and Political Questions*. BCCW. London: Equinox, 2007.
Römer, Thomas. *Dark God: Cruelty, Sex, and Violence in the Old Testament*. Translated by S. O'Neill. New York: Paulist, 2013.
———. "Joshua's Encounter with the Commander of Yhwh's Army (Josh 5:13–15): Literary Construction or Reflection or a Royal Ritual?" Pp. 49–64 in *Warfare, Ritual, and Symbol in Biblical and Modern Contexts*. Edited by B. E. Kelle, F. R. Ames, and J. L. Wright. Ancient Israel and Its Literature 18. Atlanta: Society of Biblical Literature, 2014.
Rosen-Zvi, Ishay. "Reading *ḥerem*: Destruction of Idolatry in Tannaitic Literature." Pp. 50–65 in *The Gift of Land and the Fate of the Canaanites in Jewish Thought*. Edited by K. Berthelot, J. E. David, and M. Hirshman. Oxford: Oxford University Press, 2014.
Ross, Allen P. *Psalms 1–41*. Vol. 1 of *A Commentary on the Psalms*. KEL. Grand Rapids: Kregel, 2011.
———. *Psalms 42–89*. Vol. 2 of *A Commentary on the Psalms*. KEL. Grand Rapids: Kregel, 2013.
Roth, John K. "Deliver Us from Evil? Kuhn's Prayer and the Masters of Death." Pp. 243–57 in *Fire in the Ashes: God, Evil, and the Holocaust*. Edited by D. Patterson and J. K. Roth. Seattle: University of Washington Press, 2005.
Rowlett, Lori L. "Inclusion, Exclusion and Marginality in the Book of Joshua." *JSOT* 55 (1992): 15–23.
———. *Joshua and the Rhetoric of Violence: A New Historicist Analysis*. JSOTSup 226. Sheffield: Sheffield Academic Press, 1996.
Sandy, D. Brent. *Plowshares & Pruning Hooks: Rethinking the Language of Biblical Prophecy and Apocalyptic*. Downers Grove, IL: InterVarsity, 2002.
Satterthwaite, Philip. E., and David W. Baker. "Nations of Canaan." Pp. 596–605 in *Dictionary of the Old Testament: Pentateuch*. Edited by T. D. Alexander and D. W. Baker. Downers Grove, IL: IVP Academic, 2003.
Schlimm, Matthew R. "Different Perspectives on Divine Pathos: An Examination of Hermeneutics in Biblical Theology." *CBQ* 69 (2007): 673–94.
———. *From Fratricide to Forgiveness: The Language and Ethics of Anger in Genesis*. Siphrut 7. Winona Lake, IN: Eisenbrauns, 2011.
———. *This Strange and Sacred Scripture: Wrestling with the Old Testament and Its Oddities*. Grand Rapids: Baker Academic, forthcoming.
Schmidt, H. H. *Das Gebet der Angeklagten im Alten Testament*. Giessen: Alfred Töpelmann, 1928.
Schwartz, Regina M. *The Curse of Cain: The Violent Legacy of Monotheism*. Chicago: University of Chicago Press, 1997.
Seevers, Boyd. *Warfare in the Old Testament: The Organization, Weapons, and Tactics of Ancient Near Eastern Armies*. Grand Rapids: Kregel, 2013.
Seibert, Eric A. *Disturbing Divine Behavior: Troubling Old Testament Images of God*. Minneapolis: Fortress, 2009.
———. *The Violence of Scripture: Overcoming the Old Testament's Troubling Legacy*. Minneapolis: Fortress, 2012.

Seitz, Christopher. "Canon and Conquest: The Character of the God of the Hebrew Bible." Pp. 292–308 in *Divine Evil: The Moral Character of the God of Abraham*. Edited by M. Bergmann, M. J. Murray, and M. C. Rea. Oxford: Oxford University Press, 2013.
———. "Old Testament or Hebrew Bible? Some Theological Considerations." Pp. 61–74 in *Word without End: The Old Testament as Abiding Witness*. Grand Rapids: Eerdmans, 1998.
———. *Word without End: The Old Testament as Abiding Theological Witness*. Grand Rapids: Eerdmans, 1998.
Seybold, Klaus. "The Psalter as a Book." Pp. 168–81 in *Jewish and Christian Approaches to the Psalms: Conflict and Convergence*. Edited by S. Gillingham. Oxford: Oxford University Press, 2013.
Shead, Andrew G. *A Mouth Full of Fire: The Word of God in Jeremiah*. NSBT 29. Downers Grove, IL: InterVarsity, 2012.
Sherwood, Yvonne. "Binding-Unbinding: Divided Responses of Judaism, Christianity, and Islam to the 'Sacrifice' of Abraham's Beloved Son." *JAAR* 72 (2004): 821–61.
———. "Emily Arndt: A Tribute." Pp. ix–xi in *Demanding Our Attention: The Hebrew Bible as a Source for Christian Ethics*, by Emily Arndt. Grand Rapids: Eerdmans, 2011.
Sparks, Kenton L. *Sacred Word, Broken Word: Biblical Authority and the Dark Side of Scripture*. Grand Rapids: Eerdmans, 2012.
Spieckermann, Hermann. "Barmherzig und gnädig ist der Herr . . ." *ZAW* 102 (1990): 1–18.
Stassen, Glen Harold. "The Prophets' Call for Peacemaking Practices." Pp. 240–64 in *Holy War in the Bible: Christian Morality and an Old Testament Problem*. Edited by H. A. Thomas, J. Evans, and P. Copan. Downers Grove, IL: IVP Academic, 2013.
Stassen, Glen Harold, ed. *Just Peacemaking: Ten Practices for Abolishing War*. Cleveland: Pilgrim, 1998.
Stern, Philip D. *The Biblical Herem: A Window on Israel's Religious Experience*. BJS 211. Atlanta: Scholars Press, 1991.
Stewart, Robert. "'Holy War,' Divine Action and the New Atheism: Philosophical Considerations." Pp. 265–84 in *Holy War in the Bible: Christian Morality and an Old Testament Problem*. Edited by H. A. Thomas, J. Evans, and P. Copan. Downers Grove, IL: IVP Academic, 2013.
Stulman, Louis, and Hyun Chul Paul Kim. *You Are My People: An Introduction to Prophetic Literature*. Nashville: Abingdon, 2010.
Suderman, W. Derek. "Wrestling with Violent Actions of God: A Response to Eric Seibert's *Disturbing Divine Behavior*." *Direction* 40 (2011): 151–62.
Sugirtharajah, R. S. *The Bible and the Third World: Precolonial, Colonial and Postcolonial Encounters*. Cambridge: Cambridge University Press, 2001.
Swartley, Willard M. *Covenant of Peace: The Missing Piece in New Testament Theology and Ethics*. SPS 9. Grand Rapids: Eerdmans, 2006.
Sweeney, Marvin A. *Reading the Hebrew Bible after the Shoah*. Minneapolis: Fortress, 2008.
———. *TANAK: A Theological and Critical Introduction to the Hebrew Bible*. Minneapolis: Fortress, 2012.
Swenson, Kristin M. *Living through Pain: Psalms and the Search for Wholeness*. Waco: Baylor University Press, 2005.
Tamez, Elsa. *Bible of the Oppressed*. Maryknoll: Orbis, 1982.
Templer, Bill. "The Political Sacralization of Imperial Genocide: Contextualizing Timothy Dwight's *The Conquest of Canaan*." *Postcolonial Studies* 9 (2006): 358–91.
Tertullian. *Adversus Marcionem*. Edited and translated by E. Evans. Oxford: Clarendon, 1972.
Thelle, Rannfrid I. "The Biblical Conquest Account and Its Modern Hermeneutical Challenges." *Studia theologica* 61 (2007): 61–81.

Thomas, Heath A. "Hearing the Minor Prophets: The Book of the Twelve and God's Address." Pp. 356–79 in *Hearing the Old Testament: Listening for God's Address*. Edited by C. G. Bartholomew and D. J. H. Beldman. Grand Rapids: Eerdmans, 2012.

———. "The Liturgical Function of the Book of Lamentations." Pp. 137–47 in *Thinking towards New Horizons: Collected Communications to the XIXth Congress of the International Organization for the Study of the Old Testament, Ljubljana 2007*. Edited by M. Augustin and H. M. Niemann. BEATAJ 55. Frankfurt am Main: Peter Lang, 2008.

———. "The Meaning of *zōlēlâ* (Lam 1:11) One More Time." *VT* 61 (2011): 489–98.

———. "A Neglected Witness to 'Holy War' in the Writings." Pp. 68–83 in *Holy War in the Bible: Christian Morality and an Old Testament Problem*. Edited by H. A. Thomas, J. Evans, and P. Copan. Downers Grove, IL: IVP Academic, 2013.

———. *Poetry and Theology in the Book of Lamentations: The Aesthetics of an Open Text*. HBM 47. Sheffield: Sheffield Phoenix, 2013.

———. "Relating Prayer and Pain: Psychological Analysis and Lamentations Research." *TynBul* 61 (2010): 183–208.

———. "Suffering." Pp. 757–66 in *Dictionary of the Old Testament: Prophets*. Edited by M. J. Boda and J. G. McConville. Downers Grove, IL: IVP Academic, 2012.

Thomas, Heath A., Jeremy Evans, and Paul Copan, eds. *Holy War in the Bible: Christian Morality and an Old Testament Problem*. Downers Grove, IL: IVP Academic, 2013.

Thompson, J. A. *The Book of Jeremiah*. NICOT. Grand Rapids: Eerdmans, 1980.

Toorn, K. van der. "Ordeal Procedures in the Psalms and the Passover Meal." *VT* 38 (1988): 427–45.

Trible, Phyllis. *God and the Rhetoric of Sexuality*. OBT. Philadelphia: Fortress, 1978.

———. *Texts of Terror: Literary-Feminist Readings of Biblical Narratives*. OBT. Minneapolis: Fortress, 1984.

Trimm, Charles. "Recent Research on Warfare in the Old Testament." *CBR* 10 (2012): 171–216.

———. *"Yhwh Fights for Them!" The Divine Warrior in the Exodus Narrative*. Gorgias Dissertations 58. Pistacaway: Gorgias, 2014.

VanGemeren, Willem A., ed. *New International Dictionary of Old Testament Theology and Exegesis*. 5 vols. Grand Rapids: Zondervan, 1997.

———. *Psalms*. Vol. 5 of *The Expositor's Bible Commentary: Revised Edition*. Edited by T. Longman III and D. E. Garland. Grand Rapids: Zondervan, 2008.

Vanhoozer, Kevin J. *Is There a Meaning in This Text? The Bible, the Reader, and the Morality of Literary Knowledge*. Grand Rapids: Zondervan, 1998.

Vogt, Peter. *Deuteronomic Theology and the Significance of Torah: A Reappraisal*. Winona Lake, IN: Eisenbrauns, 2006.

Volf, Miroslav. "Christianity and Violence." Pp. 1–17 in *War in the Bible and Terrorism in the Twenty-First Century*. Edited R. S. Hess and E. A. Martens. BBRSup 2; Winona Lake, IN: Eisenbrauns, 2008.

———. *The End of Memory: Remembering Rightly in a Violent World*. Grand Rapids: Eerdmans, 2006.

———. *Exclusion and Embrace: A Theological Exploration of Identity, Otherness, and Reconciliation*. Nashville: Abingdon, 1996.

———. *Free of Charge: Giving and Forgiving in a Culture Stripped of Grace*. Grand Rapids: Zondervan, 2006.

Waldow, H. Eberhard von. "The Concept of War in the Old Testament." *HBT* 6 (1984): 27–48.

Walsh, Michael. *Warriors of the Lord: The Military Orders of Christendom*. Grand Rapids: Eerdmans, 2003.

Walton, John H. *Ancient Near Eastern Thought and the Old Testament: Introducing the Conceptual World of the Hebrew Bible*. Grand Rapids: Baker Academic, 2006.

Watson, Natalie K. *Feminist Theology*. Guides to Theology. Grand Rapids: Eerdmans, 2003.

Weaver, J. Denny. *The Nonviolent God*. Grand Rapids: Eerdmans, 2013.
Weber, Beat. "Von der Psaltergenese zur Psaltertheologie: Der nächste Schritt der Psalterexegese?! Einige grundsätzliche Überlegungen zum Psalter als Buch und Kanonteil." Pp. 733–44 in *The Composition of the Psalms*. Edited by E. Zenger. Leuven: Peeters, 2010.
———. "Zur Datierung der Asaph-Psalmen der 74 und 79." *Bib* 81 (2000): 521–32.
Weber, Cornelia. *Altes Testament und völkische Frage: Der biblische Volksbegriff in der alttestamentlichen Wissenschaft der nationalsozialistischen Zeit, dargestellt am Beispiel von Johannes Hempel*. FAT 28. Tübingen: Mohr Siebeck, 2000.
Weems, Renita. *Battered Love: Marriage, Sex, and Violence in the Hebrew Prophets*. Minneapolis: Fortress, 1995.
Wenham, John. *The Enigma of Evil: Can We Believe in the Goodness of God?* Grand Rapids: Zondervan, 1985. Reprint of *The Goodness of God*. Downers Grove, IL: InterVarsity, 1974.
Westermann, Claus. *Basic Forms of Prophetic Speech*. Translated by H. C. White. Louisville, KY: Westminster John Knox, 1991.
———. *Die Klagelieder: Forschungsgeschichte und Auslegung*. Neukirchen-Vluyn: Neukirchener Verlag, 1992.
Wiesel, Elie. *Night, Dawn*, and *Day*. Night Trilogy. New York: Hill & Wang, 2006.
Williams, Stephen N. "Could God Have Commanded the Slaughter of the Canaanites?" *TynBul* 63 (2012): 161–78.
———. "'Holy War' and the New Atheism." Pp. 312–31 in *Holy War in the Bible: Christian Morality and an Old Testament Problem*. Edited by H. A. Thomas, J. Evans, and P. Copan. Downers Grove, IL: IVP Academic, 2013.
Wolff, H. W. "Swords into Plowshares: Misuse of a Word of Prophecy?" Pp. 110–26 in *The Meaning of Peace: Biblical Studies*. Edited by P. B. Yoder and W. M. Swartley. Louisville, KY: Westminster John Knox, 1992.
Wolterstorff, Nicholas. "If God Is Good and Sovereign, Why Lament?" *CTJ* 36 (2001): 42–52.
———. "Comments on 'What about the Canaanites?'" Pp. 283–88 in *Divine Evil: The Moral Character of the God of Abraham*. Edited by M. Bergmann, M. J. Murray, and M. C. Rea. Oxford: Oxford University Press, 2013.
Wright, Christopher J. H. *The God I Don't Understand: Reflections on Tough Questions of Faith*. Grand Rapids: Zondervan, 2008.
Wright, G. Ernest. *The Old Testament against its Environment*. London: SCM Press, 1950.
Yoder, Perry B. *Shalom: the Bible's Word for Salvation, Justice, and Peace*. IMS 7. Nappanee: Evangel, 1987.
Younger, K. Lawson Jr. *Ancient Conquest Accounts: A Study in Ancient Near Eastern and Biblical History Writing*. JSOTSup 98. Sheffield: Sheffield Academic Press, 1990.
———. "Some Recent Discussion on the *ḥērem*." Pp. in *Far from Minimal: Celebrating the Work and Influence of Philip R. Davies*. Edited by D. Burns and J. W. Rogerson. London: T. & T. Clark, 2012.
Zenger, Erich. *A God of Vengeance? Understanding the Psalms of Divine Wrath*. Translated by L. M. Maloney. Louisville, KY: Westminster John Knox, 1996.
Zenger, Erich. "Psalmenexege *und* Psalterexegese: Eine Forschungsckizze." Pp. 17–66 in *The Composition of the Book of Psalms*. Edited by E. Zenger. BETL 238. Leuven: Peeters, 2010.
Žižek, Slavoj. *Violence: Six Sideways Reflections*. London: Picador, 2008.

Index of Authors

Adam, K.-P. 80
Admirand, P. 2, 9, 10, 123, 130
Albright, W. F. 69
Allen, L. C. 85, 136
Ames, F. R. 9, 56
Andersen, F. I. 129
Anderson, B. W. 132, 135
Appleby, R. S. 9, 10
Arndt, E. 6, 29
Avalos, H. 2, 42

Bacote, V. 10
Baer, D. A. 141
Bainton, R. 50
Balentine, S. 104
Barker, K. 78
Barker, P. A. 140
Bartholomew, C. G. 3, 10, 12, 114, 117
Barton, J. 3, 121, 122
Bauckham, R. 89
Beal, T. 49
Bekkum, K. van 64, 66
Beldman, D. J. H. 3, 10, 114, 117
Bellis, A. O. 5
Berger, D. L. 1
Berges, U. 93, 103
Bergmann, M. 8, 43
Berlin, A. 15, 96, 107
Beyerlin, W. 82
Birkeland, H. 84
Block, D. I. 39, 40, 45, 48, 70, 130
Boase, E. 96, 101
Boda, M. J. 101
Boecker, H. J. 97, 100
Boutros, V. 122
Brett, M. G. 4
Briggs, R. S. 11
Bright, J. 75
Broyles, C. C. 86
Brueggemann, W. 9, 10, 126, 127, 141
Budin, S. L. 68
Burgess, J. P. 10
Burns, J. B. 68
Byrd, J. P. 4

Calvin, J. 52, 55, 65
Carroll R., M. D. 111, 112, 114, 122, 126, 130, 131, 146
Cavanaugh, W. T. 3, 7, 8
Chapman, S. B. 140
Childs, B. 104
Chilton, B. 20, 19, 21, 23, 24, 25, 26, 27, 28
Claassens, L. J. M. 142, 143
Clark, G. R. 141
Clines, D. J. A. 112
Coetzee, J. H. 85
Collins, J. J. 5, 41
Coote, R. B. 124
Copan, P. 8, 43, 50, 60, 66, 68, 69, 70, 71, 95, 100, 137, 142, 145
Cosgrove, C. H. 6
Cowles, C. S. 8, 11, 45
Creach, J. F. D. 8, 42, 51, 54, 57, 64, 65, 89, 95, 121, 131, 140, 143
Crenshaw, J. L. 2
Croatto, J. S. 111
Cross, F. M. 69, 99
Crouch, C. L. 9, 120, 123
Crowell, B. L. 4

Dallaire, H. M. 55, 59
Davies, A. 112
Davies, E. W. 6, 115, 117
Davies, J. 2
Dawkins, R. 3, 7, 70, 77, 145
Day, J. N. 81, 89
Deijl, A. van der 120
Delekat, L. 82
Dell, K. J. 115
Del Monte, G. F. 45
Dempsey, C. J. 112, 113
Dempster, S. 117, 119
Derrida, J. 131
Dobbs-Allsopp, F. W. 99, 106, 110
Dussel, E. 131

Eagleton, T. 7
Earl, D. S. 7, 8, 10, 42, 43, 44, 48, 49, 50, 51, 52

Ebel, J. H.   4
Eberhard, H.   47
Ellacuría, I.   111, 114
Elliff, L.   53, 56
Eph'al, I.   115
Ericksen, R. P.   1
Evans, J. A.   91, 95, 100, 145
Exum, J. C.   5, 112

Fales, E.   45, 50
Firth, D. G.   73, 83
Flannagan, M.   60
Flesher, P. M.   20, 23, 24, 25, 27
Franke, J. R.   42
Freedman, D. N.   129
Fretheim, T. E.   10, 49, 101, 120, 122, 123, 127, 128, 129, 133, 134, 137, 140, 139, 142
Fretz, M.   48
Friedman, R. E.   26

Gangloff, F.   64
Gaposchkin, M. C.   50
Garrett, S. M.   10
Gemeren, W. A. van   76
Girard, R.   131
Goldingay, J.   10, 74, 80, 88, 122
Gordon, R. P.   132, 141
Gossai, H.   2
Gottwald, N. K.   69, 109
Gray, M.   112
Greenberg, M.   41, 69
Green, D. H.   50
Green, J. B.   10
Gunkel, H.   84
Gunn, D. M.   13
Gutiérrez, G.   111

Hackett, J.   68, 69
Hamborg, G. R.   124
Hamilton, V.   22
Hanks, T. D.   119, 122
Harnack, A. von   3, 42
Hasel, G. F.   130
Hasel, M. G.   9, 115
Hawkins, R. K.   59
Hawk, L. D.   50
Hayes, M. A.   130
Hays, C. B.   21
Hays, R. B.   149
Hedges, C.   11
Heimbach, D. R.   50, 62, 63
Heschel, A.   127, 130

Heschel, S.   1
Hess, R. S.   7, 9, 69, 70, 71, 147
Hillers, D. R.   70
Hobbs, T. R.   9
Hogan, G. A.   122
Holladay, W. L.   135, 142, 146
Hossfeld, F.-L.   74, 87
Houston, W. J.   112

Ilany, O.   52, 53, 54

Jacobs, A.   11
Janzen, W.   113
Jenkins, P.   4, 108, 131
Josephus   23
Juergensmeyer, M.   2

Kaminsky, J. S.   44
Kang, S.-M.   119
Kant, I.   14, 27
Kauffman, Y.   69
Kelle, B. E.   9, 56
Kellner, M.   67, 68
Kierkegaard, S.   27
Kim, H. C. P.   126, 127
Kitts, M.   2
Klingbeil, M.   100
Kreider, A.   147
Kuan, K-J. J.   72

Labahn, A.   99
Lamb, D. T.   8, 114, 121, 136
Laney, J. C.   81
Lee, N. C.   99
Leiter, D. A.   9
LeMon, J. M.   81
Lessing, R. R.   116
Levenson, J.   17, 20, 22, 23, 27, 29
Lewis, C. S.   139, 144
Lindström, F.   102, 104
Linville, J. R.   131
Longman, T. III   61, 62, 63, 76, 119
Lyons, W. L.   63

MacDonald, N.   40, 42
Markham, I. S.   139
Martens, E. A.   7, 9, 14, 132, 143, 146, 147
Martin-Achard, R.   99
Matties, G.   137
McCann, J. C.   83
McConville, J. G.   40, 132, 135
McCoy, B.   51

McDonald, P. M.   3, 9
McEntire, M.   10, 147
McKenzie, S. L.   132
McNamara, M.   23
Meister, C.   139, 149, 150
Merrick, J.   10
Merrill, E. H.   45
Mesters, C.   111, 112
Miller, P. D. Jr.   62, 63, 99
Mintz, A.   96
Miranda, J. P.   111
Moberly, R. W. L.   41, 42, 64, 114, 132, 140
Möller, K. A.   123
Moll, S.   3
Moltmann, J.   127
Monroe, L. A. D.   44, 45
Morris, D.   55
Mowinckel, S.   84
Murphy, M. J.   8, 43

Nelson, R. D.   57, 58
Niditch, S.   9, 50, 64
Noll, K. L.   134
Noll, M. A.   4

O'Brien, J. M.   5, 113
O'Connor, K. M.   126, 127, 143
Ogden, D. K.   115
Origen   53, 51, 52, 54

Paas, S.   119
Patrick, D.   114, 122
Paul, S. M.   116, 121, 128, 129
Peels, E.   81
Peters, B. J.   11
Philo   23
Plotz, D.   136
Preuss, H. D.   119
Prior, J. M.   55
Prior, M.   4
Provan, I.   8

Ramage, M. J.   6
Ray, L.   94
Rea, M. C.   8, 43
Re'emi, S. P.   99
Reid, D. G.   61, 62, 119
Reimer, H.   123
Rivas, P. J.   122
Rodd, C. S.   37, 112
Rogerson, J. W.   5, 6, 44, 64
Römer, T.   8, 42, 47, 50, 55, 56, 61, 93

Rosen-Zvi, I.   66, 67
Ross, A. P.   74, 88
Roth, J. K.   105
Rowlett, L. L.   55, 58

Sandy, D. B.   120
Schlimm, M. R.   8, 114, 127
Schmidt, H. H.   82, 85
Schwartz, R. M.   2, 132, 131
Seevers, B.   115
Seibert, E. A.   4, 5, 6, 7, 9, 10, 42, 49, 52, 57, 61, 95, 113, 114, 116, 131, 134, 140, 148
Seitz, C. R.   3, 42, 50, 64, 109
Seybold, K.   80
Shead, A. G.   10
Sherwood, Y.   28, 29
Siebert, E. A.   13, 22, 28, 57, 148
Sparks, K. L.   5, 6, 7, 10
Stassen, G. H.   9, 145
Stern, P. D.   44, 61, 63, 64
Stewart, R.   145
Stulman, L.   126
Suderman, W. D.   113
Sugirtharajah, R. S.   4
Swartley, W. M.   147
Sweeney, M. A.   2
Swenson, K. M.   90, 94

Tamez, E.   119, 122
Templer, B.   53, 54
Thelle, R. I.   54, 55, 60, 62, 68
Theologians, K.   111, 112
Thomas, H. A.   90, 93, 95, 94, 97, 100, 101, 103, 106, 108, 109, 117, 145
Thompson, J. A.   141
Tombs, D.   130
Toorn, K. van der   83
Trible, P.   5, 142
Trimm, C.   9, 61

Vanhoozer, K. J.   12, 78
Volf, M.   7, 124, 130, 137

Walsh, M.   4
Watson, N. K.   5
Weaver, J. D.   5, 6, 148
Weber, B.   80, 87
Weber, C.   1
Weems, R.   112
Westermann, C.   103, 107, 121
Widjaja, P.   147
Wiesel, E.   2, 105

Williams, S. N.   43, 45
Wolff, H. W.   147
Wolterstorff, N.   43, 78, 93
Wright, C. J. H.   8, 10, 46, 70, 134
Wright, G. E.   69
Wright, J. L.   56

Yoder, P. B.   147, 148
Younger, K. L., Jr.   9, 44, 59, 60, 63, 64, 120

Zenger, E.   74, 79, 80, 83, 87
Žižek, S.   94, 109

Index of Scripture

Genesis
1:26–31   43
2:15   43
4:23–24   89
6–9   47
6:11   121
11:27–25   14
12:1   14
12:1–3   58, 71
12:6   71
13:7   71
14:18–20   26
14:24   22
15   49
15:6   26
15:16   46, 70, 71
15:18–21   45
18   16, 50
18:25   45, 114
21:12   22
22   12, 18, 20, 19, 23, 24, 25, 28
22:1–19   13, 14
22:2   14, 15
22:5   22, 23
22:9   13
22:10   27
23   25
25:11   14
32:2   20
34:19   22
37:2   22
41:12   22
43:8   22
44:22   22
45:10   58
46:28–34   58
48:16   22

Exodus
3:8   46
4:21   30
4:22   17
6:8   46
7:3   30

Exodus (cont.)
10:1   30
13:12b–15   19
14:4   30
14:13–14   63
14:14   63
15–18   104
15:1–18   61
15:3   61
15:6   100
17:8   72
17:16   53
19–24   49
19:5   58
19:9   99
20:3–5   65
20:3–6   48
20:5   50
23   65
23:20–33   65
23:27   63
23:29–30   66
27:21   98
28:31   48
28:43   98
29:4   98
29:10   98
29:11   98
29:30   98
29:32   98
29:42   98
29:44   98
30:16   98
30:18   98
30:20   98
30:26   98
30:36   98
31:7   98
32   19, 50
32–34   140
34:5–6   99
34:6   50, 93, 102, 140
34:6–7   48, 125
35:21   98
38:8   98

Exodus (cont.)
38:30   98
39:22   48
39:32   98
39:40   98
40:2   98
40:6   98
40:7   98
40:12   98
40:22   98
40:24   98
40:26   98
40:29   98
40:32   98
40:34   98
40:35   98

Leviticus
1:1   98
1:3–13   17
6:15–16   48
18:19–30   37
18:20–30   68
18:21   18
20:1=5   18
26:18   88
27:21–29   44

Numbers
3   17
4:6   48
10:9   62
11:1   50, 104
14   50
16:28   102
21:1   72
21:1–3   65
21:2   62
21:21–32   72
21:33   72
23:20   121
31   47
33:52   65
34:12   34

171

Index of Scripture

Deuteronomy
1:3   29
1:4   30, 31
1:27   30, 33
1:28–29   32
1:30   63
2:1–23   34
2:2–23   35
2:5   35, 45
2:7   34
2:9   32, 35
2:9–11   45
2:12   45
2:19   35
2:19–21   45
2:22   30, 45
2:24   31, 32, 41
2:25   30
2:26–30   72
2:30   30, 32
2:32–35   33
2:33   31
2:34–35   32
3:1   72
3:2   33
3:3   31
3:11   31
3:17   41
3:18–22   41
4:1–2   29
4:3   33
4:5–8   41, 50
4:7–8   58
4:10   37
4:16   40
4:19   40
4:23   40
4:25   40
4:27   30
4:28   40
4:32   38
4:34   30, 31
4:37–38   41
4:38   30
4:45   29
5:7   40, 48
5:7–9   65
5:7–10   40
5:8   40
5:8–9   40
5:9   30, 36
5:25–26   48
5:29   37

Deuteronomy (cont.)
5:33   37
6:2   37
6:4   40
6:4–5   40, 58
6:14   40
6:14–15   41
6:18–19   41
6:19   30
6:20–25   41
6:24   37
7   42, 51, 65, 66, 69
7:1   35, 47
7:1–5   48, 54, 57, 64, 65
7:1–11   41
7:2   31, 44, 65
7:2–5   46
7:2–16   100
7:4   40
7:5   40
7:6   34, 37, 39, 41, 58
7:6–8   49
7:7   58
7:7–8   138
7:7–10   136
7:10   30
7:12–13   138
7:16   31
7:16–26   53
7:17   33
7:22   66
7:23   30, 63
7:24   33
7:25   40, 48
7:25–26   41, 44
8:5   92
8:6   37
8:19   40
8:20   30, 41
9   50
9:1   33
9:1–6   41
9:1–24   46
9:3   30, 33
9:4   30, 46
9:4–5   70
9:12   40
9:14   30
9:16   40
9:28   30
10:12   37, 37, 58
10:15   34
10:17–19   37

Deuteronomy (cont.)
10:20   37
11:2   92
11:2–4   31
11:16   40
11:16–17   41
11:22   37
11:23   33
11:23–25   41
11:28   40
11:29–32   45
12:1–4   41
12:3   40, 66
12:29   30
12:29–31   46
12:29–32   41
12:31   18, 37
13:1–18   36
13:2–18   41
13:3   40
13:6   31, 35, 37, 36
13:6–7   40
13:9   40
13:11   31
13:12   40
13:12–17   48
13:15   37
13:15–16   48
13:16   31, 33
13:17   48
14:1   37
14:1–2   49
14:2   34, 37, 39, 41, 58
14:3   37
14:21   37, 39, 41, 49
14:23   37
15:21   39
16:20   34
17:1   37
17:1–7   41
17:2–7   31, 36
17:3   40
17:4   37
17:5–7   37
17:6   31
17:7   35, 37, 36
17:8–13   82
17:12   35, 36
17:12–13   36
17:13   40
17:19   37
18:9–12   41
18:9–22   41

Index of Scripture

Deuteronomy (cont.)
18:10   18, 71
18:12   46
18:20   36, 40
19:1   30
19:1–13   36
19:9   37
19:11   39
19:11–13   31
19:13   37, 36, 40
19:15–21   82
19:16–19   84
19:19   34, 37, 36
19:20   40
19:21   40
20:1–18   63
20:3   63
20:4   62
20:10–17   32
20:10–18   47, 53
20:10–20   64
20:13   30, 31
20:14   48
20:15   32
20:16–18   48, 66
21:9   37, 36
21:18   31
21:18–21   31, 36, 37
21:21   35, 37, 36, 40
21:22   31, 37
21:22–23   39
21:24   37
22:5   37
22:18   31
22:20–21   36, 37
22:20–24   31
22:21   35, 37, 36
22:22   35, 36
22:23–24   36
22:24   36
22:25   36
23:3–4   94
23:9–14   62
23:13–15   63
23:18–19   37
24:1–4   39
24:4   37
24:7   35, 37, 36
24:16   31
25:1–3   31
25:7–10   31
25:11–12   31, 40
25:16   37

Deuteronomy (cont.)
25:17–19   35
26:1–11   41
26:8   30
26:17   37
26:18   37, 39, 41, 58
26:19   37, 41, 49, 50
27   45
27:1–26   45
27:15   40
28:1   41
28:1–14   133
28:9   37
28:9–10   50
28:14   40
28:15   41
28:15–68   133
28:20   30, 40
28:22   30
28:36   40
28:37   30
28:64   30, 40
28:65   30
28:67   30
29:13–20   41
29:16   40
29:19   30
29:25   40
30:2   29
30:3   30
30:16   37
30:17   40
31:3   41
31:4   30
31:9–13   43
31:12–13   37
31:16   40
31:18   40
31:20   40
32:1–14   41
32:4   34
32:16   37
32:19–25   41
32:22–25   47
32:23   100
32:25   30
32:39   30
33:3   138
33:10   48
33:27   30, 33
34:13   65

Joshua
1:6–9   62
1:7   57
1:7–8   59
1:10–18   62
2   69
2:8–11   48
2:9   63, 72
2:9–11   69
3:5   62, 63
3:10   61
3:17   57
5   63
5:1   63, 72
5:2–9   62
5:5–8   62
5:10–12   57
5:13–15   56, 61, 62, 63
5:20   61
6   59
6:2   62
6:2–5   62
6:6–9   63
6:8–9   62
6:15–25   43
6:17–20   44
6:18   63
6:19   44
7   43, 59, 65
7:6–26   48
7:13   63
7:24   57
8:1   62, 63
8:24   57
8:26   63
8:30–35   45, 57
8:33   57
9:9–10   61
10   61, 72
10:1–2   63
10:8   62
10:11   61
10:14   63
10:20–26   52
10:25   52
10:29–43   57
11   60, 72
11:11   59
11:14   59
11:16   59
11:43   59
13:1   57
13:13   59

Index of Scripture

Joshua (cont.)
15:63   59
16:10   59
17:12   59
22:1–6   63
23:2   57
23:3   61
23:10   63
23:12–13   58

Judges
1:21   57
3:37   62
4:14   62
5:4   62
6:34   62
7:2–25   62
7:22–25   63
11:36   62
19   5
20:13   37, 62
20:40   48

Ruth
4:15   97

1 Samuel
1–15   134
7:9   48, 62
13:3–4   62
13:9–10   62
14:6   62
14:6–14   62
14:15–23   63
14:23   63
14:24   62
15:3   63, 100
15:29   50
17   87
17:10   87
17:26   87
17:36   87
17:45   62
17:46   87
21:4–5   62
21:5   62
21:6   63

2 Samuel
1:21   62
4:11   37
5:17–25   47
7:14   92

2 Samuel (cont.)
11:11   62, 63
20:1   63
24:1   25

1 Kings
4:10   37
9:20–22   67
12:6   63

2 Kings
6:11–23   146
22:2   57
23:2–3   57
23:4–20   57
23:21–23   57

1 Chronicles
21:1   25

2 Chronicles
3:1   20

Nehemiah
1:2–8   125

Job
6:4   100
34:6   100

Psalms
1   79, 80
1–2   80
1:80–81   80
2   74, 80
2:9   74, 80
3   73, 76, 82
5   76
5:10   76
7   80
7:13   76
8   43
9:19–20   76
10:1   90
10:15   76
11:1   140
12:3   76
14   80
17:1   90
18:14   100
18:42   80
21:12   100
22:2   90

Psalms (cont.)
23:3   97
23:4   92
25:7   136
28:4   76
31:1–9   82
31:17–18   76
34:8   136
35:4–8   76
35:26   76
38:2   100
40:13–17   80
40:14–15   76
44:23   90
46–48   86
46:10   140
50:6   114
51–100   87
51:21   48
52:9   136
53   80
54:5   76
55:1–19   82
55:15   76
55:56   82
55:57   82
55:59   82
57:7–11   80
58:6–7   76
59:11–12   76
60:5–12   80
64:7   100
68   61
68:1   76
68:1–2   61, 76
69   83, 85
69:22–28   76
70   80
70:2–3   76
71:13   76
72   74
72:12–14   74
73:1   136
74:2   90
74:4–8   73
77:17   100
79   86, 87
79:6   76
79:12   76
83:13–17   76
86:5   136
88:7   85
93:4   92

Index of Scripture

Psalms (cont.)
94:2–7 74
94:3–7 73
94:16–23 82
96:13 114
100:5 136
101 74
101–150 74
101:8 74
104:35 76
106:1 136
108 80
109 79, 86
109:6–20 76
118:1 136
119:68 136
119:78 76, 79
120:4 100
129:5–8 76
135:4 58
136:1 136
137 75, 78, 86, 87
137:7–9 76
139:19–22 76
140:9–11 76
141:10 76
143:12 76
144:6 100
145:9 136
146–150 80
149:4–9 78

Proverbs
3:11–12 92
6:23 92
13:24 92
22:15 92
23:13 92
29:15 92

Isaiah
2:1–4 147
2:18 48
11 147
11:1–5 129
11:1–9 147
11:6–11 129
13:16 87
14:4–23 128
14:21 87
16:9–11 127
28:21 129
33:14–16 129

Isaiah (cont.)
34:2 43
40–66 109
41:2 100
45:23 121
54:8 142
55:8–9 49
55:11 121
60:10 142
65:17–24 129

Jeremiah
1:4–19 143
2–9 127
2:2 138, 144
2:4–3:20 144
2:6 138
2:7 138
2:13 138
2:14–19 136
2:16–18 145
2:17 136
2:19 136
2:29–31 135
3:5 137
3:11 144
3:12 137
3:19–20 135
4:4 133
4:8 143
5:7–9 134
6:1–12 143
6:11 143
6:19 137
7:5–7 135
7:17–19 134
7:20 132, 134, 143
7:22 138
8:2–4 136
8:4–7 135
8:12 136
8:14–17 143
8:18–20 135
8:21–9:1 143
9:1 127
9:3 143
9:10 135
9:17–19 135
11:4 138
11:5 138
11:7–8 135
11:9–13 136
11:9–14 143

Jeremiah (cont.)
11:10 132
12:2 133
12:7–13 137
12:13 132
13:20–27 136
15:14 132
15:18 144
15:19 145
16:14 138
18:1–10 125
18:6–10 45
18:8 128
20:7 144
21:6 133
21:7 133
23:1–6 129
23:19–20 133
23:31 138
24:7 138, 139
25:3–4 138
25:4 146
25:9 43
25:11 137
25:37 132
26:1–11 136
27:2 146
27:12 146
28:15–16 136
29:7 146, 149
30:14 134
30:18 146
30:24 132
31:3 138, 140, 141, 144, 146, 150
31:6–7 147
31:8 141
31:8–9 147
31:9 141
31:10 141
31:10–14 141
31:12 147
31:12–14 141
31:15–17 143
31:15–22 141, 147
31:17 141
31:18 92
31:20 141, 150
31:22 142
31:23 146
31:24 147
31:31–34 138
31:32 135

Jeremiah (cont.)
32:22 138
32:31 137
32:41 136
32:44 146
33:1–13 138
33:5 132
33:6 147
33:7 146
33:11 136
33:26 146
38:17 146
42:1–10 129
48:29 139
48:29–33 127
48:30 139
48:35 139
48:42 139
49:5 137
49:37 143
50:13 143
50:25 137
50:31–32 137
51:24 137

Lamentations
1 108
1:2 97, 103
1:5 103, 106
1:9 106
1:10 93, 96, 110
1:11 97
1:13–15 97
1:16 95, 97, 98, 110
2 99, 107
2:1 98, 99, 106, 110
2:1–9 93, 98, 99, 100, 107, 108
2:2 98, 100
2:3 98, 100
2:4 98, 99, 100
2:4–5 100
2:5 98
2:6 98, 99
2:7 98, 99, 102
2:8 98
2:9 98, 99
2:10 99
2:11 106
2:11–12 99
2:14 107
2:15 48
2:20 106

Lamentations (cont.)
2:20–22 105, 106, 107, 108, 110
2:21 106
2:22 106
3 95
3:1 92
3:21 95
3:21–24 93
3:24 101
3:25 101
3:25–39 90, 95, 101, 104, 105
3:26 105
3:29 102
3:31 102
3:31–32 140
3:32 103
3:32–33 142
3:33 103
3:34–36 103
3:36 104
3:37 104
3:39 104
3:42 105
3:42–59 105
3:43 105
3:44 105
3:49–50 98
3:50 105, 111
3:58 95
3:59 98, 105, 106
4:13–14 107
5:1 106
5:1–22 105
5:19–22 105

Ezekiel
4–24 47
16:14 48
18:20 50
26:17 128
27:3 48
28:11–19 128
28:12 48

Hosea
1–3 144
3:1 138
3:1–2 144
9:5 138
11:1 138

Joel
2:12–14 125

Amos
1–2 120
1:1 115, 125
1:2 118, 127, 131
1:3 118, 119, 121
1:4 118
1:5 118, 125
1:6 121
1:7 118
1:8 118
1:9 121
1:10 118
1:11 121
1:12 118
1:13 121
1:14 118, 127
2:1 121
2:2 118
2:3 118, 119, 125
2:5 118
2:5–16 124
2:6 119, 122, 125
2:7 122
2:8 122, 125
2:9 122
2:13 115, 118
2:16 118
3:1 122, 125
3:4 118
3:6 118
3:7 119
3:10 122, 125
3:11 118
3:12 118
3:13 119
3:14 115, 130, 131
3:15 125
4:1 122, 125
4:3 118
4:4–5 131
4:4–16 125
4:6 128
4:6–9 115
4:6–11 122, 131
4:10 116, 121
4:11 115
4:12 131
4:13 119
5:1–3 127, 128
5:1–17 128

Index of Scripture

Amos (cont.)
5:2   116
5:4–6   125, 131
5:6   118
5:8   119
5:11   122
5:11–13   125
5:12   122
5:14   131
5:14–16   119
5:15   116, 130
5:16–17   116, 127, 128
5:17   131
5:18   130
5:18–20   116, 131
5:21   127
5:21–25   131
6:1–3   131
6:3   130
6:3–6   122
6:3–7   125
6:7   118
6:8   116, 119, 127
6:9–10   127
6:9–11   115, 116
6:13   121, 125
6:14   116, 125

Amos (cont.)
7   50
7:2   121
7:3   128
7:4   118
7:7–8   116
7:9   123, 131
7:9–10   125
7:10   125
7:10–14   125
7:13   130
7:17   116
8:3   116, 130, 131
8:4   122
8:4–6   125
8:5   122
8:6   122
8:7   127
8:8   115
8:10   127
8:10–14   116
9:1   115, 116, 131
9:2–4   119
9:5   119
9:5–6   119
9:6   119
9:7   49, 122

Amos (cont.)
9:8–10   119, 123
9:10   131
9:11   130, 131
9:11–15   129
9:14   130
14:5   115

Obadiah
1:15   101

Jonah
3:10   50, 128
4:2   125, 128

Micah
4:13   44
6:9   92

Habakkuk
2:6–20   128
3:9   100

Zechariah
1–2   109
9:9–10   140
9:13   100
14:31   43

New Testament

Matthew
1:5   43, 48
3:17   15
5:21–48   148
5:39   150
5:43–48   77, 81
5:44–45   149
7:1   149
19:7   149
23:1–36   81

Mark
14:12–26   26
15:34   89

Luke
3:22   15
6:29   150
18:19   149

John
1:18   150
3:16   149
11:50   39

Acts
1:20   83

Romans
5:2–4   92
5:8   149
7:16   149
8:6   148
8:28   149
8:32   30
14:17   148
15:33   148
16:20   148

1 Corinthians
5:7   26
12:7   149
16:22   81

2 Corinthians
13:11   148

Galatians
3:22   148
4:21–31   149

Ephesians
4:3   148
4:26   150
5:22–32   149
6:15   148

Philippians
3:10   92
4:9   148

Colossians
1:24   92

1 Thessalonians
4:6   81
5:23   148

2 Thessalonians
1:7–8   149
3:16   148

1 Timothy
4:4   149

2 Timothy
1:12   92
3:16   148
4:14   81

Hebrews
8–9   149
13:20   148

James
1:2   92
5:7–10   92

1 Peter
1:6–9   92

1 Peter (cont.)
2:3   149
3:8–22   92
4:1–19   92

1 John
3:16   149
4:7–8   149

Revelation
6:10   90
11:17–18   81
15:2–4   81
16:5–7   81
18:1–8   81

Deuterocanonical Literature

1 Maccabees
2:52   25

2 Maccabees
6   26
6:10   26
7   26

4 Maccabees
7:13–15   24
14:20   24
16:16–20   24

www.ingramcontent.com/pod-product-compliance
Lightning Source LLC
Chambersburg PA
CBHW021956090426
42811CB00001B/55